浙江工商大学省级重点专业（英语）建设经费资助成果

Western Culture

A Discussion of Its Evolution, Noteworthy Personalities, and Prominent Ideas

西方文化论

■ 邹　颉　著

浙江工商大学出版社
ZHEJIANG GONGSHANG UNIVERSITY PRESS

图书在版编目(CIP)数据

　　西方文化论 / 邹颉著. —杭州：浙江工商大学出版社，2013.12
　　ISBN 978-7-5178-0065-1

　　Ⅰ．①西… Ⅱ．①邹… Ⅲ．①西方文化－文化史 Ⅳ．①K500.3

　　中国版本图书馆 CIP 数据核字(2013)第 266872 号

西方文化论

邹　颉　著

责任编辑	黄静芬　　王黎明	
封面设计	王妤驰	
责任印制	汪　俊	
出版发行	浙江工商大学出版社	
	（杭州市教工路 198 号　邮政编码 310012）	
	（E-mail：zjgsupress@163.com）	
	（网址：http://www.zjgsupress.com）	
	电话：0571 - 88904980，88831806（传真）	
排　　版	杭州朝曦图文设计有限公司	
印　　刷	杭州恒力通印务有限公司	
开　　本	710mm×1000mm　1/16	
印　　张	16.25	
字　　数	307 千	
版 印 次	2013 年 12 月第 1 版　2013 年 12 月第 1 次印刷	
书　　号	ISBN 978-7-5178-0065-1	
定　　价	38.00 元	

PREFACE

This book is intended for students of English at college level in China, aiming to help them to explore the key ideas, values, and ideals upon which Western institutions have been built and by means of which Western people guide their lives. The format is chronological. The historical development of Western Culture—from ancient Greece to contemporary Europe and America— is set forth in twelve topics: ancient Greece, ancient Rome, the Middle Ages, the Renaissance, the Reformation, Scientific Revolution, the Enlightenment, the French Revolution and the Industrial Revolution, Romanticism, Socialism, Psychoanalysis, and Contemporary Western World. Although the book's general arrangement is historical, moving closer to the present day as it proceeds, the main chapters are fairly self-contained, and can be read selectively or out of the present order.

This is not a definitive work on Western Culture, but a kind of map by which interested readers can find their way along some of the main roads of Western Culture. I hope it is clear and concise enough for this purpose. At the same time, I have tried to give enough information and interpretation to serve as a point of departure for further reading and research.

I hope the book will be useful for those interested in Western Culture, but I feel it necessary to add a word of caution. The reader should always keep in mind that this is an overview, a broad discussion. Any generalizations drawn from the material contained in these pages will be just that—generalizations.

I am grateful to College of Foreign Languages of Zhejiang Gongshang University for funding the publication of the book. My gratitude goes to Prof. Zhang Xin from School of Marxism Studies of Zhejiang Gongshang University for her insightful criticism and many comments. I should also like to thank Ms Huang Jingfen for her editorial assistance and those who encouraged and helped me in one way or another with this project. For the mistakes or inadequacies which remain, the blame is entirely mine.

Zou Jie

Zhejiang Gongshang University

CONTENTS

Chapter 1　Ancient Greece:
Fountainhead of Western Culture

The civilization of the Greeks goes back to about 6500 BC, when nomad farmers crossed into the European continent from the fertile river valleys of Mesopotamia in the Middle East. By 3000 BC these settlers had fortified cities on the European mainland and on the nearby islands in the Mediterranean that would become the isles of Greece. About 1900 BC an Indo-European people called the Achaeans migrated to the area, founded their own towns, and brought with them a language that became Greek.

1.1　Homer's Epics

To understand the Greek experience, it is helpful to start with Homer, the poet whose epics the *Iliad* and the *Odyssey* preserve for us a brilliant and well-rounded picture of the time. An epic is not "true" in the sense that it accurately portrays a specific time and place or a particular series of events. It is, rather, a narrative woven out of the collective memory of a people. The particular circumstances in which the *Iliad* and the *Odyssey* were composed are not known, but it is likely that the *Iliad* appeared somewhere on the coast of Asia Minor in the eighth century BC, and the *Odyssey*, at least two generations later.

Both epics describe events that took place in Mycenaean Greece from the fifteenth to eleventh century BC, but some scholars believe the society described in the poems existed later, probably during the tenth and ninth century BC. The epics tell us a great deal about the economic and social life of the agrarian society in which they were produced—its warrior cult, its religious beliefs, its customs, its standards of behavior—and they illuminate the thought world of a primitive civilization.

1

The *Iliad*, a story about warriors, is set in the tenth year of the Trojan War. Paris, the son of King Priam of Troy, had seduced Helen, the wife of King Menelaus of Pylos, and abducted her to Troy. Such an insult had to be avenged, and the Greeks—called Achaeans by Homer—had held Troy under siege for nine years, unable to storm into the city for a total victory. The central figure of the poem is Achilles, the son of Peleus, king of the Myrmidons in Thessaly, and the sea nymph Thetis, who rendered him invulnerable, except for the heel by which she held him, by dipping him in the river Styx. Wise, courageous, and handsome, Achilles is the prototype of the Homeric hero.

As the epic begins, a plague was ravaging the Greek camp. Agamemnon, the leader of the Greek expedition against Troy, had angered the god Apollo by insulting one of Apollo's priests. Apollo had awarded Agamemnon by giving him the priest's daughter. When the priest tried to bargain for her return, Agamemnon sent him away, and the plague began. The gods agreed to end the devastation only if Agamemnon returns the prize. He obeyed, but demanded in her place Achilles' war prize, a girl called Briesis, and Achilles was outraged.

While the gods watched and took sides, Achilles withdrew his powerful troops, the Myrmidons, and was in a sulk in his camp. Without Achilles' support, the Greeks were sufficiently weakened to allow the Trojans, led by Hector, the eldest son of King Priam of Troy, to venture from the safety of their city and very nearly destroy the Greek fleet. Although Achilles couldn't be persuaded to help, Patroclus, his best friend and companion since childhood, donned Achilles' armor intending to frighten the Trojans, only to be killed in combat by Hector. It is only the death of his friend, a death he watched from the sidelines, that finally moved Achilles to action. He made peace with Agamemnon and then, in armor forged by the gods, entered the combat, although he knew he would meet his death. Accepting his fate, he slaughtered countless Trojans and drove the rest back within the walls of Troy. But he was not satisfied until he had killed Hector and dragged his body three times around the walls of Troy.

The *Iliad* ends when Achilles, at the order of Zeus, accepted a ransom for the body of Hector so that the Trojans could bury him with honor. He was left to await the fate he knew he couldn't escape: He would die in battle. He was killed by Paris, who shot a poisoned arrow into his heel. Achilles died young, but his glory goes on forever.

As the sequel to the *Iliad*, the *Odyssey* was composed later and is concerned with the homecoming of the Achaeans after their victory in the Trojan War. Its hero is the warrior Odysseus, known for his prowess and cleverness. It is his fate to endure ten years' delay in his homecoming—to be shipwrecked, lost, held captive, and subjected to various trials. Finally, twenty years after his departure from home, the goddess Athena helped him to return to the island of Ithaca.

The *Odyssey*, like the *Iliad*, starts *in medias res* and describes the voyage home of Odysseus after the fall of Troy, and the vengeance he took with his son Telemakos on the suitors of his wife Penelope on his return. Believing Odysseus to be dead, a large band of noblemen from Ithaca and other kingdoms were asking for his wife's hand, but the faithful Penelope, who still mourned for Odysseus, steadfastly refused to wed any of the suitors. Meanwhile, the gods had decided to restore Odysseus to his kingdom, and he was released by the demigoddess Kalypso, who had held him captive as her lover for seven years. After a dangerous voyage and a shipwreck, he was washed up on the shore of Phaiakia. Appearing as a beggar, he revealed himself to his young son Telemakos, and they planned to avenge themselves on the suitors. Coming to his own home at last, Odysseus and his son slaughtered the suitors. Telemakos proved himself a man in aiding his father, Odysseus regained his kingdom, and order was restored to Ithaca.

Violence and honor are the dominant themes in the two great epics. Together, the epics depict a tribal society that revolved around the family. Kinship counted for almost everything. The most important dividing line in social, economic, and military relationships—the line between the aristocracy and the common people—was set according to the kinship group a man was born into. Not only was a man's status dictated by his lineage, but his very nature—even his personal standards of behavior—were determined and ruled by it.

The gods were ever present in Homer's world. Every meaningful action had to be preceded by a libation or sacrifice in honor of the appropriate god. Wine was poured on the ground, or a sheep, goat, or cow was slaughtered and its thigh bone wrapped in fat and burned on the fire. Feasting followed and the god was pleased. Failure to sacrifice to the gods met swift and sure retribution.

But one could not be absolutely sure of a favorable outcome even after proper ceremonies. It was easy to give offense to the gods unawares, and aside from this, there was sometimes the intervention of fate, from which there was no escape and no appeal.

Homer's gods differed in one important respect from the gods of most primitive peoples. For Homer, the forces of nature were not in themselves divinities. He seldom saw gods in rocks or trees or animals. The gods, rather, were anthropomorphic, that is, they were supermen. A god might control the sea or some other natural force, but except for his immortality and the fact that he lived high on Mount Olympus, he was similar in behavior and appearance to man. The gods were subject to human passions and they actively participated in human affairs. Humans could be descendents of gods, could look like gods, and could act like gods, but were removed from the gods, like Achilles, only because of their mortality. Homer's idea of the gods was revolutionary, because he envisaged the gods so much like man and made man nearly divine. The idea that man is "like a god" stands very near the heart of the Greek humanism of the fifth century BC Athens.

From the archaic period of Homer to classical Greece, these three centuries saw profound changes in the social and political forms of society, but Homer's picture of the gods remained the accepted standard. The Greeks never ceased to emulate the Homeric ideal of honorable human behavior. The aristocratic ideal of Homer's time, the conviction that man must seek honor through excellence, was adapted to local social and political forms to provide a standard for Greek ethical behavior that prevailed for centuries.

1.2　The Polis

By the time Homer's epics were written down in the eighth century BC, great changes were taking place in Greece, out of which emerged a world far different from the world described by Homer. Not long after Homer's time, Ionia, an area not far away from the site of the city of Troy, developed into an urbanized and prosperous cultural and commercial center. It led the Greek world into contacts with the Near East and other forms of civilization that heralded the emergence of Greek society from the Dark Ages. Ionian culture contributed not only to the works of Homer but also to the revival and refinement of writing and the development of early science, philosophy, and lyric poetry.

As communication between various areas in Greece became more frequent, the Aegean Sea became the center rather than the boundary of the Greek world. The Mediterranean, with the revival of trade, became once more the highway of the Greeks. Eastern techniques and motifs in pottery and art again exerted a wide influence on Greek forms. At this time, the Phoenician alphabet was imported by the Greeks and adapted to the Greek language, making written literature possible. The Greek world was settled down to a more ordered, more civilized existence.

With its dramatic increase in population, Greece called for a higher level of agricultural production. But the land of Greece could not support a large population. Therefore, the Greek world underwent a period of rapid expansion through colonization. The colonists took with them a constitution and the gods and customs of the home community, but the new settlement was essentially independent. In a movement of expansion that lasted for more than a century, the Greeks dotted the eastern Mediterranean with colonies, from Sicily and the French coast in the west to the Black Sea in the east.

Such profound changes in the conditions of life were sure to have a major impact on the old tribal society. The end of eighth and beginning of the seventh century BC saw the transformation of the old community based on the family and tribe into the polis, the so-called "city-state". Although there were many similarities between the two, the bases of the polis implied an important departure from the old tribal relations. The polis was like a tribe in that its citizens were usually born into it and in that it dominated all aspects of life. It differed from the tribe in that it came to control a specific territory and in that its social and economic bases had little to do with the old kinship relationships.

The center of the polis in the earliest days was not even a town, let alone what we would call a city. It was merely a settlement of houses of the farmers who worked the land in the surrounding area. It was originally organized on the basis of tribal relationships, but later it became more a territorial division as the polis took on the characteristics of a town. Public buildings, temples, and meeting places appeared. As the economy grew more complex, the polis became a marketing center for the exchange of goods as well as a home and a meeting place. Gradually people came to be conscious of the polis as an entity independent of family relationships. Religious cults associated with particular polis grew up, and a feeling similar to patriotism developed.

The new form taken by the polis led, among other things, to the disappearance of kingship, for kingship did not fit the new society. The king had no effective means to tax the community at large, and his financial position therefore was very weak. In addition, more settled conditions and the development of the hoplite formation made the old warrior kings obsolete, and their place was taken largely by groups of aristocrats. Often the executive function of government was divided among a priest, a military leader, and a judicial officer; sometimes a council of aristocrats ruled. On the whole, the new political arrangements did not keep pace with the development of society. In the seventh and sixth centuries BC, much of Greek history revolved around the attempts of the polis to find forms of government that would satisfy, first, the need for justice and impartial public authority and, second, the desire for a public authority responsive to new social and economic groups.

1.3 Religion

The Athenian polis was not only a community involving the political, social, and economic lives of its citizens, but also the center of their cultural life, which was intimately connected with religion. The process of religious development by which the religion of the tribe or family was transformed into the religion of the polis was shaped by two fundamental trends. The major trend was toward the gradual absorption by the state of the religious beliefs and practices of the family and locality. Second, the polis tended to adopt the more rational and aristocratic versions of the gods as they were presented by Homer in his epics and by Hesiod in his systematic account of the gods' origins.

Greek religion never incorporated a code of behavior or a coherent body of theological beliefs. It was, rather, a medley of myths, of stories that accounted for particular phenomena. For example, the explanation for the changing of the seasons was given in the story of Kore, who was abducted by Hades to the underworld. Kore's mother, Demeter, goddess of crops, was overcome by sadness and wandered the barren earth until Zeus pacified her by arranging that her daughter would spend only part of the year with Hades and part with her. Thus, the earth was barren for part of the year, but when Kore returned to her mother every spring, life returned to the earth.

Another type of religious cult operated primarily outside the state. These cults were characterized by wild, ecstatic behavior on the part of participants, behavior that might include hallucinations, orgies, and the sacrifice of animals and even sometimes of human beings. The typical cult of this sort was the worship of Dionysus, god of wine and fertility. Its participants were from all levels of society, even including slaves, and the ritual, carried out at night, apparently consisted mainly of wild orgiastic dancing to music. Dancers wound their ways across the mountainsides in a frenzy, the object of which apparently was to lose oneself, to escape from reality. The cult of Dionysus was eventually taken over by the polis of Athens and transformed into a solemn religious festival that featured the recitation of choral odes. In time, these odes developed into full-scale plays; the festivals thus gave birth to the classical Greek tragedy.

One of the most important aspects of polis religion was the worship of heroes. The idea of hero-veneration grew naturally out of the Greek view that a man's immortality consisted mainly in how he was remembered by other men. Thus, it was an important duty of the polis to honor its heroes. The spirit of the hero, as of all ancestors, resided in his tomb, which thus had to be properly revered. In return, the hero, through his spirit, could help protect the polis. The dead Athenian hero Theseus, for instance, was said to have been seen fighting in the Athenian ranks against the Persians at the battle of Marathon. Neglect of a hero, however, could bring disaster to a polis.

Although most religious observances took place within the polis, there were Panhellenic religious institutions in which all Greek participated. The most important of these was the Delphic oracle, located at Delphi in central Greece. The Greeks believed that northerners had brought Apollo to Delphi, where he established his oracle and then shared it with Dionysus, who took possession during the three winter months when Apollo was absent. The god spoke through a priestess, who, in a trance, answered questions asked by official emissaries from the Greek cities. The oracle was also visited by common people with personal problems and by foreign emissaries from Asia. Apollo was the god of justice, and the oracle gave advice that ranged from instructing poleis when and where they should found colonies to telling murderers whether and how they could purify themselves. Lycurgus was thought to have received his Spartan constitution from the oracle, and many cities took care to gain the advice of the oracle whenever new laws were issued. In addition, in each polis emissaries from the oracle acted as overseers of all religious observances in their polis. They saw that rituals were duly followed and that crimes were punished in the correct manner, and they gave advice when the proper course of action for the polis was in doubt. When the matter was especially serious, the emissaries were sent to the oracle for advice directly from Apollo himself.

All these facets of Greek religion were parts of a messy body of myths, cults, rituals, and beliefs, which grew up side by side in various localities in a haphazard fashion. Such a religious climate could find room—along with its huge number of gods and goddesses—for a mixture of ideas about supernatural phenomena. Conceptions of the afterlife and the underworld, for instance, varied widely, and there were vastly divergent notions about such fundamental beliefs as the nature of the spirits of the dead and the location of the underworld itself. Nothing was excluded simply because it was incompatible with any existing deity or tale. Greek religion could and did absorb anything that interested and attracted the Greeks.

It is only within this framework that we can comprehend the achievement of Homer and Hesiod. Working in the midst of this complex and often contradictory body of myth, the two poets attempted to formulate and describe an ordered conception of the gods and their relationship to man. Homer gave the gods a dwelling place (Olympus), a father (Zeus), and assigned them places in the hierarchy of beings in the universe. Gods were like man, except that they were physically flawless, immortal, and able to foresee human events; in short, they were man perfected. Because of their superior nature, they exercised power over human events in much the same way that the nobles of the Dark Ages possessed authority over the commoners, who were inferior to them. The gods' anger could breed affliction for man, while their blessing promised success. In Homer, the gods were ever present in human affairs, especially at moments of human decision. They might speak aloud to a man, avert a spear to save his life, or put in a personal appearance at any time and in almost any guise. Above all, the gods were to be seen at work in actions that surpassed the normal behavior of man. Transcendent wrath were hints that the gods had intervened. In addition, the gods had control over natural forces and could bring them to bear either for or against a man. Sailors, for instance, had to be careful to retain the good will of Poseidon, god of the sea. It was Poseidon who, when offended by Odysseus, delayed his passage home. Zeus not only exercised his persuasive thunderbolt at certain decisive moments but also gave out good or evil fortune variously to each man at birth.

In Homer, there is never any question as to whether one should believe in the gods; nor will obedience to the divine ever be questioned. The will of the gods is inescapable, and therefore they simply cannot be ignored. If punishment is not visited upon a man who insults the gods, it will surely strike his children or children's children. But when a man unknowingly commits an offence against a divinity, it is possible, by observing the proper rituals and by behaving properly, to remain on good terms with the gods. To behave correctly is to act in accord with one's nature. Just as a commoner could be humiliated for speaking out of turn in the assembly, so the suitors in the *Odyssey* could be punished for behavior inappropriate to their position.

The ideal man never forgets his humanity and his mortality, but at the same time he has to emulate the gods. The gods were supposedly deserving of this emulation by reason of their perfection, although the myths are full of instances where the gods tell a lie, cheat, commit adultery, and generally act in less than a god-like fashion. A hero is a man who possessed godlike qualities, and he is given immortality in the only way that is meaningful or appealing to the Greeks. To live forever in the memory of one's polis is the incentive to proper human action. The gods look with favor upon lofty human behavior. For example, Heracles was a man the gods found so worthy that they accepted him as a god. Heracles represented the closest thing the Greeks ever had to a universal symbol of a hero, and he belonged to all the Greeks.

Homer created the Greek image of the gods and gave them personality and function. It remained for Hesiod in his *Theogony* to attempt to systematize the family of deities and depict the genealogy of the gods and their roles. His system was Greek, of course, but it shows some Near Eastern influences. Hesiod's major contribution was to explain the conception that the gods were a moral force. He achieved this by making them champions of justice.

The Greek polis adopted Homer's and Hesiod's conceptions of gods, and despite the variety of local practices, a distinctive Greek religion was developed. This religion was always complex and never consistent in all its details; still, its view of man and the world lies at the center of Greek culture.

1.4　Philosophy

In the fifth century BC Greek lived a large group of intellectuals who were primarily concerned with explaining the nature of the universe in physical terms. The outcome of their inquiries was the discovery of abstract thinking and the birth of philosophical thought.

The early philosopher-scientists like Thales of Miletus, rejected myth and anthropomorphic gods as ultimate causes of events. Instead, they began to look for explanations in material terms. They tried to find the basic substance out of which all other materials were formed. Thales (624—545 BC) thought it was water, and others said it was air or fire or earth. The Pythagoreans founded both a mystical sect, who believed in reincarnation, and a philosophical school, which asserted that the principle of all things was number. Instead of thinking in terms of substances such as air and water, they reduced reality to spatial units that could be understood logically and mathematically. They regarded the point, the line, and the plane as the constituents of reality, and they were therefore the first to think of reality in purely abstract terms.

For thinkers such as Heraclitus (540—470 BC), change, the basic element in human sensory experience, was the result of external motion acting in accordance with the inner, constant reason (Logos) in the universe. Parmenides (515—450 BC) extended this idea to assert that there were two separate realities: the way of Truth, which was external to human experience and could be grasped only through the uncompromising application of reason; and the way of Seeming, which could be perceived by the senses but was a false way. Zeno (490—430 BC) perpetuated the Parmenidian tradition in his argument for the unity of the universe by showing through a paradox that plurality was logically impossible. He used similar arguments to prove that motion and change were impossible. This meant that reality was immutable and, at least theoretically, rationally accessible to human comprehension.

The writers who followed Parmenides and Zeno got around the objection that plurality cannot evolve from unity by positioning an ultimate plurality.

Empedocles (493—433 BC) held that there were four elements—fire, air, earth, and water—and that these were moved by Love and Strife. Man could perceive these because he had the senses to experience each element. Anaxagoras (500—428 BC), the teacher of Pericles (495—429 BC), carried the idea further when he held that creation came from an infinite number of seeds which contained the elements of all things in their diversity. Ultimately, Leucippus (450—420 BC) and Democritus (460—370 BC) combined the idea of a basic material with the Pythagorean idea that reality is composed of geometric units. They held that all things were made up of indivisible units, called "atoms", which were all similar, and that different combinations of these led to the apparent differences in nature. According to different thinkers, the particular combinations were ordered by a divine Mind or were the result of change, but the scientific dimensions of the Greek analysis of reality was firmly established.

The development of abstract thought had far-reaching implications. The gods of the polis, still to a large extent the Homeric anthropomorphic gods, had no place in such systems, which explained the universe in purely physical terms. The same was true for the conventional ideas of mortality: What had seemed the transcendent laws of the polis given to man by the gods were now no more than conventions that could be changed. There grew up in Athens, among some thinkers, the idea that the laws of nature—what was thought to be naturally good for man—might actually be in conflict with the laws of the polis.

In addition, the knowledge of the intellectuals was specialized and highly abstracted, quite outside the normal Greek educational systems. It did not even seem useful to society. Most of the early philosophers conducted rudimentary experiments and made minor inventions. But technology advanced relatively little after 600 BC in Greece, and the theoretical achievements of the scientists were seldom put to socially or economically beneficial uses. Medicine was a partial exception, and the Hippocratic school was quite advanced in its investigation into the causes of disease. In spite of this, the Greeks generally put as much faith in the worship of the healing god Asclepius as in scientific medicine.

On the whole, science and philosophy remained pastimes for aristocrats, a world apart from the experience and the concerns of the rest of society. In 500 BC, there was a movement designed to overcome this aloofness. Formerly, such high education as was necessary for philosophical thought was conveyed by means of a purely private relationship between a wise man and the younger pupils he happened to gather around him. Then, a new group, the Sophists, began to offer education to anyone—for a price. Furthermore, they would not waste their pupils' time with speculations as Zeno's inquiries. Education was to be put to use in society; it was to help the educated people get on in the world. Since they believed that there was no absolute truth, the Sophists and their pupils did not seek truth but that which was to their advantage. Sophists were trained in methods of rhetoric and arguments—especially in the Athenian assembly, where the most convincing speaker carried the day. Thus, along with theoretical logic, the Greeks also invented practical logic-chopping.

1.5 Classical Philosophers

Socrates (469—399 BC) opposed both the natural scientists and the Sophists. He found the conclusions of the philosophers about the nature of the universe unsatisfying. He not merely wanted to know the succession of physical changes which had resulted in the present order, but also wanted to know *why* things were ordered as they were. He sought not what substance things came from but what purpose they served. It appeared to him that the world must be ordered to fulfill some moral end.

Socrates turned the tools of science and logic to the examination of man. The subject of his search was the nature of the good, that is, what is appropriate to man's nature and to the nature of the universe, since he believed that if man knows the good, he would pursue it. Socrates asserted that man would not commit an act that he feels to be wrong; evil conduct is the consequence of ignorance. In order to search out the good, Socrates spent his life in discussion with anyone who was interested in his questions. His method was rigorous self-examination; the first prerequisite for good action was to "know thyself". Socrates argued that "the unexamined life is not worth living". He felt that every individual and social belief has to be examined and justified by reason, and no subject, including the gods and the law, is exempt from his ceaseless inquiries. This attitude made Socrates a prime target for the criticism of the traditionalists, like Aristophanes, who felt threatened by what they saw as the breakdown of the old Athenian morality at the end of the

Peloponnesian War (431—404 BC). Socrates was tried for corrupting the youth of Athens and for not believing in the gods of the polis, although in fact he carried out all the customary religious observances. The Athenian jury condemned him to death by poison from his own hand. Although he could have escaped into exile, Socrates chose to die for his belief and behavior. He refused the dishonor of fleeing from the laws of his polis, even when they were used unjustly against him.

Socrates left no written record of his teachings, but his greatest pupil, Plato, made Socrates the major speaker in many of his dialogues, which present the outlines of his philosophy. Plato went beyond his teacher. His inquiry began with ethics, but at one point or another he considered most of the questions that have been of concern to philosophers since his time. All of Western philosophy, as the eminent twentieth-century British philosopher A. N. Whitehead has said, is but "a series of footnotes to Plato".

Plato (427—347 BC) grew up during the last years of the Peloponnesian War and was a young man when Socrates was condemned by the state. At an early age, he entered a life of writing and teaching, after a period of involvement in the politics of both Athens and Syracuse. He had witnessed the Athenian democracy at its worst, during the postwar period, and his concern for discovering the essentials of a well-ordered state never left him. In what may have been his last work, the *Laws*, he attempted to draw up a constitution of the "best possible" state, with a view toward putting it into actual practice.

Plato's view of the correct ordering of the ideal state is best seen in the *Republic*, in which Socrates discusses the nature of justice with three Sophists. Since justice is found only in the good state, he has to begin by outlining what sort of state that might be. Plato's conception of the ideal form of government was derived from his view of the nature of man. The human soul has a three-part nature comprised of wisdom, honor, and appetite. Whichever characteristic predominated determines the nature of each particular man. The best man is governed by reason or wisdom, the worst by his appetites; only the former could be truly free or truly happy. States governed by democracy are not immune to the rule of appetite. Governments devoted to the pursuit of honor he called "timocracies".

The ideal state would be governed by wisdom. It would be characterized by true justice—that is, everyone fulfilling his function within a harmonious whole. Those who were controlled by the appetitive soul would provide the labor of the state, while those who were governed by the search of honor would defend it and perform executive functions. The wise would rule as philosophers and kings.

Wisdom does not consist of expertise in governmental affairs; it is rather the ability to perceive the good. This ability could be achieved by those few men who possessed the best sort of soul and who underwent long years of education—rigorous physical as well as philosophical training.

For Plato, knowledge involved going beyond particular transitory objects, which can be perceived with senses, to the ultimate reality in the universe—the world of pure ideas. Reality is not contained in those things which come into being and pass away but rather in eternal form, which although they resemble the things we see, are outside time and space. Everything that exists—that can be seen and felt—was for Plato but an imperfect reflection of its ideal form. Beyond the particular pure forms, there is one highest form, the idea of the good. It is the knowledge of this transcendent reality that separates the truly wise people from the rest of mankind.

Unlike Socrates, Plato established a formal school, the Academy, where he lectured throughout the latter part of his life. His greatest pupil was Aristotle (384—322 BC). After Plato's death, Aristotle began increasingly to diverge from his master's doctrines, and the basis of this disagreement was Plato's doctrine of ideal forms. Aristotle came to believe that all reality can be perceived with senses; there are for Aristotle no perfect forms outside time and space. Instead, Aristotle held that the image we have of a class of objects is no more than a generalization based on all the particular objects in that class that we have perceived.

In accordance with the empirical attitude, Aristotle believed there is no essence of the state, no perfect form of justice. If we want to determine the nature of the best state, we must carefully compare all the states that exist and see which of their qualities help them to maintain smooth functioning and which tend toward instability. Aristotle held that there are naturally three types of government: rule of one, or monarchy, which tends to become tyranny; rule of the few, or oligarchy, which easily turns into timocracy; rule of the many, or democracy, which tends to degenerate into anarchy. Aristotle decided that the most stable and therefore the best form of government is a mixture of the three extremes in a balanced constitution.

The goal of both the state and the individual life, in Aristotle's view, is human happiness. In his conception of happiness, Aristotle was governed by the Greek ideal of moderation. Excess of pleasure would ultimately bring as much unhappiness as pain itself. The best life, like the best state, is characterized by balance and harmony. The happiest man is he who spent his life in contemplation; the philosopher fulfilled man's highest potential and is therefore the happiest of man.

Aristotle's method of investigation was based on observation and experiment, and he applied himself to almost all possible fields of inquiry. He and his students, through collection and examination of specimens, undertook an extensive biological classification. The definition and categorization of all aspects of physics, astronomy, logic, metaphysics, and even poetry also occupied his attention. In every field, his contribution was not surpassed for many centuries.

1.6 History

History as the systematic analysis of past events was a Greek creation. Herodotus (484—425 BC) was the author of *The Persian Wars*, a work commonly regarded as the first real history in Western civilization.

The central theme of Herodotus' work is the conflict between the Greeks and the Persians, which he viewed as a struggle between Greek freedom and Persian despotism. Herodotus traveled widely for his information and was dependent for his sources on what we today would call oral history. Although he was a master storyteller and sometimes included considerable fanciful material, Herodotus was also capable of exhibiting a critical attitude toward the materials he used. Regardless of its weaknesses, Herodotus' *History* is an important source of information on the Persians and our chief source on the Persian Wars.

Thucydides (460—400 BC) was a far better historian; in fact, historians consider him the greatest historian of the ancient Western world. Thucydides was an Athenian and a participant in the Peloponnesian War. He had been elected a general, but a defeat in battle led the Athenian assembly to send him into exile, which gave him the opportunity to concentrate on writing his

History of the Peloponnesian War.

Unlike Herodotus, Thucydides was not concerned with divine forces or gods as causal factors in history. He saw war and politics in purely rational terms, as the activities of human beings. He examined the causes of the Peloponnesian War in a clear and objective fashion, placing much emphasis on the accuracy of his facts.

1.7   Poetry and Drama

In the two centuries after Homer, the most important form of poetry was lyric, that is, poetry composed to be sung by an individual or by a chorus to the accompaniment of the lyre. The new poetry tended to be very personal in nature, especially when it was meant for an individual performer. One of the best-known lyric poets was Sappho (610—580 BC). Her large body of love poetry illustrates the worlds of difference, in both content and form, between this type of poetry and the earlier epics.

Lyric also took the form of choral epics, written to be performed at private celebrations like weddings, or at public festivals. The greatest of the poets who wrote choral works of this nature was Pindar (522—443 BC), most famous for his "victory odes". These choral odes dealt with the victor and his victory, but contained Pindar's own views on life and the gods.

The seminal development in the history of Greek poetry was the evolution of the choral odes performed at the festival of Dionysus at Athens. Originally the odes were about the god Dionysus and took the form of a dialogue between the chorus and the chorus leader. When the poet Thespis, in the late 600 BC, allowed the chorus leader to impersonate the character whose actions he had formerly just reported, drama was born. At about the same time, the tyrant Pisistratus (605—527 BC) initiated a drama contest at the annual festival. Officials chosen by the state selected three tragedians to submit plays to be performed before the Athenian populace. Each tragedian submitted a trilogy of tragedies and a satyr play to be performed without intermission. In the afternoon, comedies were presented. Each of ten judges, one from each tribe, wrote his choice of the best tragedian on a ballot. Five of the ballots were then drawn by lot, and the tragedian who received the most votes received an honorary award. The production of the plays involved a very large number of men and boys (women did not participate) and extensive rehearsals. The enterprise was financed by rich sponsors chosen by the state. Drama, like everything else, was a polis affair.

Tragedy became very popular all over Greece, but the Athenian festival, where no play could be performed twice, was the greatest stimulus for the creation of new plays. Of all the playwrights who submitted tragedies, the works of the only three have survived: Aeschylus, Sophocles, and Euripides. In their plays, we can see how the old poetic tradition was transformed to give expression to the classical Athenian ideal.

Aeschylus (525—456 BC) began writing in the early 500 BC. By adding a second actor to the single choral leader, he brought tragedy into existence as true drama. Dialogue between individual characters was till then possible and the intricacy and subtlety of the plays were vastly increased. The subject matter of his plays ranged from the myths of Greek religion to contemporary events like the Persian Wars. The purpose of his drama was not to tell a story but to explore a problem. For example, Aeschylus took as his subject the story of King Agamemnon—how he returned victorious from Troy only to be killed by his unfaithful wife, and how Orestes, their son, avenged his father by killing his mother. Aeschylus' purpose was not to describe a series of interesting events, nor to portray the character of Orestes. He took for his subject the problem of justice, the cessation of the destructive and never-ending series of retributions for murder with more murder. His answer to this problem was the divinely ordained but essentially human institution of law.

Sophocles (496—406 BC) was younger than Aeschylus but still his contemporary and often his rival at the annual content. In his earliest extant play, *Ajax*, the Sophoclean conception of tragedy is evident. In this play, the army of the Achaeans had voted to give the armor of the dead Achilles to Odysseus rather than to Ajax. Overcome with anger born of injured pride, Ajax decided to murder all the leaders of the army. But the goddess Athena diverted him with madness, and he killed the army's animals, thinking they were the generals. A failure, and debased by his action, Ajax committed suicide. Agamemnon and Menelaus, the leaders of the army, forbade the burial of the body. It is Odysseus, Ajax's archenemy, who convinced the generals that the greatness of Ajax required that he be properly buried in spite of his crimes. Through his contrast of Ajax's primitive concept of honor with

Odysseus' higher ideal, Sophocles was able to contrast sharply two human attitudes.

In the play *Oedipus Rex*, Sophocles goes even further in his exploration of human character. Before the action of the play begins, King Oedipus, through an inescapable fate, commits two terrible crimes: He kills his father and marries his mother. The action of the play revolves around the gradual unfolding of Oedipus' past before his eyes, until the immensity of his guilt drives him to blind himself. Tragically, it is his own uncompromising pursuit of the truth that illuminates his gruesome past. Although he is repeatedly warned not to hasten his fate by uncovering the truth, Oedipus presses his inquiries in the false and presumptuous hope that the truth will give him control of his destiny. This is hubris—the excessive pride that leads a man to believe that he can do something that is denied to him by his very humanity. To the Greeks, hubris was a crime greater than patricide or incest. Oedipus' punishment is to wander the earth as an exiled beggar, unable to see anything around him but forever conscious of the reality he dared to expose.

These plays illustrate Sophocles' conception that tragedy is played out within the individual. In *Ajax*, the character of the hero is revealed by the reactions of others to him—his brother, his concubine, his son, Odysseus, and the leaders of the army. In *Oedipus Rex*, the character of the tragic hero is revealed by the reports of other characters about his past life, a past whose meaning has been hidden from him. Given the order of the universe, each character is fated to pay the penalties for his own crimes—to suffer because of the limitations of his own nature.

Euripides (480—406 BC) has yet another approach to tragedy, differing from that of Aeschylus or Sophocles. In his play *Hippolytus*, for example, the tragedy stems from the unbalanced personality of the tragic hero. Hippolytus worships Artemis, the goddess of chastity, to the exclusion of Aphrodite, goddess of love. Aphrodite revenges herself by making his stepmother, Phaedra, fall in love with him. Phaedra kills herself in despair, claiming in a note to Theseus, her husband and Hippolytus' father, that his son has raped her. In his anger, Theseus calls down the wrath of Poseidon, god of the sea, who kills Hippolytus. In this play, all three major characters sin against the gods: Phaedra through an excess of passion, Hippolytus through an excess of purity and his devotion to one goddess to the exclusion of another, and

Theseus through his excessive anger. Each of the three represents an extreme in human character. These extremes are also reflected in the gods—Aphrodite, Artemis, and Poseidon—who represent psychological forces that possess man against his will.

In general, the classical tragedians took their material from traditional Greek mythology, but they altered that material to suit their purposes—to convey in a dramatic way the moral and rational potentialities of man. For example, Orestes, who in mythology is the prototype of the honorable avenger, was used by Aeschylus as the subject for a play whose theme is really the futility of private vengeance rather than the preservation of honor. In the play *Ajax*, Sophocles transformed Odysseus from the Homeric trickster into a truly wise man and used Ajax to exemplify a conception of honor far in advance of that of Achilles in the *Iliad*. In his epics, Homer characterized the gods in terms of their jealousies; but in Euripides' *Hippolytus*, the gods were enlarged and abstracted to become embodiments of universal psychological forces.

1.8　The Heritage of the Greeks

The civilization of the ancient Greeks is the fountainhead of Western culture, because the ancient Greeks are considered the first people to think critically about the dimensions of human nature. Socrates, Plato, and Aristotle established the foundations of Western philosophy. Herodotus and Thucydides created the discipline of history. Western literary forms are largely derived from Greek poetry and drama. Greek notions of harmony, proportion, and beauty have remained the touchstones for subsequent Western art. A rational method of inquiry, so important to modern science, was conceived in ancient Greece. Many political terms are of Greek origin, and so are Western concepts of the rights and duties of citizenship, especially as they were conceived in Athens, the first great democracy in world history. Athens gave the idea of democracy to the Western world. Especially during their classical period, the Greeks raised and debated the fundamental questions about the purpose of human existence, the structure of human society, and the nature of the universe that have concerned Western thinkers ever since.

Chapter 2   Ancient Rome:
Pragmatic Rationality

About 1000 BC, the Etruscans—a people of sailors, traders, farmers, cattle herders, and horse tamers—settled in where is Italy today. They were attracted by the warm weather and rich soil; they found tin, iron, clay, and timber there. They became, like the Greeks across the Adriatic Sea, a civilized people.

2.1   Roman Law

In many ways, Roman culture is a continuation of Greek culture. But the Romans had made their own contribution to Western civilization. One of Rome's chief gifts to the Mediterranean world of its day and to succeeding generations was its development of law. The Twelve Tables of 450 BC were the first codification of Roman law. The Twelve Tables, though inappropriate for later times, were never officially ended, and gave birth to Civil Law.

The Early Empire (14—180) experienced great progress in the study of and codification of the law. The second and early third centuries AD witnessed the "classical age of Roman law", a period in which a number of great jurists classified and compiled basic legal principles that have proved extremely valuable to the Western world. The identification of the law of nations with natural law led to a concept of natural rights. According to the jurist Ulpian (170—228), natural rights implied that all men are born equal and therefore be equal before the law. In practice, however, that principle was not applied. The Romans did, however, establish standards of justice applicable to all people, many of which we would immediately recognize. A person was regarded as innocent until proved otherwise. People accused of wrongdoing were allowed to defend themselves before a judge. A judge was expected to weigh evidence carefully before arriving at a decision. These principles lived on in Western civilization long after the fall of the Roman Empire.

2.2   Literature and Art

The Romans produced little literature before the third century BC, and the Latin literature that emerged in that century was strongly influenced by Greek models. The demand for plays at public festivals eventually led to a growing number of native playwrights. One of the best known was Plautus (254—184 BC), who used plots from Greek New Comedy for his own plays. The actors wore Greek costumes and Greek masks and portrayed the same basic stock characters: lecherous old man, skillful slaves, prostitutes, young men in love. Plautus wrote for the masses and became a very popular playwright in Rome.

In the last century of the Republic, the Romans began to produce a new poetry, less dependent on epic themes and more inclined to personal expressions. Latin poets were now able to use various Greek forms to express their own feelings about people, social and political life, and love. The finest example of this can be seen in the work of Catullus (87—54 BC), Rome's "best lyric poet" and one of the greatest in world literature.

Catullus became a master at adapting and refining Greek forms of poetry to express his emotions. He wrote a variety of poems on, among other things, political figures, social customs, the use of language, the death of his brother, and the travails of love. The ability of Catullus to express in simple fashion his intense feelings and curiosity about himself and his world had a noticeable impact on later Latin people.

The development of Roman prose was greatly aided by the practice of oratory. Romans had great respect for oratory since the ability to persuade people in public debate meant success in politics. Oratory was brought to perfection in a literary fashion by Cicero (106—43 BC), the best exemplar of the literary and intellectual interests of the senatorial elite of the late Republic and, indeed, the greatest prose writer of that period. For Cicero, oratory was not simply skillful speaking. An orator was a statesman, a man who achieved his highest goal by pursuing an active life in public affairs.

Later, when the turmoil of the late Republic forced him into semiretirement politically, Cicero became more interested in the writing of philosophical treatises. He was not an original thinker but served a most valuable purpose for Roman society by popularizing and making understandable the works of Greek philosophers. In his philosophical works, Cicero, more than anyone else, transmitted the classical intellectual heritage to the Western world. Cicero's original contributions came in the field of politics. His works *On the Laws* and *On the Republic* provided fresh insights into political thought. His emphasis on the need to pursue an active life to benefit and improve humankind would greatly influence the later Italian Renaissance.

The high point of Latin literature was reached in the time of Augustus. The literary accomplishments of the Augustan Age were such that the period has been called the golden age of Latin literature.

The most distinguished poet of the Augustan Age was Virgil (70—19 BC). The son of a small landholder in northern Italy, he welcomed the rule of Augustus and wrote his greatest work in the emperor's honor. Virgil's masterpiece was the *Aeneid*, an epic poem clearly meant to rival the work of Homer. The connection between Troy and Rome is made explicitly. Aeneas, the son of Anchises of Troy, survives the destruction of Troy and eventually settles in Latium; hence Roman civilization is linked to Greek history. The character of Aeneas is portrayed as the ideal Roman—his virtues are duty, piety, and faithfulness. Virgil's overall purpose was to show that Aeneas had fulfilled his mission to establish the Romans in Italy and thereby start Rome on its divine mission to rule the world.

Another prominent Augustan poet was Horace (65—8 BC), a friend of Virgil's. Horace was a very sophisticated writer whose overriding concern was to point out to his contemporaries the "follies and vices of his age". In the *Satires*, a medley of poems on a variety of subjects, Horace is revealed as a detached observer of human weaknesses. He directed his attacks against movements, not living people, and took on such subjects as sexual immorality, greed, and job dissatisfaction. Horace mostly laughed at the weaknesses of humankind and called for forbearance.

The last of the great poets of the golden age was Ovid (43 BC—AD 18). He belonged to a youthful, privileged social group in Rome that liked to ridicule old Roman values. In keeping with the spirit of this group, Ovid wrote a frivolous series of love poems known as the *Amores*. Intended to entertain and shock, they achieved their goal. Another of Ovid's works was *The Art of*

Love, which was essentially a handbook on the seduction of women.

The most famous Latin prose work of the golden age was written by the historian Livy (59 BC—AD 17). Livy's masterpiece was his *History of Rome* from the foundation of the city to 9 BC. Only 35 of the original 142 books have survived. Livy perceived history in terms of moral lessons. For Livy, human character is the determining factor in history.

Livy's history celebrated Rome's greatness. He not only revealed the character of the chief figures but also demonstrated the virtues that had made Rome great. Though not concerned about the factual accuracy of his stories, he is an excellent storyteller, and his work remained the standard history of Rome for centuries.

The century and a half after Augustus is often labeled the "silver age of Latin literature" to indicate that the literary efforts of the period, though good, were not equal to the high standards of the Augustan golden age. The popularity of rhetorical training encouraged the use of clever literary expressions at the expense of original content. A good example of this trend can be found in the works of Seneca.

Educated in Rome, Seneca (4 BC—AD 65) became strongly attached to the philosophy of Stoicism. In letters written to a young friend, he expressed the basic tenets of Stoicism: living according to nature, accepting events dispassionately as part of the divine plan, and universal love for all humanity. His letters show humanity, benevolence, and fortitude, but his sentiments are often undermined by an attempt to be clever with words.

The greatest historian of the silver age was Tacitus (56—120). His main works included the *Annals* and *Histories*, which presented a narrative account of Roman history from the reign of Tiberius through the assassination of Domitian (14—96). Tacitus believed that history has a moral purpose. As a member of the senatorial class, Tacitus was disgusted with the abuses of power perpetrated by the emperors and was determined that the "evil deeds" of wicked men would not be forgotten. His work *Germania* is especially important as a source of information about the early Germans. But it is colored by Tacitus' attempt to show the Germans as noble savage in comparison with the decadent Romans.

The Romans were also dependent on the Greeks for artistic inspiration. During the third and second centuries BC, they adopted many features of the

Hellenistic style of art. The Romans developed a taste for Greek statues, which they placed not only in public buildings but also in their homes. Once demand outstripped the supply of original works, reproductions of Greek statues became fashionable. The Romans' own portrait sculpture was characterized by an intense realism that included even unpleasant physical details. Wall paintings and frescoes in the houses of the rich realistically depicted landscapes, portraits, and scenes from mythological stories.

The Romans excelled in architecture, a highly practical art. Although they continued to employ Greek styles and made use of colonnades, rectangular structures, and post-and-lintel construction, the Romans were also innovative. They made considerable use of curvilinear forms: the arch, vault, and dome. The Romans were also the first people in antiquity to use concrete on an enormous scale. By combining concrete and curvilinear forms, they were able to construct massive buildings—public baths and amphitheaters, the most famous of which was the Coliseum in Rome, capable of seating fifty thousand spectators. These large buildings were made possible by Roman engineering skills. These same skills were put to use in constructing roads (the Romans built a network of 50,000 miles of roads throughout their empire), aqueducts (in Rome, almost a dozen aqueducts kept a population of one million supplied with water), and bridges.

2.3 The Heritage of the Romans

The Roman Republic had created one of the largest empires in antiquity, but it suffered from overexpansion. The Western Roman Empire eventually collapsed in the face of invasions by the Germanic peoples, but Roman achievements were bequeathed to the future. The Romance languages of today (French, Italian, Spanish, Portuguese, and Romanian) are based on Latin. The Roman legal code, the Twelve Tables, began the sophisticated legal system to which Western practices of impartial justice and trial by jury owe so much. As great builders, the Romans left monuments to their skills throughout Europe, some of which, such as aqueducts and roads, are still in use today. Aspects of Roman administrative practices survived in the Western world for centuries. The Romans also preserved the intellectual heritage of the Greco-Roman world of antiquity.

Chapter 3　The Middle Ages:
Duty of Conscience

The great civilizations of Ancient Greece and Rome are usually taken as the starting points of Western culture. Although these civilizations encompassed vast territories, their intellectual, political, and creative centers were two cities—Athens and Rome. Following the collapse of the Roman Empire in 476, however, Western civilization took a radically different course and entered the period we now call the Middle Ages.

The Middle Ages comprise roughly the thousand years between 500 and 1500, during which Greco-Roman culture fused with the Christian religion. Beginning with the fall of Rome and ending with the turmoil of the Protestant Reformation, the medieval centuries were shaped by the Christian Church and the political and socio-economic structures of feudalism and divine monarchy. Throughout the Middle Ages, Christianity became the unifying force in Western civilization, and the Western world regarded itself as a Christian kingdom—"Christendom".

3.1　The Rise of Christianity

The rise of Christianity marks a fundamental break with the dominant values of the Greco-Roman world. Christian views of God, human beings, and the world were quite different from those of the Greeks and Romans.

In Hellenistic times (from the death of Alexander the Great in 323 BC until the accession of the Roman emperor Augustus in 27 BC), the Jewish people had been granted considerable independence by their Seleucid rulers. Roman involvement with the Jews began in 63 BC, and by AD 6, Judaea had been made a province and placed under the direction of a Roman procurator. But unrest continued, augmented by divisions among the Jews themselves.

The Sadducees favored a rigid adherence to Hebrew law, rejected the possibility of personal immortality, and favored cooperation with the Romans. The Pharisees followed a strict adherence to Jewish ritual, and although they wanted Judaea to be free from Roman control, they did not advocate violent means to achieve this goal. The Essenes were a Jewish sect that lived in a religious community near the Dead Sea. As revealed in the Dead Sea Scrolls, a collection of documents first discovered in 1947, the Essenes, like many other Jews, awaited a Messiah who would save Israel from oppression, usher in the kingdom of God, and establish a true paradise on earth. The Zealots were militant extremists who advocated the violent overthrow of Roman rule. A Jewish revolt in AD 66 was crushed by the Romans four years later. The Jewish Temple in Jerusalem was destroyed, and Roman power once more stood supreme in Judaea.

In the midst of the confusion and conflicts in Judaea, Jesus of Nazareth (6 BC—AD 29) began his public preaching. Jesus grew up in Galilee, an important center of the militant Zealots. Jesus' message was straightforward: The Kingdom of God is imminent and the individual has to turn away from all extraneous demands and put himself in complete obedience to the will of God. God's command is simple—to love God and one another. In the Sermon on the Mount, Jesus presented the ethical concepts—humility, charity, and brotherly love—that would form the basis for the value system of medieval Western civilization. As we have seen, these were not the values of Classical Greco-Roman civilization.

Although some people welcomed Jesus as the Messiah who would save Israel from oppression and establish God's kingdom on earth, Jesus spoke of a heavenly kingdom, not an earthly one. In this he disappointed the radicals. At the same time, conservative religious leaders believed Jesus was another false Messiah who was undermining respect for traditional Jewish religion. To the Roman authorities of Palestine and their local allies, Jesus was a potential revolutionary who might transform Jewish expectations of a messiah kingdom into a revolt against Rome. Therefore, Jesus found himself denounced on many sides and was given over to the Roman authorities. The procurator Pontius Pilate ordered his crucifixion. But that did not solve the problem. A few loyal followers of Jesus spread the story that Jesus had overcome death, had been resurrected, and had then ascended into heaven. The belief in Jesus' resurrection became an important tenet of Christian doctrine. Jesus was now hailed as the "anointed one", the Messiah who would return and usher in the kingdom of God on earth.

Christianity began, then, as a religious movement within Judaism and was viewed that way by Roman authorities for many decades. Although tradition holds that one of Jesus' disciples, Peter, founded the Christian church at Rome, the most important figure in early Christianity after Jesus was Paul of Tarsus (5—67). Paul reached out to non-Jews and transformed Christianity from a Jewish sect into a broader religious movement. Called the "second founder of Christianity", Paul was a Jewish Roman citizen who had been strongly influenced by Hellenistic Greek culture. He believed that the message of Jesus should be preached not only to Jews but to Gentiles (non-Jews) as well. Paul was responsible for founding Christian communities throughout Asia Minor and along the shores of the Aegean.

It was Paul who provided a universal foundation for the spread of Jesus' ideas. He taught that Jesus was, in effect, a savior-God, the son of God, who had come to earth to save all humans who were basically sinners as a result of Adam's original sin of disobedience against God. By his death, Jesus had atoned for the sins of all humans and made it possible for all men and women to experience a new beginning with the potential for individual salvation. By accepting Jesus Christ as their Savior, they too could be saved.

Although some of the fundamental values of Christianity differed markedly from those of the Greco-Roman world, the Romans initially did not pay much attention to the Christians, whom they regarded at first as simply another sect of Judaism. The structure of the Roman Empire itself aided the growth of Christianity. Christian missionaries, including some of Jesus' original twelve disciples, or apostles, used Roman roads to travel throughout the empire spreading their "good news".

As time passed, however, the Roman attitude toward Christianity began to change. The Romans were tolerant of other religions except when they threatened public order or public morals. Many Romans came to view Christians as harmful to the social order of the Roman state. Because Christians held their meetings in secret and seemed to be connected to Christian groups in other areas, the government could view them as potentially dangerous to the state.

Some Romans felt that Christians were overly exclusive and hence harmful to the community and public order. The Christians did not recognize other gods and therefore refused to join in public festivals honoring these divinities. Finally, Christians refused to participate in the worship of the state god and imperial cult. Since the Romans regarded these as important to the state, the Christians' refusal undermined the state security and hence constituted an act of treason, punishable by death. But to the Christians, who believed there was only one real God, the worship of state gods and the emperors was idolatry and would endanger their own salvation.

Roman persecution of Christians in the first and second centuries was only sporadic and local, and had little to stop the growth of Christianity. It had, in fact, served to strengthen Christianity as an institution in the second and third centuries by causing it to shed the loose structure of the first century and move toward a more centralized organization of its various church communities. Crucial to this change was the emerging role of the bishops, who began to assume more control over church communities. The Christian church was creating a well-defined hierarchical structure in which the bishops and clergy were salaried officers separate from the laity or regular church members.

Christianity grew slowly in the first century, took root in the second, and had spread widely by the third. Why was Christianity able to attract so many followers? First of all, the Christian message had much to offer the Roman world. The promise of salvation, made possible by Jesus' death and resurrection, had immense appeal in a world full of suffering and injustice. Christianity seemed to imbue life with a meaning and purpose beyond the simple material things of everyday reality. Second, Christianity was not entirely unfamiliar. It could be viewed as simply another eastern mystery religion, offering immortality as the result of the sacrificial death of a savior-God. At the same time, it offered advantages that the other mystery religions lacked. Jesus had been a human figure, not a mythological one, such as Mithras. Moreover, Christianity had universal appeal. Unlike Mithraism, it was not restricted to men. Furthermore, it did not require a painful or expensive initiation rite as other mystery religions did. Initiation was accompanied simply by baptism—a purification by water—by which one entered a personal relationship with Jesus. In addition, Christianity gave new meaning to life and offered what the Roman state religion could not—a personal relationship with God and a link to the higher worlds.

Finally, Christianity fulfilled the human need to belong. Christian formed communities bound to one another in which people could express their love by helping each other and offering assistance to the poor, the sick, widows, and orphans. Christianity satisfied the need to belong in a way that the huge, impersonal, and remote Roman Empire could never do.

Christianity proved attractive to all classes. The promise of eternal life was for all—rich, poor, aristocrats, slaves, men, and women. Although it did not call for revolution or social upheaval, Christianity emphasized a sense of spiritual equality for all people.

As the Christian church became more organized, some emperors in the third century responded with more systematic persecutions, but their schemes failed to work. The last great persecution was by Diocletian at the beginning of the fourth century. But even he had to admit what had become apparent in the course of the third century—Christianity had become too strong to be eradicated by force.

In the fourth century, Christianity flourished after Constantine became the first Christian emperor. According to the traditional story, before a crucial battle, he saw a vision of a Christian cross with the writing, "In this sign you will conquer. " Having won the battle, Constantine was convinced of the power of the Christian God. Although he was not baptized until the end of his life, in 313 he issued the famous Edict of Milan officially tolerating the existence of Christianity. Under Theodosius the Great (378—395), it was made the official religion of the Roman Empire. Christianity had triumphed.

3.2 Patristic Writers

The victory of the Christian Church was not confined to the religious sphere. One of the greatest battles of the fourth century was fought in the realm of ideas. The adversaries were pagan classical culture, with all its beauty and sophistication, and the new teachings of the Christian Church. For many, the contradictory, unsophisticated writings in the Bible and in the early church literature were no match for the logic of Plato or the beauty of expression of Virgil. In the fourth century the Church made great advances toward a truce with pagan thought. Church leaders succeeded in winning over the educated elite of the Roman world, not by denying the validity of Platonic doctrine or the beauty of classical poetry but by showing that the classical tradition was merely the forerunner of a higher truth. By casting their defense of Christianity in classical terms, by accepting classical education as the basis for Christian education, and by incorporating some elements of pagan thought into Christian orthodoxy, they put Christian doctrine into terms which were appealing to the Roman elite. At the same time, church scholars also perpetuated the classical tradition, so that when Roman political power was submerged in the barbarian invasions, the works of the classical writers were passed on into the culture of the Middle Ages and eventually preserved for the modern world.

Fortunately for the Church, there appeared in the fourth century a group of Christian writers who were capable of undertaking the task of explaining and justifying Christianity in the eyes of pagan world. Eusebius (264—340), the biographer of Constantine, was an ardent admirer of the great emperor as well as a devout Christian. He saw history as proof of the validity of the Christian position. The Empire and the Church had been born at the same time, and their destinies were joined. Constantine was the agent of God, sent to save the Empire. Just as the paganism of the Empire was seen as the source of its woes, so Christianity was hailed as the source of its rebirth.

The great scholars and thinkers of the late fourth century did not share Eusebius' optimistic view of the world, but they did see Christianity as the source of salvation for mankind. St. Jerome (347—420) was trained in classical humanism and became a master of the Latin language. After a dream in which he was castigated by God for his love of Cicero, Jerome repented his devotion to classical literature and retreated to the desert to do penance. When he returned to civilization, he resumed his reading of classical authors, but he also translated the Bible into Latin, in the Vulgate version that became authoritative for the Catholic Church.

St. Augustine (354—430) suffered many intellectual crises and passed through several spiritual stages—including adherence to heretical Manichaeism and to neo-Platonism—before he resigned his position as a teacher of rhetoric to become a great Christian bishop in northern Africa. His *Confessions* related his great struggles of conscience, and his numerous other writings encompass almost every phase of Christian concern. St. Ambrose (339—397) was a Roman aristocrat who was bishop of Milan during the reign of Theodosius the

Great. He had been an imperial official until he was acclaimed bishop by the people of Milan. He not only wrote in defense of Christianity but disciplined the emperor himself from his pulpit. The work of these Latin Church Fathers—Augustine, Ambrose, Jerome—and other great writers of the late Roman Empire laid the foundation upon which the medieval Church built its elaboration of Christian doctrine.

The first task of the patristic writers was to justify the Christian Scriptures, which the Church held to be the absolutely true word of God. The Jewish philosopher Philo Judaeus (30 BC—AD 50) had been a pioneer in the attempt to reconcile classical philosophy and the Old Testament. The patristic writers continued this approach through their commentaries on the Old and New Testaments. Allegorical interpretations were used to show that in most cases there was agreement between the two traditions. In some cases it was shown that the assertions of classical authors had been superseded by the higher authority of the word of God.

Far from denying classical literature, the Church used it as the basis of its educational system. The writings of Virgil and Cicero were considered the first steps to Christian education. Christian children of the Roman nobility attended the classical schools. The study of rhetoric and other parts of the classical curriculum were transmitted to the Middle Ages, where they continued to form the basis of a Christian education. After a Christian student had mastered the prescribed classics, he went on to study theology.

Just as it was necessary to show the ground for the authority of the Scriptures, the authority of the Church also had to be justified. In the absence of a clearly defined orthodox position, a wide divergence of views about theological matters and the question of the nature of the Church threatened to break fourth-century Christianity into a multitude of different groups. The question of the nature of the Church was resolved in the attempt to deal with the Donatist heresy. Diocletian had conducted a short-lived but intense persecution of the Christians, and a number of Christian clerics had chosen to accept the rather easy terms offered to those who denied their Christian beliefs. The Donatists held that these priests, or any priests who had sinned, were no longer capable of administrating the sacraments, and that a priest must be in a state of grace in order that a sacrament be valid. Donatism was especially widespread in Africa, where St. Augustine, who was bishop of Hippo, was faced with a possible schism.

Augustine held that any sacrament was valid as long as the priest was ordained by the Church. Even if he was sinful, he could still administrate the sacraments. Augustine further held that if the Donatist would not come back into the Church voluntarily, the power of the state should be used to compel them to do so. The Donatists regarded the Church as a community of the elect, while Augustine and the orthodox position viewed it as a universal institution which would necessarily have within it some sinners. The division between saints and sinners would be made by God at the Last Judgment. This became the doctrine of the medieval Christian church.

The Christians had a great advantage over pagan religions in that they could claim historical validity for the otherwise supernatural constituents of religious belief. The birth of Christ necessarily came to be viewed by Christian writers as the most significant event in history. The Christian view also necessarily had to divorce itself from a nationalistic view of history or from any history written within narrow chronological limits. For many Greek and Roman thinkers, history was essentially a repeating cycle of events. The classical world also tended to view history as a record of one particular nation or people. Every act in history was important, either because it was typical of mankind in general or because it revealed the destiny of a nation. But the Christian idea of history was a theory of universal history: The history of the world was a linear progression from the beginning to the end of time. Each event was unique, and while it might represent universal human experience, it was non-repeatable. At the same time, Christian history was the history of all men; it was not attached to any one nation or institution.

The Christian conception of history which was accepted in the Middle Ages was essentially that of St. Augustine. While Eusebius could write early in the fourth century of the reconstruction of the Empire as the fruit of Christian victory, in Augustine's time at the end of the century there was chaos and disaster on every hand. The pagans said that the gods were angry because of the triumph of Christianity. In *The City of God*, Augustine set out to prove that it was the sinfulness of the Empire, not the neglect of pagan gods, which brought disaster. More important, he outlined a highly sophisticated philosophy of history as the basis for his views. History, according to Augustine, was the working-out of God's divine plan in the temporal world. It began with the creation of Adam, the first man, and had passed through six stages based on the Old Testament version of history. The beginning of the last stage was marked by the birth of Christ. After the reign of Antichrist would come the Last Judgment.

The significance of history lay in the working-out of the destinies of the two cities, the heavenly city populated by those chosen by God, and the earthly city, loyal to the devil. At the Last Judgment the heavenly city would be resurrected to an eternal life, while the earthly city, the city of the devil, would suffer the terrors of hell. Augustine held that man could never know the details of God's divine plan, but all would be revealed on the Last Day. Thus Augustine answered the pagan view of history by offering an alternative view based on the Scriptures.

The Christian view of the state had been relatively simple in the days before the conversion of Constantine. For Paul, the state was merely a necessary institution irrelevant to Christianity. But Constantine was a Christian emperor, the representative of God on earth. The Christian Roman Empire presented a more complicated problem to the thinkers of the fourth century. Eusebius had held that Constantine was God's representative on earth, and that his actions, which were carrying out God's will, were good. Constantine called church councils, presided at them, and pronounced decisions on church doctrine. He considered himself the priest of those outside the Church. For Eusebius, church and state were irrevocably joined in a common cause—the fight against devil and error. They were inseparable, and at the top stood the emperor. This was the beginning of the so-called Caesaropapist view of the relations between church and state that was perpetuated in medieval Constantinople.

Augustine, who lived in a different period, held a much more complex view. In *The City of God* he vehemently claimed that the state, in and of itself, was a "band of robbers". Augustine did believe that the state might provide a kind of temporal order necessary to peace and security, but he was convinced that it was a purely functional institution with no ultimate end in itself. It could be the product of an evil as well as a good human will. For Augustine, even the Church was no guarantor of salvation; salvation was a matter between God and the individual conscience. The institution was incidental to the fundamental relationship between God and each man.

St. Augustine's view of the relationship between church and state, when further defined, became the basis for the medieval view. When Theodosius I had seven thousand civilians in Thessalonica executed as punishment for the lynching of an imperial official, Ambrose refused to allow the emperor to take communion until he repented and did a long penance. Theodosius accepted Ambrose's authority and his judgment. Ambrose was called to discipline the pious Theodosius on other occasions, and he justified his actions on the grounds that in spiritual matters even the emperor was no more than a layman subject to the authority of a priest. Since he, as priest, was responsible for Theodosius' soul, he had the right to discipline him. Thus Ambrose established a precedent for ecclesiastical intervention in affairs of state.

The Christian concept of morality was also shaped by the patristic writers. Their ideal Christian was a saint who coupled chastity and asceticism with deep and unwavering faith in God. Augustine's view of predestination presented certain difficulties for the view that man had a sinful will: How could God have willed the damnation of the majority of mankind? It was held that while God knew in advance all that would happen, man acted according to his own free will and was therefore responsible for his actions. Humans were responsible for their own damnation, God for their salvation.

Early Christians had held that the commission of sin after baptism necessarily brought damnation. As a result, many Christians waited until they were near death before receiving the sacraments. To replace this rather unworkable doctrine, the Church, at Augustine's urging, substituted the practice of penance. Baptism was undertaken while the Christian was still a child, and subsequent sins were atoned for by repentance and penance. This practice helped to transform the ecclesiastical structure from a community of saints to a universal Church, since it was possible to err and still return to the Church.

By the end of the fourth century, Christian writers had explicated Christian theology in terms which were understandable and appealing to the world of the fourth century. While pagan philosophy languished with the decline of the vitality of the Empire, the cultural achievement of the Christian writers, their brilliant style, and their intellectual merit made Christianity an attractive alternative to the pagan view of the world. They also laid the groundwork for medieval theology and culture.

When St. Augustine died at Hippo in 430, the city was about to fall to the Vandals. The Roman Empire in the West was in its last fight for survival, but the Christian Church was a dynamic institution which was just beginning to exercise its potential leadership in Western civilization.

3.3 Thomas Aquinas

The importance of Christianity in medieval society probably made it certain that theology would play a central role in the European intellectual world. Beginning in the eleventh century, the effort to apply reason or logical analysis to the Church's basic doctrines had a significant impact on the study of theology. The word *scholasticism* is used to refer to the philosophical and theological system of the medieval schools. A primary preoccupation of scholasticism was the attempt to reconcile faith and reason—to demonstrate that what was accepted on faith was in harmony with what could be learned by reason.

Scholasticism had its beginnings in the theological world of the eleventh and twelfth centuries but reached its high point in the thirteenth century. The overriding task of scholasticism in the thirteenth century was to harmonize Christian revelation with the work of Aristotle. The most famous attempt to reconcile Aristotle and the doctrines of Christianity was that of Saint Thomas Aquinas.

Thomas Aquinas (1225—1274) studied theology at Cologne and Paris and taught at both Naples and Paris, and it was at the latter that he finished his famous *Summa Theologica*. Aquinas resolved the problems of late twelfth-century theology in a paradoxical way; he arrived at the conclusion propounded by St. Augustine and the Christian neo-Platonists, but he reached them by way of Aristotelian science and logic. His enemies accused him of Averroism, but Aquinas believed that the study of Aristotle need not lead to the conclusions reached by the Arabic philosopher and commentator on Aristotle. Averroes (1126—1198) had concluded that the teachings of Greek science and philosophy could not be reconciled with revelation, and this Aerroist doctrine gained important adherents in Christian Europe. St. Thomas denied the "double truth" of science and faith; he insisted that Christian theology was compatible with rational logic and could in fact be proved by it.

The Thomistic system rests on the belief that man's knowledge is building out of his sense experience, not by his mystical participation in "pure" Platonic ideals. Since human knowledge is firmly based in the facts of the real world, man can trust his logic to prove various theological principles. Aquinas admitted that not all Christian doctrine can be proved by logic, but he insisted on the validity of his proofs of the existence of God and some of His attributes. Aquinas' five proofs for the existence of God are based on the Aristotelian necessity of a "first cause", and his teaching of Christian morality is based on Aristotelian ethics.

Although Thomism is the official philosophy of the modern Roman Catholic Church, the contemporaries of St. Thomas did not readily accept his work. Chief among his critics were the Franciscan philosophers. St. Bonaventura (1221—1274) reasserted the Platonic-Augustinian position in a great treatise which denied Aquinas' "mechanistic" Deity and reemphasized the grace of God and the primacy of will—or love—over intellect. St. Bonaventura and the other Franciscan philosophers expressed a persistent anti-intellectual strain. The New Piety had been taken into the Church and had found expression in the Franciscan order.

The Franciscan movement was enormously popular in the thirteenth century; it attracted able minds as well as mass devotion. Its dissatisfaction with Aristotelianism gave the movement considerable influence on men who have been considered the first modern scientists. Men like Robert Grosseteste (1168—1253) and the Oxford friar Roger Bacon (1214—1294) were inclined to separate faith and science, and with their Platonic view of a universe of perfect, mathematically proportioned forms, they eventually followed paths of inquiry more fruitful than those of Aristotelian science, which had been firmly linked to Christian revelation by the work of Thomas Aquinas.

Aquinas departed from the Augustinian position in political as well as theological philosophy. Early Christian thinkers viewed the state as morally negative, and throughout the early Middle Ages the state had been valued only for the help it might give in the establishment of *The City of God*. Church political theory was Augustinian: The state was viewed as the servant of the Church. As the realities of royal power became more obvious, however, political thinkers tried to find justification for the continuing entrenchment of the secular arm. Again, Aquinas' starting-point was the work of Aristotle; he accepted the Greek view of the state as a moral necessity and of man as a political being. St. Thomas attempted to integrate the moral quality of the state with aspects of the Augustinian tradition, that is, to preserve the supremacy of the Church. This he accomplished through his philosophy of law: He believed that secular law which conformed to natural law (a reflection of divine law) had the moral sanction of God's will.

The relations between monarchy and church in the thirteenth century seemed to uphold political Thomism; the saintly kings, Henry Ⅲ of England and Louis Ⅸ of France, were ideal Christian monarchs whose law clearly reflected the divine will. Church and state appeared to be successfully working together to express God's will, but within the careful equilibrium were weakness and discrepancies which would reveal themselves in the years to come.

Chapter 4   The Renaissance:
Human Life in This World

From 1350 to 1600 Western civilization went through a period called the Renaissance, which is traditionally seen as ending the Middle Ages and beginning modern times. It was the era of European culture that saw the death of feudalism and the growth of nationalism. It witnessed the end of the unilateral power of the medieval church and the beginning of the modern nation-state.

4.1   The Italian Renaissance

The Renaissance started in Italy in the fourteenth century, where many were conscious of a decisive break with the past and where wider social circles were affected by the changes. The revival of interest in classical rhetoric (particularly Ciceronian), Roman history, and ancient poetry marked a break with the medieval world view, as did the flowering of vernacular literature and the discovery and exploitation of natural (not allegorical), spatial, and human dimensions in art. During the Renaissance, intellectual and artistic achievements were appreciated for their own sake, not with a view to any spiritual end. The quality of the art, not only its message, was what the Italians valued. A few outstanding artists and writers, such as Giotto di Bondone (cf. 1267—1337), Dante Alighieri(1265—1321), Francisco Petrarch (1304—1374), and Giovanni Boccaccio (1313—1375), pioneered the study of ancient art and letters and the creative expression of subjective feelings, and their work developed into a cultural style which was eagerly emulated by the Italian upper classes.

The essentials of the Italian cultural style of the fourteenth, fifteenth, and sixteenth centuries are closely identified with the movement known as humanism. The term *humanism* has been used to denote many kinds of ideas and activities, but it has two major and compatible meanings. First, there is social or civic humanism, which describes the outlook of the upper middle class in the Italian cities during the Renaissance. The upper bourgeoisie, glorying in its new political power, expressed its independence by placing great emphasis on human autonomy and on the value and grandeur of the city-state. The new class imitated the French aristocracy of the thirteenth century, taking up the aristocratic education, style, and courtly life which they considered suitable to their own emancipation and to their equality with the northern aristocrats. Social humanism inspired a passionate civic patriotism, a belief that all urban resources should be applied to the defense and beautification of the republican commune.

The second major aspect of humanism developed in both northern Europe and Italy. This was the intellectual movement, based on neo-Platonic philosophy, which emphasized the primacy of human values and intellectual creativity over feudal and ecclesiastical traditions and institutions. Humanist philosophers believed the human mind to be capable of defending for itself without reliance on traditional authority. In both its social and its intellectual aspects, humanism drew strength and inspiration from the Greek and Roman classics, which taught the value of the city-state and its self-governing urban elite and upheld the critical powers of the individual human mind.

Both northern and Italian humanists applied their learning and philosophy to study of the Scriptures as well as the ancient classics, bringing their individual intellectual powers and broad education to theological problems hitherto left to ecclesiastical authorities. Contrary to common assumptions, most Italian humanists were devout Christians, enthusiastic about the possibility of applying critical methods to Biblical studies. Many of them aimed at some form of Christian Platonism. The humanist emphasis on individualism did not necessarily result in secularism; it was also directed toward mysticism, which emphasizes an individual, personal relationship to God. Humanists were not necessarily antipapal; in fact, Rome became an intellectual and artistic center during the Renaissance. In the late fifteenth and the sixteenth century, several popes—notably Pius II —were humanists themselves as well as patrons of the arts.

Thus the term *humanism*, which is used to characterize an international intellectual and philosophical movement that was particularly suited to the Italian elite, denoted not only the study of the humanities but certain assumptions about man's place in the universe and the proper direction of human moral and rational capacities. Scholars in the Middle Ages became familiar with the classical tradition but saw it ultimately as an alien and pagan view of the world. People of the Renaissance were able to study that tradition fully for the first time. Humanism advocated an educational system in which classical studies were the curriculum for moral as well as intellectual training.

The culture of the Italian Renaissance was closely tied to conditions in fourteenth-century and fifteenth-century Italy. The wealth of Italy, the matrix of social relationships, the character of political life in the Italian city-state, and the more remote impact of Roman cultural traditions all played important roles in shaping the character of the Italian cultural revolution. The character of Italian society allowed the Renaissance to develop as a pervasive cultural mode rather than the isolated expression of a few geniuses. For every Petrarch or Giotto, there were hundreds of lesser men who studied and imitated their works or served as patrons of art and letters.

The two aspects of Italian society that most clearly distinguished Italy from the rest of Europe were wealth—its quantity and the means by which it was amassed—and the political structure of the city-state. By the latter part of the thirteenth century, Italy possessed a money economy based on trade and finance. The late thirteenth and early fourteenth centuries saw the rise of the great banking houses. The Pope was the bankers' largest single customer in Europe, since he needed an agency for the deposit and transfer of vast church funds. Money was lent in sometimes staggering sums to kings and merchants and nobles. Often the banks had widespread trading connections in addition to their purely financial interests.

Next to the bankers in magnitude of wealth were the international merchants, and below them the lesser traders and merchants. The merchant-artisan was in a separate and lower class, although he prided himself on his superiority to the wretched workers, living on the wages of industry, whose misery made them a frequent source of disorder. The man of means invested in land—often extensively—but land was not a primary source of the fortunes of the wealthy Italian families of the fourteenth and fifteenth centuries.

The elite of Italian society differed in many ways from the feudal nobility of northern Europe. Neither a life of leisure nor the security of heredity played as pervasive a role among the upper class in Italy as it did in northern Europe. French noblemen had for centuries lived as courtiers on the income from landed estates and offices, but Italian wealth was not so stable. One generation, or even a few years, could destroy a mercantile enterprise which had been built up with endless pains. Furthermore, the vicissitudes of business had a powerful impact on the income of wealthy Italian families—economic disasters were common liabilities in Italian life. This means that even the wealthiest families needed heirs with the ability to handle family finances, and sons of great magnates were trained for business enterprise. Careers in civil or canon law or international commerce were considered important, for they were the necessary foundation for economic and social prominence.

The fluid and sometimes fortuitous nature of wealth had a profound impact upon social relationships. While at any one time a few great families held sway at the top of Italian society, there was a fair amount of social mobility in Italian life. The oldest families with the "best blood" were not always the wealthiest and often traded their good breeding for the cold cash of the nouveaux riches through marriage. Every city had its share of self-made men who in a single lifetime were able to amass wealth and power through ability and energy. There might also be vast disparity between the wealth and prestige of different branches of the same family. Few men felt secure enough to consume the family fortunes placidly: The life of an Italian noble was filled with activity and struggle.

The political structure of the Italian cities also had a significant effect on social and cultural life. In the tyrannies established in the late fourteenth and the fifteenth century, effective political and military power in a city-state rested in the hands of one man. The political stability so essential to the well-being of the merchant could collapse overnight with the tyrant's death or defeat. At the same time, the ordinary merchant was isolated from political life. Policy and power were the domain of the prince and his personal associates—his court. The prince gathered around him those who were useful because of their practical abilities or desirable because of the luster they could add to his image.

The general character of Italian courtly life has been preserved in Castiglione's *The Book of the Courtier*, which was published in 1528. It is set in the court of Urbino, where the ladies and gentlemen of the court settle upon the task of describing the perfect courtier. The dialogue itself illustrates the value put upon style in speech and behavior. The courtier was above all a gentleman—a man of good breeding, physically attractive, and accomplished in all things. He was a good warrior, proficient at games and tournaments, and a man of art and letters. Good at everything, he yet must refrain from obvious effort, from an excess of enthusiasm, and from boasting. It was quite respectable to finish the race in the middle of the field, though never last. The search for honor and glory must not mar the effect of graceful speech and conduct.

The Renaissance gentleman in Castiglione's portrait differs from the chivalric knight of medieval tradition in his intellectual pursuits, the careful rhetorical style of his speech, his easy reference to Cicero, Aristotle, and the ancient heroes, and his sophisticated opinions on the writings of Petrarch and Dante and the paintings and sculptures of Giotto, Michelangelo, and Raphael. He differed from the ideal Christian knight in his preoccupation with finite rewards: his own glory and advancement and that of his patron. The ultimate function of the courtier was to guide his patron by personal excellence and sound advice.

The late fifteenth-century popes, many of whom were noted humanists, established great Renaissance courts peopled with leading writers and artists. St. Peter's Church and the papal library, among other Roman monuments, attested to the wealth and the exquisite taste of the popes who were poets and patrons rather than saints.

Both the princely courts and the Italian republics regarded themselves as continuators of the Roman political tradition. While the princes were the heirs of the Caesars, bringing peace and civilization out of chaos and ignorance, the republics sought to restore the glories of the Roman Republic, so beautifully idealized in the writings of Cicero. The greatest flowering of the Renaissance came not in the princely states, nor even in the papal court with its vast resources, but in republican Florence.

In the fourteenth century, Florence survived the ravages of plague, civil war, the fall of the major banking houses, and the revolt of the lower classes to rebuild republican institutes and expand its trade once again. The old oligarchy, the magnates, lost leadership to new wealth, that is, the bankers, lawyers, and international merchants in the greater guilds. The offices of government were placed in the hands of a series of councils, in which membership was for the most part restricted to members of the guilds. The lower middle class and the magnates were given minor roles in government, where they were neither so frustrated as to rebel nor so powerful as to seriously hinder the ruling oligarchy. In practice, the offices of government rotated among the members of a hundred or so wealthy and respectable families, the precise position of any family depending upon its wealth, ability, and political connections at any given time.

In the early fifteenth century, diplomatically and militarily isolated, Florence stood alone against the attempts of the dictator of Milan to reduce all of northern and central Italy to subjection. The members of ruling oligarchy restrained their habitual factional bickering to meet the threat and imposed a system of direct, graduated taxes on themselves. Workers who lived off their wages were classed as paupers and not taxed. The result of the struggle was the victorious assertion of the republican institutions and ideology of Florence.

Civic patriotism and humanist ideals characterized political and intellectual life in Florence in the first half of the fifteenth century. Participation in government was a necessary condition for economic success, because the unrepresented or unpopular family found that it bore the full burden of taxation. The sons of the oligarchs sought to excel in business, government, or church administration; and for success in any one of these, the tastes of the time required a humanist man of letters with the proper oratorical style. Leading artists and writers became public heroes.

The houses of wealthy Florence humanists gave tangible proof of the wealth and refinement of their owners. Artistic masterpieces, classical and modern, were supplemented by manuscript libraries with beautiful copies of Cicero, Seneca, Aristotle, and other great classical authors. The household staff was often adorned by a Greek or Latin tutor, a highly respected addition to the usual array of servants. Wealthy private citizens and the city government commissioned works of art to commemorate great persons and events. This was the great age of ecclesiastical building in Florence, as well as in Rome and other Italian cities. Civic patriotism demanded beautiful buildings, the finest Latin style in public documents, and literary works describing the long and glorious history of the city. Admirers clustered about the famous learned people of the day to share in their intellectual discussions. While many such

Western Culture

gatherings centered round laymen, professional scholars of the highest renown taught at the university in Florence, which was known throughout Europe as the greatest center of the New Learning.

The height of the Renaissance spirit in Florence was reached during the reign of the Medici family. Their wealth came from the famous Medici bank, which was founded in the late fourteenth century and had branches all over Europe. The Medici family was able to get the banking business of the papacy, which had been left without an adequate banker by the fall of the great Florentine banks earlier in the century. At that time the Medici were known as supporters of the popular party in Florence and were thus political enemies of powerful houses in the ruling oligarchy. For many years the Medici family was forced to pay outrageously high taxes, and opposition to the Medici continued to grow—but so did their power.

The outstanding manager of the bank and the architect of the political take-over of the government of Florence was Cosimo de' Medici (1389—1464). After a year in exile he returned to Florence as the effective power behind the workings of the Florentine government. Commissions and councils continued to sit, and new officials continued to be drawn from a rigged lottery. The difference was that no man could rise in office nor any family continue in prosperity without the sufficient support of Cosimo de' Medici. Families which had once used the taxing power of the government to lash the Medici found themselves taxed into ruin and denied the credit essential for their commercial enterprises.

The rule of the Medici fostered Florentine humanism. Cosimo was the patron *par excellence*; cultural life reached new heights under his sponsorship. And if Cosimo was liberal, his grandson Lorenzo the Magnificent, the last great Medici ruler of Florence, was lavish. Lorenzo was not the banker or the statesman that Cosimo had been, however, and he was unable to reverse the decline in the fortunes of the family bank—although he covered it for a time with funds drawn from the public treasury. In the early sixteenth century, a Medici pope continued the tradition of patronage begun by his predecessors, but the wealth and finally the real power of the Medici had disappeared by the end of the fifteenth century. In 1500, Renaissance culture had just begun to suffer from the financial blight which eventually would relegate Italy to a secondary place in European life.

The situation in Florence was in many ways a typical example of the

44

Renaissance environment of all Italian cities. Professional and amateur humanists existed side by side. Professors, tutors, and professional artists were inseparable from Renaissance gentlemen, who often made outstanding contributions to art and letters while conducting their more mundane political and mercantile affairs. Although a large part of the Italian contribution to classical studies, art, and letters was absorbed by academic circles in northern Europe, the Renaissance as a comprehensive cultural mode found its full expression only in the Italian cities.

The Italian Renaissance was a diversified cultural outpouring which extended to every facet of the intellectual and artistic life of the Italian elite. It was a cultural movement rather than an intellectual revolution as such—it did not contribute to Western civilization a new paradigm for ordering man's conception of the universe or his experience, as did the scientific revolution of the sixteenth and seventeenth centuries. Rather it contributed a new style of life and a new educational ideal. By revitalizing certain aspects of the Western tradition, the Renaissance created a new cultural mode which was to dominate the ideas of the European elite for centuries and which accelerated the erosion of the medieval world view. Insofar as the Renaissance was a general rebirth of learning, its roots lie in the social, political, and economic environment of the Italian cities. Its particular character and direction, however, were due in large measure to the formative influence of a few great men such as Dante, Petrarch, and Boccaccio.

Dante was in many ways a transitional figure; his work is inconsistent in outlook and full of contradictions. He retained his belief in a hierarchically ordered universe and argued in syllogism. *The Divine Comedy*, his greatest work, is essentially religious in theme. However, he wrote his greatest poem in the vernacular rather than in proper clerical Latin; he was obsessed with his personal, if somewhat idealized, love for Beatrice; he admired the Romans and asserted that the pagan Roman Empire had won the world by right according to the will of God. Dante was a member of a leading Florentine family, and although exiled from his beloved native city as a result of a political conflict, he remained at heart a loyal Florentine. He was also a layman who made his living by his pen. His love sonnets, focusing on his love for Beatrice, show an intense awareness of personality. They and his great epic description of heaven, purgatory, and hell—*The Divine Comedy*—raised the use of the

Italian languages as a poetic medium to new heights.

The Divine Comedy, which is thoroughly medieval in outlook, is one of the great syntheses of the Christian faith. The characters whom Dante encounters on his journey through the three spheres—heaven, purgatory, and hell—illustrate both his scholastic outlook and his love of the classics. Virgil is his first guide; the other great poets of antiquity exist in limbo—they lived before Christ and thus could not be saved, although they were good men. Other classical characters abound in the various levels of hell; those in the lowest circle include Brutus and Cassius, the murderers of Julius Caesar, as well as Judas and a political enemy of Dante in Florence. Dante's guide through purgatory and the lower circles of heaven is Beatrice, who stands for the Church, and his guide to the highest glories of heaven is the medieval mystic St. Bernard.

Petrarch is much more than Dante as a man of the Renaissance. His love sonnets were written to Laura, the object of his unending but unreturned love, but they deal above all with his own state of mind. Petrarch was constantly connected with his soul, emotions, intellect, and reputation. He epitomized the self-consciousness of the Renaissance man. Yet Petrarch was also deeply religious, concerned about his own salvation and the defense of orthodoxy. His writings were often marked by reference to Christian literature—Augustine's *Confessions* was one of his favorite works—and Christian dogma. For Petrarch, however, piety did not mean self-denial or self-abasement before the mystery and majesty of God; he saw self-fulfillment as a Christian duty. Petrarch did not consider the things of the world to be works of the devil. Like others of his day, he valued worldly things and man himself but his concern with humanity is truly Christian.

Petrarch was more than a writer of love sonnets in Italian. As a classicist he gained an unparalleled reputation in his own day, and although by the refined standards of the later Renaissance his Latin was less than pure Ciceronian, he was the foremost man of letters in fourteenth-century Italy. He was an avid manuscript hunter and possessed an impressive library. Unable to learn Greek for lack of a teacher, he nonetheless valued his manuscripts of Plato's writings and was active in search of translators and teachers of Greek. Petrarch was not merely concerned with the language and style of the classics, however; he found the stoicism and civic patriotism of Cicero and other great Romans wholly in keeping with the ideal behavior of a Christian gentleman and citizen.

The greatest of Petrarch's associates was Boccaccio, another eager manuscript hunter and Latin stylist. Like Petrarch and Dante, Boccaccio had his perpetually unsuccessful love affair—with Fiammetta. But Boccaccio's love, even more than Petrarch's, was a love of frustrated desire involving little idealization. His passion was expressed not only in admiration of his beloved but in the bitterness of betrayal.

Boccaccio thought of himself as primarily a Latin poet, but his greatest contribution to European literature was the *Decameron*. Written in vernacular prose, the *Decameron* is a series of stories told by a group of young ladies and gentlemen who have gone to the hills outside Florence to escape the plague. There is little apparent didactic purpose to the tales. Some are funny, some are sad, and many are marked with satire or ribaldry. Their major purpose was not to educate but to entertain.

Writings in the vernacular did not play the major role in the literature of the time. Both Petrarch and Boccaccio spent the greater part of their energies in cultivating their Latin and their knowledge of classical literature. Throughout the fourteenth and fifteenth centuries the main drive of Italian culture was in the direction of classical studies, or the humanities. In the universities, chairs of rhetoric were established so that scholars might lecture on the classical masterpieces, on the style and grace of the language and the worthiness of the ideas set forth by the great classical authors. The ability to speak and write properly was the distinctive mark of an educated man, and in the hands of people like Petrarch, classical Latin once more became a supple and graceful vehicle of expression.

The study of Greek was more difficult for the Italians, since teachers were rare and complete Greek texts almost unknown at the beginning of the Renaissance. After 1400, chairs for the study of Greek were established in most Italian universities, and subsequently good Latin translations of Greek works began to appear. Later, after Constantinople fell to the Turks in 1453, many Greek scholars fled to Italy. Their learning and the manuscripts they brought with them made a substantial contribution to classical studies.

The rarity of complete and accurate manuscripts of the most important works of antiquity led to a search for manuscripts which took scholars to Byzantium and to monasteries all over Europe. When manuscripts were located, they were often in very poor condition—having been copies, perhaps, by an obscure monk in the early Middle Ages. Classical scholars were forced to become experts in textual criticism, collecting and collating available manuscripts to put together as complete and accurate a text as possible. Perhaps the greatest expert on the critical evaluation of manuscripts was Lorenzo Valla (1405—1457), who would make no compromise with the evidence presented in the texts. He proved conclusively, for example, that *The Donation of Constantine* was a medieval forgery. Even the rage of ecclesiastical officials did not deter Valla from publishing the conclusions derived from his study of textual evidence. The groundwork of modern philology and textual criticism was laid by the scholars of the Renaissance.

Classical literature as we know it today was first assembled by Renaissance scholars. The possession of complete and accurate manuscripts of many ancient thinkers, including Cicero, Plato, and Aristotle, had a profound impact on the study of the classical authors. Many writers had previously been known to the Middle Ages only through one or two of their works, and even Aristotle, whose major works had been translated in the thirteenth century, now became better known as the full corpus of his writings was made available. With full texts at hand, it was possible for the first time for scholars to evaluate critically the writings of the great authors of antiquity. The result was often a revolutionary change in attitude toward their works.

The outstanding example of the impact of the New Learning was the enhancement of the reputation of Plato, who had been known to the Middle Ages only through his *Timaeus* and through the works of such neo-Platonic writers as St. Augustine. In the mid-fourteenth century, the Platonic corpus was successfully assimilated into humanist thought through the work of Marsilio Ficino (1433—1499). Under the patronage of Cosimo de' Medici, Ficino became the founder of the Florentine Academy, an informal school of writers and artists which was devoted above all else to the full comprehension and assimilation of the works of Plato. Ficino himself made the most successful synthesis of the philosophy of Plato, asserting that there is one universal truth and that all valid philosophies partake of at least a part of it. Ficino's interpretation of the Platonic universe was ideally suited to give philosophical underpinning to the humanist view of man. He believed that the soul of man is the center of motion and decision, and that the human soul lies midway between the carnal and the divine, with the ability to choose between the lower and higher course.

The greatest follower of Ficino, Pico della Mirandola (1463—1494), carried to a new extreme his teacher's belief in the compatibility of all great philosophical and theological systems. Pico's life was short but he became one of the most learned men of his day, mastering Hebrew as well as Greek and Latin. He then embarked upon a synthesis of all knowledge into one system, asserting that Christian, Jewish, and pagan thought did not contradict one another in essentials.

The neo-Platonic view of the universe taught at the Florentine Academy is uniquely suited to the humanist philosophy. It developed partly in response to the simultaneous growth of Aristotelian studies in the Italian universities. The study of Aristotle was often accompanied by Averroist teachings that struck at the humanist view of man. The Averroist doctrine of the unity of the intellect asserted that the soul is given individually only through its temporary union with the body. After death, the Averroists believed, the individual soul is united with the universal soul; personal immortality and blessedness or punishment after death are impossible.

Pietro Pomponazzi (1462—1525) reconciled the unity of the intellect with the Aristotelian concept of the universe and with humanist values. Pomponazzi held that belief in the immortality of the individual soul rested on faith rather than on nature or reason. For him, the intellect or soul was an organic part of the body, and its operations were explicable in natural terms. While accepting on faith the immortality of the soul, he held that reason irrefutably demonstrates that the soul perishes at death with the body.

Pomponazzi emphasized moral behavior for its own sake, not for otherworldly goals, and the effect of his argument was to place upon man the responsibility for good or evil actions. This view accorded with the humanist traditions. Pomponazzi particularly disliked the objection that his theory precluded divine punishment and reward as operative forces in human morality; he asserted that virtue is its own reward and morality a purely temporal affair.

In general, while they did not develop a new view of the universe, Renaissance thinkers did dig deep into ancient philosophy to derive a philosophical synthesis in accord with the humanistic view of the nature of man. Both Ficino's interpretation of the Platonic system and Pomponazzi's description of the nature of the human soul gave strength to the belief that man's mortal existence is an end in itself. As devout Christians, Pomponazzi and the majority of Renaissance thinkers were quick to accept on faith what they denied on philosophical grounds, but they were in fact developing a secular attitude toward human affairs. Those humanists influenced by neo-Platonism held views that diminished the uniqueness of Christianity by stressing the fundamental compatibility of all religions. The humanistic attitude itself was not antireligious, but separation of the natural from the spiritual realm was its essential consequence. Further, the strength of the secular intellectual and cultural activities of the humanists undermined the Church's monopoly on learning.

The humanist philosophy was wholly compatible with the outlook of the Italian upper classes. The secular educational system developing in Italian cities was directed toward education in the humanities—in art and letters—to prepare the young man of good family to take his place in society. The goal was not to cultivate a highly trained scholar but to inculcate the proper social values and the right forms of expression. It was more concerned with morality than with philosophy or theology. The search for truth was an accepted value, but it was not isolated from secular concerns. Rather, the student was supposed to become a man of affairs, a citizen who took an active part in public matters. With a few notable exceptions, even professional scholars and teachers did not exclude themselves from public life; they were in great demand as secretaries and ambassadors.

The beginning of art history and of historiography as modern disciplines can be credited to the Italian humanists, who applied their critical powers and wide learning in these fields as in literature and philosophy. The Florentine artist Giorgio Vasari (1511—1574) published the first history of art, *The Lives of the Most Excellent Architects, Sculptors, and Painters*, in the mid-sixteenth century. Machiavelli's writings reveal men in conflict for power, motivated by personal ambition; he attributed historical change to the clash of human wills. His *History of Florence* is a great achievement of humanist historiography.

The secular and classical attitudes which characterized humanist thought, and the examples of the Italian city-states, exerted a profound influence on the development of political theory in the fourteenth and fifteenth centuries. In medieval political theory the state was part of the divine organization of the universe. To St. Augustine, it was a necessary coercive limitation on the evil, dark forces of human nature, with no intrinsic moral end. His was the predominant medieval view, existing side by side with the ideal of the Christian emperor, first put forward by Eusebius (264—340), biographer of the emperor Constantine. The central issue in medieval political thought was the relationship between the "two swords"—ecclesiastical and secular authority. Did the unquestioned jurisdiction of the Pope in ecclesiastical affairs extend to the secular sphere, or did the king's authority come directly from God?

Renaissance political theory from Dante to Machiavelli answered decisively in favor of the autonomy of secular political authority. Thinkers like Marsilio da Padova so completely assimilated the Aristotelian tradition of government as a potential force for good into their view of the state that Aristotelian concepts played a central role in European political theory until the nineteenth century. The Thomist synthesis, based on Aristotle, had revised the Augustinian view of the state. St. Thomas asserted that the state plays a positive role in human affairs. More than a mere peace-maker, it serves the common good and thereby enables men to live well. Positive law—in other words, law enacted by man— was a partial manifestation of natural law, which was in turn the temporal aspect of divine law. Aquinas thus asserted a fundamental harmony between the temporal state and the divine. Renaissance thinkers amended Aquinas to perceive the state as an end in itself, with its own purpose.

The first treatise on political theory by a Renaissance thinker was the *Monarchia* of Dante. The form of argument and the primary assertion of the treatise—that universal monarchy is a necessary and good form of government—are thoroughly medieval. Dante, however, saw the state as an essentially secular institution whose independence from spiritual authority was essential to its well-being. He not only attacked the argument from the doctrine of the two swords (that the spiritual is intrinsically superior to the secular) but refused to accept either the Donation of Constantine or the Petrine doctrine as valid arguments for the secular authority of the pope. The radical tendency explicit in Dante's statements about ecclesiastical authority and his glorification of the Roman Empire were not completely new, but they were an early indication of the attitude which marked the political thought of the Renaissance.

In 1324 the appearance of the *Defensor Pacis* (*Defender of the Peace*) of Marsilio da Padova (1275—1342) brought forth a storm of controversy that did not die down for over a century. Marsilio's beliefs were tinged with

Averroism, leading him to assert the absolute separation of the secular and the spiritual, and he was vehemently anticlerical. He denied the authority of the Pope and of the Church in secular affairs on the ground that these were purely temporal concern, outside the jurisdiction of the papacy. He further held that the absolute authority of the Pope was a tyrannous usurpation and that supreme authority in the Church lay with the entire community of believers.

In the more positive aspects of his work, Marsilio relied heavily upon Aristotle's *Politics*, asserting that the proper end of the state is the provision of peace and security for its citizens. Marsilio was a thoroughgoing republican, defining the law as the expression of the will of the weightier (that is, worthier, wealthier) part of the citizenry and the true expression of the common good. He believed men as individuals are prone to evil, but the collective opinion of the citizens must necessarily result in the common good.

In his concept of law, Marsilio recognized the necessity for providing some other principle upon which the state could demand obedience if it did not claim to be the expression of divine will. He asserted that the transcendent end of the state—the common good—commanded the obedience of the citizen and that the consent of the citizens bound them to obey the laws, in theory and in practice. Echoes of Marsilio's doctrines can be found throughout the political thought of the fifteenth, sixteenth, and seventeenth centuries.

The political experience of the Italian cities, while departing from the clerical view of the state preoccupied much of Renaissance thought, exerted another important influence on the Renaissance concept of government. After Florence had successfully withstood the invasion of the Milanese tyrants, for example, the Florentine Republic became the subject of numerous works which glorified its history and propounded the political principles of republican Rome. Florentine writers believed that the public spirit of the citizens—inherited from their distant ancestors in the Roman Republic—and the excellence of the republican constitution were responsible for the political strength and cultural glories of the city. The writings of Cicero and the example set by Brutus and Cassius, the murderers of the tyrant Caesar, were woven into the political ideology of the Florentine government.

This concept of the high moral aim of the state in republican Florence had its parallel in the political ideology of the tyrants of Italy, who claimed to be perpetuators of the Pax Romana of the age of Augustus. The tyrants held that only a universal monarchy (or at least a national Italian monarchy) could ensure the peace necessary for the earthly well-being of mankind. Neither Florence nor the tyrannies, however, consistently practiced their high-sounding principles.

Despite the theoretical pronouncements of humanist writers, the political life of the Italian cities was as sordid as any in Europe, and a much more pessimistic view of the state dominated the writings of the greatest political thinker of the Renaissance, Niccolo Machiavelli (1469—1527). Machiavelli lived through the depressing years of the rise and fall of Florentine fortunes at the end of the fifteenth century. In spite of a rather unsatisfactory family background for public life, he spent many years in the service of the Florentine state, achieving moderate success but failing to gain the kind of political position he desired. When the republic was overthrown and the Medici returned to power, he was forced into exile.

Machiavelli spent the rest of his life trying to regain a place in the political life of Florence. At the same time he began his career as a writer. Some works, like the *Prince*, were written in an attempt to exhibit his political abilities to those who could give him back his position in public life, while others record the bitterness of his forced retirement.

Machiavelli, then, wrote about politics from first-hand experience as a Florentine diplomat and administrator. In addition, he had read the works of Aristotle and the writings of Latin authors on the history of Rome and the political ideals of republican Rome. His works—among them the *Prince*, dedicated to Lorenzo the Magnificent as a manual of government, *The Discourses*, a commentary on Roman history written to illustrate the political principles which could be learned from the past, and the *History of Florence*—express a purely secular attitude. Beyond that, they show Machiavelli as a man who distrusted all ideals. He strove to show things as they were, not as they ought to be.

Machiavelli's views on religion play a small part in his writings. He felt that religion was necessary in the state in order to secure the obedience of subjects and that the corrupt example of the papal court had destroyed the morals of the Italian people.

For Machiavelli, the struggle for power is the essence of politics. The only constant in human affairs was perpetual change. The most adaptable political organism is the most durable. The state is not a reflection of hierarchical order or theological principles; its appropriateness and durability depends not upon the moral purpose but on the successful monopoly of power.

Machiavelli had a fundamentally pessimistic—or realistic—view of human nature, tempered by a firm belief that man was the most creative force in the universe and, in fact, the only hope for bringing about change. He did not commit himself on the ideal form of government any more than on its moral end, since any government of a transient organism would eventually disintegrate through its own weakness or the challenge of a superior force. In the *Prince* he asserted that only the strong government of a single man could save Italy from the throes of the political chaos, but in the *The Discourses* he seemed to favor a republican form of government, suggesting that government by the people is more likely to be free from abuse than government by a prince. But nowhere did he give a formula for the ideal constitution of a government.

To Machiavelli, it was not the form of authority but its techniques that determined the durability of a state. Governmental decision must be based solely on the interest of the state. Machiavelli's open advocacy of the use of evil methods if they are necessary to preserve the state brought him notoriety as a political thinker, but more important for the development of Western political theory was his conception of a state as an independent entity with its own principles of operation. In addition, his interpretation of human motivation in political affairs as fundamentally concerned with the pursuit of power has been one of the most important ideas in modern political thought. Machiavelli as the theorist of *Realpolitik* represented a decisive break with the medieval tradition.

4.2   The Northern European Renaissance

Not only in art but in all phases of Renaissance culture, the achievements of Italy in the fourteenth, fifteenth, and sixteenth centuries could not fail to have an impact in northern Europe. However, the impact of the Italian Renaissance was not widely felt in northern Europe until the end of the fifteenth century, and even then it did not bring about a general cultural revolution but an intellectual movement. The persistence of local and national traditions in the North—the essential continuity of cultural life—and the much greater intensity of the Italian movement are the most decisive differences between the Renaissance in northern Europe and the Italian Renaissance.

As in Italy, the lay scholar who lived off his wits or a private income became increasingly prominent in the intellectual life of northern Europe. Such men were often primarily international personalities, but some were no more than occasional scholars who traveled to Italy or some other center of learning once or twice in their lives. In addition, patronage played an important role in the cultural life of the North: Rich men, kings, and cities provided financial support for men of learning and talent. By the beginning of the sixteenth century, humanism had become fashionable in court circles, especially in England and France.

The differences between the cultural milieus of northern and southern Europe can be illustrated by examining the impact of classicism upon northern Europe. In Italy, the humanist ideal had coexisted with Christian piety through the careful separation of the two aspects of human life, the temporal and the spiritual. Efforts were made to integrate pagan culture and Christian theology, but these were not entirely successful. In northern Europe, such a solution proved to be impossible, and while classical studies were incorporated into the intellectual and educational apparatus of the North, it was necessary to establish carefully their compatibility with Christian theology.

The study of ancient languages and texts was responsible for the most revolutionary aspect of the absorption of humanism into northern academic life. The study of original texts—of the Scriptures as well as the classics—revolved around philology, and Scriptural exegesis was based not on scholastic logic and dialectics but on a literal and historical approach which differs so much from the medieval tradition. In France, Lefevre d'Etaples (1466—1536) published his Greek text of the Bible with a Latin translation which ran counter to the accepted Latin tradition, the Vulgate, and aroused a storm of controversy. In England, John Colet (1466—1519) dared to preach and lecture without a theological degree and based his interpretation of St. Paul on a literal rather than an allegorical reading of the original texts.

The northern humanists applied the techniques of the Italian humanists to the Scriptures, and they also shared the Italians' admiration for classical literature. While many Italian humanists had concerned themselves with the discrepancy between pagan and Christian ethics, most northern scholars carefully selected those parts of ancient learning compatible with Christian teachings, asserting Christianity as the fulfillment rather than the denial of the true spirit of antiquity.

The impact of humanist learning in the northern universities was severely limited by the firm grasp of the traditional scholastic disciplines on academic chairs and curricula. It was outside the great universities that the greatest impact of humanism was felt. The humanists formed an international circle of intellectuals whose writings in Latin were bound by no national literary traditions and whose correspondence provided the spirit of cohesion and the cross-fertilization of ideas.

The universally acknowledged leader of the humanist circle is Desiderius Erasmus (1469—1536), paramount in learning and in his Latin writing style. Erasmus came from a poor Dutch family, was orphaned as a boy, joined a religious order but found it confining and unacceptable, and was thus forced to worry about his means of support. In spite of his lack of means, he became proficient in Latin and Greek. He never found a university career compatible with his humanist interests and remained a free-lance scholar. His wanderings all over Europe and the tremendous volume of his correspondence communicated his ideas to his contemporaries. Although the humanist circle which revolved around Erasmus was too amorphous to form a cohesive cultural movement, at the end of the fifteenth century it gained the adherence of leading intellectuals—men who were important in education, the Church, scholarship, and even political life.

While the classical scholarship of this circle had a profound intellectual impact as an alternative to scholasticism, the educational activities of the humanists and their ethical writings exerted the most significant effect on European society in the early sixteenth century. The most important humanist grammar school was set up in the cathedral school of St. Paul's in London through the patronage of John Colet. The curriculum featured the study of Greek and Latin grammar, with a view to producing not classical scholars but well-educated young gentlemen whose command of rhetoric would equip them to live well. Elements of the humanist ideal in education were also incorporated into the most traditional schools of the Brethren of the Common Life. In the course of the sixteenth century, the grammar school based on the study of the classics became predominant in the education of the youth of Europe, a position it was to retain until the twentieth century.

Humanists were as concerned with the framework of classical studies as with the classics themselves, and the books by Erasmus were written with profound didactic purpose. Textbooks of Latin grammar were imbued with the humanist concern for education in general and with the preoccupation with ethical behavior which led the humanists into the fields of social, political, and religious criticism. The two greatest works to arise out of the social criticism of the humanist were More's *Utopia* and Erasmus' *Praise of Folly*. Sir Thomas More (1477—1535) was a learned English lawyer and government official with first-hand knowledge of the political affairs of his day. His *Utopia* juxtaposed the economic and political evils of sixteenth-century European society with the virtues of a pagan society whose concern for basic human values produced an ethical and social world far superior to the Christian Europe of More's day. His concern was not to attack the Church but to assert the values of a constructive social and legal order. More's main question was: If pagans could do so well, why can't a Christian society do even better?

Erasmus' social commentary was much more closely tied to ecclesiastical abuses, and perhaps for that reason he was careful to avoid the explicitness characteristic of More. The most popular of his critical works was the *Praise of Folly*, in which Folly extols the obvious evils of Church and society. In addition, Erasmus contributed more positive guides to the Christian life, which exhibited his deep religious feeling.

In general, the humanist movement did not translate criticisms of scholasticism or clerical abuses into explicit protest but operated within the established political and religious framework of northern European society. Humanist learning made significant inroads into the medieval world view, but the humanists themselves were not reformers. Neither Erasmus nor More had the temperament or the fanaticism of a social or religious revolutionary.

4.3 The Heritage of the Renaissance

It is difficult to find in Renaissance culture a particular theory or principle that is wholly original. But the Renaissance sifted and scrutinized the classical and medieval traditions for the best that had been thought and said in the world; it synthesized the ideas that seemed most in accordance with the nature of humanity into an integrated philosophy and style of life that dominated the culture of the early modern world. Western civilization during the three centuries after 1450 lived off the intellectual capital of the Italian Renaissance, and the philosophy, political theory, art, and literature of the early modern world were extrapolation from one or another aspect of Renaissance culture.

The most significant achievement of the Italian Renaissance is its establishment of a culture that suited the way of life of the now literate nobility and the now leisured high bourgeoisie and at the same time perpetuated most of what was valuable in classical and medieval civilization. Put another way, Renaissance culture allowed the lord or businessman to feel that his pursuit of power, status, and wealth was justified, that he had a right to indulge his personal feelings, but at the same time Renaissance culture placed these private interests and individual sensibilities within the context of universal and political order and directed them to social needs. This balance is fundamental to modern life and is why the Italian Renaissance may rightly be regarded as the dawn of the modern world, even though the humanist scholars failed to reach modern science and the Italian merchants and entrepreneurs did not attain the Industrial Revolution.

Renaissance culture deserves to be termed "secular", although not in the sense that the humanists were unbelievers or even, in fundamental matters, anticlerical. From Petrarch to Erasmus, the humanists were very vocal in their criticism of theologians and scholastic philosophers—even though many of the humanists were themselves well trained in theology and scholasticism. They felt that the intellectuals of the Church had become abstract and narrow, divorced from the reality of human love for God. They believed that many bishops were corrupt and disgracefully ignorant. This did not make the humanists enemies of the Church; it made them passionate advocates of church renewal and modernization.

Renaissance culture gave value to man's secular concerns and finally justified worldly endeavor not as a regrettable weakness but as something fundamental to and glorious in human life. Modernity required this celebration of man's involvement with his feelings and his participation in nature and society. Medieval men could never quite escape from a sense of guilt, or at least regret, about their natural, secular actions; Renaissance culture was a liberation from this guilt and restraint.

In Dante's writings we find an explicit attitude toward a new secular culture. *The Divine Comedy* explicates the medieval scheme of salvation, and for the most part the structure of the poem runs parallel to Thomist theology. But Dante, internalizing the doctrines of the Church, made them expressions of his own feelings. Paradoxically, *The Divine Comedy* is at the same time a summation of the medieval world view and the communication of the poet's personal sensibility. *The New Life* is Dante's closest approach to Renaissance humanism. He was concerned with placing his love for Beatrice within a perspective of Christian theology, but it is the yearnings of his "secret self" that form the theme of the work.

More directly than Dante, Petrarch confronted the antagonism between soul and body, between the spiritual and secular worlds, between the Christian and classical traditions. Although he described this conflict in apologetic and guilt-ridden terms, he could not deny that he was intensely conscious of his total humanity. For Petrarch, classical culture became the road to emancipation from the restraints that medieval theology placed upon human nature. For him, ancient Rome was the generator and symbol of a better society and a more humane philosophy than that which prevailed in his own day. His desire for a fuller and finer appreciation of human life is expressed in a longing for return of the Golden Age of the Roman Empire.

By the fifteenth century the philosophy of humanism expressed paradoxically by Dante and defensively by Petrarch was unequivocally enunciated in Florentine intellectual circles. Never before or since has the dignity of man been more emphatically stressed than by Pico. Pico has retained the ancient and medieval doctrine of the great chain of being, but he has completely rejected the implication of that doctrine by using it to point not to man's limitations but just the opposite. Since man stands at the center of the chain of being, he combines all things in the universe in himself. Man is the most wonderful and complete of all creatures. To understand human nature is to know all things. Man is not only the measure of all things; he is an end in himself, and to cultivate human qualities is to feel and understand the universe. No more radical celebration of humanity has ever been made.

Here we have arrived at the theory of liberal humanism, which holds that the resources of human society are so vast as to be virtually unlimited. There is no need for violence, poverty, and misery in society because the human mind is powerful enough to find remedies for these ills and establish a community where all men will have the freedom to cultivate the sublime and beautiful which are potential in every human being. This is, essentially, what Sir Thomas More is saying in *Utopia*. Considering what human beneficence and reason can achieve, it is disgraceful and outrageous, he argued, that in a society that has received the additional grace of divine revelation, greed and injustice and exploitation should be so prevalent. He puts before his readers the ideal of commonwealth, by which he means a society that in its institutions fulfills at the political level the dignity of man. Even Machiavelli, who was much more pessimistic about the degree of moral action that could be expected at the political level, believed that men have a great amount of freedom to improve the condition of their lives. Machiavelli's hopes for a prince who would act as the "deliverer" of Italy from disunity and invasion were not fulfilled. More's expectation that England would become the perfect commonwealth was even more cruelly disappointed. The secularized millenarianism, the utopianism, of the Renaissance humanists played a small role in the actual political and social development of sixteenth-century Europe. But the humanists had clearly stated a liberal philosophy that would be a permanent part of the heritage of Western civilization and that would gain important adherents in succeeding generations, finally becoming, in the eighteenth and nineteenth centuries, the dominant philosophy of man and society in Western Europe and North America.

Renaissance liberal humanism did not have significant impact on the political and social structure of early modern Europe. But the Italian influence on European literature, art, and education was immense, and it was through these aspects of higher culture that the Renaissance philosophy continued to shape the outlook of succeeding generations. The most widely read and influential belletristic literature that came out of Renaissance Italy emphasized feeling and individual personality: Dante's *The Divine Comedy*, Petrarch's love sonnets, Boccaccio's *Decameron*, biography such as Vasari's *The Lives of the Most Excellent Architects, Sculpotors, and Painters*, autobiography like Cellini's, and historical writing, which in the Renaissance mode was focused on great individuals. What is common to all these forms of literature is a complete turning away from the vestiges of medieval didacticism: Literature becomes the means of communicating personal experience, and it is addressed to a relatively large and highly literate public that wishes to share the author's sensibility. These would be the main characteristics of European literature in the following four centuries.

Renaissance art parallels the progression of thoughts that we have traced from Dante to the beginning of the sixteenth century. An identifiable Renaissance school of painting was inaugurated at the end of the thirteenth century by Giovanni Cimabue (1240—1302) and Giotto di Bondone (1267—1337). With some help from the Byzantine revival of a more classical style and strongly influenced by the Franciscan-bourgeois proclivity for a more realistic style, these painters achieved a markedly intensified humanization of traditional Christian iconology. In Giotto's later work and the paintings of the early Flemish school, a quasi-naturalistic style was employed to communicate religious motifs directly to a semi-literate but highly aggressive middle-class audience. In the fifteenth century, in the famous works of Leonardo da Vinci (1452—1519), Michelangelo Buonarroti (1475—1564), and Raphael Sanzio (1483—1520), this pragmatically developed naturalism was replaced by a self-conscious, classical naturalism and a humanistic celebration of the human body and the natural world. The Renaissance school thereby attained its highest development, which set the model for all subsequent neoclassical revivals in Western civilization.

Both the theory and the curriculum that prevailed in Italian humanist circles in the fifteenth century exclusively dominated European education to the middle of the nineteenth century, and the humanist influence is still crucial in Western schools and universities. As against the medieval university, the humanists contended that the liberal arts should be, not a cursory preparation for advanced professional studies, but the main concern of any educational institution. Through development of the mind in literary—chiefly classical—studies, the student would be so equipped with broad knowledge and wisdom, and his reason and feelings would be so finely tuned, that he could undertake any further investigation he wanted. In short, universities should be concerned with teaching and communicating with undergraduates. Professors should be excellent teachers, with very broad interests. The curriculum should be concerned with the culture of the past and problems of the present and should be directly relevant to the student's personal experience and social commitment. Research and professional training should either be assigned a decidedly secondary role on the campus, be relegated to separate institutes or professional schools, or be abandoned altogether as socially useless or reactionary. The struggle in the universities between the humanists and the scholastics has continued well into the present day, and perhaps will go on forever.

Chapter 5   The Reformation:
Split Within Western Christendom

As the Renaissance waned in the early sixteenth century it was superseded by a movement which, although in part its product, nevertheless departed markedly from it in spirit. This was the Reformation, which originated in northern Europe. The first important figure of the Reformation was Martin Luther, an Augustinian monk and a professor of theology at University of Wittenberg in Saxony-Anhalt, Germany.

5.1   Martin Luther

In 1517, Martin Luther (1483—1546) published his *The Ninety-five Theses* in Wittenberg. His action was an invitation to scholarly debate; neither Luther nor the Pope at Rome recognized it as the beginning of the Protestant Reformation. The posting of the theses was a commonplace event, but the response turned Luther's simple act into a crisis which shook Christendom to its roots. The monk Luther proved himself to be a great spiritual and revolutionary leader. Before the end of the revolution which began in Wittenberg, the authority of the Pope had been successfully denied in many parts of Europe, and a number of independent churches were competing for the spiritual allegiance of Christians.

The recorded facts of Luther's life as a monk indicate that he was a good one: He was ordained a priest and launched in the study of theology. In 1511 he went to Rome on a mission from his monastic house to the head of the Augustinian order. In Rome he visited as many famous shrines as possible, saying masses for his relatives and engaging in the pious works which were the dream of every pilgrim to the holy city. Eventually Luther was transferred to the Augustinian house at Wittenberg, where he took the degree of Doctor of

Theology and began the career of preaching and teaching which was to occupy him for most of his life.

The outward placidity of Luther's monastic career concealed inner turmoil. Luther believed that even his sincere efforts and the rigors of monastic discipline could not make him righteous enough to deserve God's grace. He heaped confession upon confession and penance upon penance, but nothing could free him from consciousness of sin and unworthiness. Although he met all the standards of piety and righteousness demanded of a holy man, his early years as a monk were spent in a desperate search for peace and for assurance of salvation.

At last, after years of study and unhappiness, Luther made peace with his soul. During the years after 1513, while teaching at University of Wittenberg, he found a satisfying intellectual framework for his religious emotion. As an adherent of the theological views of the fourteenth-century English philosopher William of Ockham (1285—1349), he rejected the Thomist idea that salvation occurred through understanding of the divine. Like William of Ockham, he believed that man could not proceed from natural knowledge to knowledge of God—that belief required a leap of faith and was accomplished through the will. Luther's interminable religious exercises in the monastery were an attempt to discipline his will in order to achieve true righteousness; but he found spiritual peace only when he came to believe that righteousness was not an achievement of man but a gift of God to the believer. Man could not triumph over the will, nor could he justify himself through good works, but he could believe in the saving grace of God—and that belief was his salvation.

Thus in the years prior to 1517 Luther worked out the doctrine of justification by faith alone which was to provide the theological basis for his attack upon the established practices of the Church. At the same time, he worked out the problem of his own salvation and achieved spiritual peace. He could preach and lecture in the confidence that he understood man's salvation. Luther's study of the writings of St. Paul and St. Augustine helped him to develop his theological views.

It was the new Martin Luther who wrote the *Ninety-five Theses*. The work was provoked in 1517 by the appearance of Tetzel, an infamous vendor of indulgence, just beyond the borders of Saxony. Indulgences—temporal remission of punishment for sin—had originally been granted to knights who went on crusade. From that limited application the practice had been expanded by the papacy; indulgences were bought and sold, and the process gradually became a major commercial enterprise. In a Europe deeply troubled by consciousness of sin, its moneymaking potential was vast. Successful salesmen often minimized the limitations of indulgences—that they required true penitence, for example—and exaggerated their efficacy, claiming that the jingle of money in the salesman's pouch winged the soul of the beneficiary straight to heaven.

Luther had often preached against the sale of indulgences, which seemed to him an obvious example of the folly of reliance upon good works for salvation. His theses described the practice on other grounds as well: as an abuse of the power of the papacy, a deception of the recipient, and a form of financial exploitation typical of the Roman tendency to bleed Germany in order to feed the appetites of corrupt Roman prelates.

By publishing his theses, Luther intended only to open the subject to debate, as was customary in the Medieval academic world; but instead they were printed and circulated throughout Germany. The countryside was thrown into an uproar, astounded at Luther's audacity, but both his audacity and his conclusions were applauded in many places. A thousand voices took up his words and carried them across Germany, and an academic dispute became a widespread religious issue. Before long, all Europe was drawn into the controversy.

In spite of its revolutionary beginning and because of its alignment with the German Prince and its adoption of a rigid Orthodoxy, Lutheranism soon settled down within the confines of its first great expansion. In princely territories and cities where rulers and oligarchies were willing to adopt the new religion, Lutheranism was instituted as an established church, but it made little headway in the lands of the Roman Catholic monarchs. Zwinglianism was strong in the German-Swiss cantons, but its influence outside of Switzerland was indirect. Although Zwinglian theology became an important part of Protestant thought, the Zwinglian Church itself was not a successful evangelical movement. Similarly, the English Reformation was primarily a national movement. The radical evangelical spirit of the Anabaptists and others was vitiated by their extremism and the systematic persecution which they faced; it was impossible for them to adapt to either exercise of, or control by, political authority. The radicals ultimately were successful only when unobtrusive passivity rendered them innocuous.

5.2 John Calvin

The second important figure of the Reformation was a younger contemporary of Luther, the Frenchman John Calvin (1509—1564), the man responsible for molding Protestant theology and ecclesiastical organization into a system with sufficient force and coherence to expand across territories governed by hostile rulers. Calvin's church at Geneva and his theology, contained in *The Institutes of the Christian Religion*, had a profound influence on the development of Protestantism in Europe and America.

John Calvin was born in France and educated in the best French schools. Like many of his contemporaries, he studied Ockhamist theology and the humanist approach to learning at the University of Paris. His study of theology was interrupted by a period spent studying law at Orleans, where he came into contact with Roman Catholic reformers whose view of the Church resembled that of Erasmus. Calvin had undertaken the study of law at the order of his father; when his father died, he soon returned to theology. Before long he was converted to Protestantism, and finally he was forced to flee France because of his association with a reformer who invited persecution by his extremist denunciation of abuses in the Church—denunciation clothed in decidedly Lutheran terms.

Calvin's theology was based on his view of God as the omnipotent creator of the universe, whose will was the source of all that happens. For Calvin, salvation, damnation, and every worldly event took place by God's express command. Apparent evil, including damnation, was evil only in the limited view of man, who could not see the higher good brought forth thereby.

Calvin was not satisfied with the Thomist assertion that faith follows knowledge. He regarded the Thomist doctrine as basically false because it allowed for a passive, intellectual relationship between Christ and man. Calvin posited a deeply emotional relationship that went far beyond mere knowledge of God. It is questionable whether Calvin was altogether fair to Thomas Aquinas; ultimately the doctrines of the two men are quite compatible. But, in any case, Calvin claimed that the man with faith "embraced" the message of God, and by surrendering his individual will to the divine will, he might receive salvation. To Calvin, salvation was more than the promise of eternal life; it meant the rehabilitation of depraved human nature.

Calvin's concept of salvation, which included the immediate regeneration of the sinner, differed from the Lutheran view of good works as the grateful response of faith. For Calvin, faith alone saved, but the man with faith must inevitably reform his life in obedience to God's will. Although the saved man might still sin while bound by his earthly existence, his soul was no longer helpless in the face of sin. Christian freedom existed in the ability to overcome sin and to live in joyful righteousness according to God's Law. The New Testament, which asserted the freedom of the Christian from Jewish laws, did not imply that the Old Testament had been superseded. It implied only that obedience to the Law had a new meaning: It was no longer a constraint but a guide, to be willingly followed by any man who was saved. Thus Christian turned for guidance to both the Old and the New Testament, which he could fully understand only after receiving grace.

The Church, for Calvin, was the community of the elect, through which those chosen by God for salvation attained to that state through faith and righteousness. While the Church was universal in the sense that it encompassed the elect, it was a gathered Church in the sense that it excluded the ungodly.

Baptism and communion bound together the members of the Church and distinguished them from outsiders. Baptism of infants was recommended because it gave them the promise of God and initiated them into the community, just as circumcision initiated a child into the Hebrew community and made him a part of the covenant between God and the community. For Calvin, the Christian Church was the heir to the covenant which the Jews had rejected when they failed to accept Jesus Christ as God.

Communion was also a manifestation of the unity of the Church; unbelievers were excluded, along with those who had fallen into sin and were temporarily separated from the community. Calvin denied the bodily presence of Christ in the sacrament, and he also condemned the Zwinglian doctrine that the communion was merely a commemorative ceremony at which Christ was spiritually present. In Calvin's view, Christ was present when the eating of the bread and drinking of the wine was taking place; the bread and wine were not the physical body of Christ, but while the body of the believer was nourished by the bread and wine, so the soul of the believer fed on Christ in the sacrament and was nourished; its sanctity barred the unfaithful while it bound the godly more closely together.

Ideally, Calvin saw the state as an extension of the Christian community. The Church was necessarily autonomous, neither controlled by the state nor exercising civil jurisdiction. However, in a community of Christians, the magistrates could be expected to exercise their duty as Christians. Thus the state might have a positive role in the ordering of a godly society.

5.3 The Heritage of the Reformation

Unlike the Renaissance whose intellectual, cultural, and artistic achievements were really products of and for the elite, the Reformation touched the lives of the masses of the people in new and profound ways. After the Reformation, Europe would never again be the unified Christian commonwealth it once believed it was.

The immediate and decisive legacy of the Reformation was the transfer of power from church to state. In this sense, the Reformation represents a stage in the evolution of the modern nation-state. The Reformation shattered the universal medieval Church into a large number of local territorial churches. The common feature of all these local churches was their control by secular rulers. Regardless of whether the church remained Catholic in doctrine or adhered to one of the Protestant faiths, it was the secular authority that controlled ecclesiastical appointments and church finances.

The Reformation led to doctrinal dissension and intolerance, which caused in a succession of bloody religious wars. But the resulting fragmentation of Western Christendom compelled the contending sects to accept the fact that the hegemony of any universal church was not feasible, hence the greater acceptance and implementation of religious toleration.

The Reformation had implications for status of the individual. Luther championed individual interpretation of the Scriptures, and the emphasis on the reading of the Bible led to greater mass literacy. Protestant leaders considered married life desirable, stressed mutual love and respect between husband and wife, though they took for granted the husband's primacy in the family.

Chapter 6 Scientific Revolution: New Conception of the Universe

Between 1500 and 1715, European aristocracy developed a new cultural style, a way of life which features good breeding, good manners, and good taste. In the process, the monolithic intellectual world of the Middle Ages was broken apart. Aristocratic education sought to produce gentlemen, not scholars. Scholastic education was replaced by the humanistic approach developed first in Italy during the Renaissance and then exported to northern Europe.

But scholarship was not destroyed with scholasticism. Scholasticism and the medieval university curriculum were simply bypassed by a new burst of scholarly investigation based outside the university. During the sixteenth and seventeenth centuries a scientific revolution took place, a revolution so far-reaching that it toppled the medieval Aristotelian view of the universe. Even more important, the new science gave birth to a methodology and a view of the universe which remained unchanged until the twentieth century. The very word *science* took on the meaning which still separates the sciences from the arts, and men learned to see the world through new eyes.

6.1 The Rise of Modern Science

The medieval explanation of nature was a blending of Christian theology and ancient science—especially the work of the scientists Aristotle, Ptolemy, and Galen. The earth was at the center of a divinely created universe made to serve man and edify him. Everything moved to a purpose in a divinely ordered scheme. The four elements—earth, water, air, and fire—each inhabited its own sphere. Natural motion, such as the movement of the stars or the propensity of a stone to fall to the ground, resulted from the inherent desire of each element to return to its proper sphere. When an object moved away from its natural sphere, it had to be propelled by an outside force. An arrow, for instance, was set in motion by the bowstring; its motion was maintained by the air displaced in flight pushing in behind it.

This view of the universe is manifestly absurd to the modern scientist, but prevailed for two millennia, and its endurance testifies to its attractiveness and usefulness to the ancient and medieval world. In fact, for centuries it was difficult, if not impossible, to see the universe in any other way. The fourteenth and fifteenth centuries revealed serious fissures in the Aristotelian synthesis but offered no real alternative to the general view of nature which a few scholars questioned. It was necessary to pose new questions before a new synthesis could be constructed.

The Renaissance itself was regrettably indifferent to scientific inquiry as such, but it did provide an indispensable impetus to scientific thought. Many early steps toward a new science resulted from attempts to explain the old. The availability of complete and accurate texts of Aristotle and other classical authorities gave rise to renewed scientific debate and offered new means of verification and investigation. It probably was no accident that Copernicus, Galileo, Harvey, and other great scientists of the sixteenth century all spent time at the University of Padua, the home of the debate over Aristotle in the fifteenth century. The New Learning was not primarily scientific in nature, but it provided new scholarly tools and a form of education free from the limitations of the scholastic outlook. The community of scientific investigators the New Learning developed gave impetus to scientific pursuits in general. As the cracks in the Aristotelian synthesis widened, new mathematical knowledge and much-improved data from observation of nature allowed alternatives to be presented, and they in turn could be challenged or verified.

Both the brilliance and the inadequacies of the new science in its early stages are exhibited in two works which appeared in 1543: *On the Fabric of the Human Body* by Andreas Vesalius (1514—1564) and *Of Revolution* by Nicholas Copernicus (1473—1543). The main contribution of Vesalius was to lay the ground work for systematic study of the human body—although he was never able to forget Galen when describing what he saw. Vesalius, who was born in Brussels but taught at Padua, was revolutionary in his method, not in the minimal adjustments he made in the prevailing view of human anatomy. He demanded direct observation, and his book was lavishly illustrated with woodcuts of every aspect of human anatomy. It remained for other men to use his techniques of dissection to construct a new overall explanation of the workings of the body.

Copernicus, on the other hand, began with the revolutionary conviction that the sun, not the earth, is the center around which the planets move. He spent his life attempting to describe the revolutions of the universe in a manner which would justify his hypothesis, but his complicated pattern of planetary motion was not a convincing paradigm. Without benefit of telescope or other instruments, which had not yet appeared, Copernicus made many errors—except in his original conviction. Despite the implications of his theory, he managed to escape notoriety. He died at his home in Poland as his book was being published and never knew that the foreword, written by the publisher, described his theory as a mere hypothesis.

Copernicus' description of the universe had little, if any, obvious superiority to that of Ptolemy. It remained for Galileo (1564—1642) to bring the controversy before the public and to launch the attack on Aristotelian physics in general. In *The Dialogue on the Two Chief Systems of the World* (1632), Galileo brought Aristotle and Copernicus face to face in a debate which left the Christian Aristotelian with nothing to stand on but his faith. The Pope himself became aroused, Galileo was forced to recant, and the Church took a firm doctrinal stand against the heliocentric theory.

Galileo's achievement was not limited to criticism of Aristotle; after all, Aristotle had survived earlier attacks. With the aid of the telescope, Galileo improved substantially on Copernican astronomy and discovered the moons of Jupiter. Yet he clung to the belief that the planetary orbits described perfect circles—evidence of the perfection of the universe. Galileo's astronomy and his humiliation by the Church have attracted attention away from his true significance in the scientific revolution of the seventeenth century. It was in physics and mechanics that his work signified real change. With improved instruments and mathematical knowledge, he was able to take an important step toward the concept of inertia. In his law of falling bodies, he finally went beyond his Greek predecessors and expressed motion in mathematical ratios. It was his conviction that the dynamic world around man—a world in which heavenly and terrestrial bodies are continually in motion—could be measured, and that the universe could be understood in mathematical terms. Galileo established that the rate of acceleration of a falling object is proportionate to the time it falls; in so doing, he introduced the dimension of time into scientific study.

Galileo's pioneering achievements look small beside the enormous accomplishments of the succeeding generation of physicists—primarily, of course, those of Sir Isaac Newton. His mathematical tools, improved as they were over those of medieval scientists, were still rudimentary and awkward. He had neither analytic geometry nor calculus to assist him in the description of his ideas and discoveries. Despite the incalculable help of the telescope in observation of the heavens, he lacked data to support his theories. Many of the experiments he described were performed only in his mind in order to illustrate theories which had been formed without them. But none of this detracts from Galileo's supreme position as a scientific revolutionary; his conception of the mathematical expression of physical facts and the abstract nature of physical laws makes his work a watershed in Western history. Galileo did not supply conclusive answers to physical questions—his experimentation and mathematics were too faulty—but, like Copernicus, he raised questions of tremendous significance.

In the observation of celestial phenomena, it was the Italian Galileo's contemporaries, Tycho Brahe (1546—1601), a Dane, and Johannes Kepler (1571—1630), a German, who provided the most accurate descriptions of the heliocentric universe. Brahe brought astronomy to a new level of accuracy through his observation of the heavens. Thanks to his highly refined telescopes and elaborate methods of recording data, and above all to his diligent nightly observations, he was able to bequeath to his assistant, Kepler, the data needed to draw an immensely improved picture of the solar system. Kepler had the mathematical ability to make sense out of the endless tables and charts. After years of trial-and-error hypotheses and computation, prolonged by the lack of trigonometric tables, Kepler derived formulas which described the elliptical orbits of the planets. Galileo had used observation as an occasional tool, but Kepler built his laws of planetary motion upon observed data.

René Descartes (1596—1650), a French contemporary of both Galileo and Kepler, applied the new power granted by mathematics in a very different approach to scientific problems. For Descartes, if the universe could be shown to obey mathematical laws, then these natural laws could be discerned more clearly through mathematical reasoning than through observation of a morass of detail. Descartes believed that the human mind could apprehend the principles inherent in nature through deductive reasoning from the simplest and most basic truths to the most complex. Celestial bodies in the Cartesian universe (the universe according to Descartes) moved in a fluid atmosphere, since he believed matter to be continuous. A devout Catholic, Descartes escaped Galileo's fate by propounding a complicated paradigm in which the planets circled the sun while the rest of the universe revolved around the earth.

Much of Descartes's system and many of his particular assertions were outmoded by the empirical findings of his contemporaries and successors. Not surprisingly, his most important contribution was in the field of mathematics. In particular, his discovery of coordinate geometry allowed much greater facility in handling problems of motion than had been possible for Galileo. Descartes was able to describe the principles of inertia accurately by showing that objects in motion tend to move in a straight line until affected by another force, a concept essential to the understanding of motion.

The anomalies in Descartes' system and the limitations in scope of Kepler's laws were overcome by Sir Isaac Newton (1642—1727), whose work represents the culmination of the scientific revolution of the sixteenth and seventeenth centuries. Newton himself was a scientific genius. In the first of two brief creative periods (1665—1666 and 1684—1687) he arrived at the principles of his monumental synthesis. In the second, he presented them to the world in *The Mathematical Principles of Natural Philosophy*. Newton combined Descartes' ability to think in mathematical terms with Kepler's grasp of data to integrate two centuries of scientific study in a comprehensive explanation upon which rests classical physics as well as modern engineering and mechanics.

Newton's particular contributions were immense; they included differential and integral calculus, the law of gravity, and a vastly improved theory of light. Above all, his conception of the universe as a huge mechanism in which all motion can be described in quantitative terms made physics before Albert Einstein (1879—1955) little more than a series of footnotes to Newton. Newton's system possesses both simplicity and utility: In the Newtonian universe, no pieces are left over, and mathematics is closely wedded to observation. The unanswerable questions (for instance, what is gravity?) are carefully excluded, and God appears as the Great Watchmaker, who has created a mechanism and then stepped back to allow it to operate in an orderly and predictable manner. The limitations of the Newtonian system are its virtues, defining both the questions which can be asked and the means to find the answers.

In fields other than physics, the scientific revolution was slower and less comprehensive. Although the groundwork for the modern system of biological classification had been laid by the early eighteenth century, the emergence of a convincing synthesis of biological data had to wait for the discoveries of Charles Darwin (1809—1882) in the nineteenth century. William Harvey (1578—1657) published his study of the circulation of the blood in 1628. His meticulous methods of dissecting different kinds of animals to observe the action of the heart in various organisms proved productive, but further understanding of the workings of the body was seriously impeded by the rudimentary state of seventeenth-century chemistry. The heritage of medieval alchemy hindered progress in chemistry; the nature of gases and of the elements was not discovered until the eighteenth century. The minute and invisible world proved more difficult to penetrate than the grander mysteries of the heavens.

Yet the revolution which culminated in Newtonian physics produced a methodology which could be applied in all fields. Not long after the telescope, the microscope appeared; and while mathematics could be applied directly to dynamics, it was useful also in biology and chemistry. Above all, the definition of science as the study of matter and motion had been accomplished. By the time of Newton, Aristotle was little more than a memory; he no longer presented a built-in mental barrier to scientific investigation.

The development of an adequate methodology was accomplished by the development of a scientific community devoted to answering the questions the scientific revolution raised. By the end of the seventeenth century the scientist had become indispensable to the intellectual world, and science an independent discipline. The scientist was no longer constrained to be a theologian or a physician as well. The scientific society and the learned journal gave formal expression to the discourse and argument which were inherent parts of the scientific revolution.

The earliest scientific society had been founded in Italy in 1603. The Royal Society in England originated during the Puritan Revolution, when men interested in science agreed to meet together to discuss nature, banishing the turbulence of politics from their discussions. The Royal Society received only blessings from the English Crown, but in France the state took a positive role in patronizing scientific investigation. By the end of the seventeenth century the Academy of Sciences had taken shape as a society which gave pensions to men in every major field of science. The growing refinement of scientific study was thus accomplished by professionalization. By the end of the seventeenth century what had seemed an open book to the educated man of the Renaissance became a complicated discipline beyond the understanding of the average gentleman.

6.2 Rationalism and Empiricism

The scientific revolution of the sixteenth and seventeenth centuries penetrated man's fundamental view of the universe systematically, explicitly, and undeniably. It gradually became impossible to assert, for example, that the earth was the center of the universe; and the role of theology in shaping scientific debate became ever more limited.

The breach between theology and philosophy had been gradually widening since the fifteenth century. In the seventeenth century, philosophical thought took as its starting point the new science rather than the old theology, and the separation between the two—especially in the vital realm of methodology—became virtually complete. For the most part, the new metaphysical systems by-passed rather than challenged the scholastic theology of the universities. Few of the great philosophers of the seventeenth century received their education primarily through university training; none of them did his creative work within the confines of the academic world. Hobbes and Spinoza were denounced as impious, but most of the seventeenth-century philosophers professed religious orthodoxy. The new philosophy simply raised new questions and answered them through new methods. The old triumvirate of Scripture, tradition, and ecclesiastical authority faded before the demands of rationalism and empiricism.

No reconstruction of Western philosophy could be simple, and no general philosophical system achieved the clarity and general acceptability of Newtonian physics. Early in the debate, two dominant modes of thought emerged: rationalism and empiricism. It is, of course, an oversimplification to consider these two approaches as distinct and opposing philosophical systems; in fact, the two were often interdependent, and a thinker's identification with either camp was often little more than a matter of emphasis. It is true that rationalism proceeded deductively, constructing a picture of nature, man, and society from first principles; but rationalists expected their picture to describe and explain the sense data of experience accurately. By the same token, the empiricists attempted to build a picture of reality from the data of observation and experiment; but they could not ignore the demands of logic and consistency, nor could they eliminate hypothesis and necessarily deductive mathematical analysis in methodology.

The founder of Continental rationalism was Descartes, whose scientific theories have already been discussed. In many ways he typified the seventeenth-century philosophers. Educated in Jesuit schools, he was a devout Catholic, but he found scholasticism hopelessly irrelevant to serious philosophical and scientific inquiry. He longed for tranquility and meditation but spent much of his life as a gentleman officer in Dutch and German armies. He enjoyed frequent contact with other men of science and letters in Paris and the Netherlands, and he died at the court of Queen Christina of Sweden, whom he had hoped to instruct in his fascinating new ideas. Although Descartes believed that the experimental approach to science was largely a waste of time, he kept abreast of scientific discoveries and attempted his own explanation of such diverse problems as the movement of heavenly bodies and the circulation of the blood. In both areas his scientific ideas suffered from his tendency to ignore experiment. In mathematics, however, he made lasting contributions; and his scientific ideas enjoyed an acceptance far beyond their intrinsic merit because of the persuasiveness of his philosophical system and his intellectual power as a mathematician.

Descartes' approach to philosophy was radical—much more so than the theological and moral principles which he ultimately derived from it. He began by abandoning the reliance upon authority and humility of medieval philosophy, asserting that man can understand the universe by means of his own intellect. Descartes' point of departure was neither the Bible nor sensory perception of nature. He adopted the method of metaphysical doubt as the basic principle of inquiry, resolving to doubt everything that could be doubted and then to build upon that foundation a system of philosophy which accepted only ideas which were "clear and distinct" to him. And the only thing which could not be doubted, he discovered, was his own existence. His famous statement, "I think, therefore I am," expressed his realization that the very process of doubting his own existence affirmed his existence as a thinking being.

But what could Descartes affirm beyond his own existence? His perception of the world, even of his own body, was certainly subject to error. Descartes solved his problem by turning to the idea of God, whose existence could be deduced from concepts of perfection and infinity which were innate in the human mind. Thus Descartes found in his own ideas the necessity for a perfect and eternal creator and sustainer of the universe. Such a God could not by His very nature be a deceiver of man; and from this assumption Descartes derived the belief that he could trust those ideas of his own which were clear and distinct. The nature of God implied a rational, ordered universe intelligible to a man who could, with his innate abilities, reason about it.

The exact nature of Descartes' epistemology—theory of knowledge—is one of the greatest problems in understanding his philosophy and has remained the subject of unending debate for subsequent philosophers and historians. It is clear that Descartes believed in two sorts of knowledge—ideas which were intrinsic to the mind, and sense perceptions which were presented to the mind by the physical world. He believed that ideas have an existence of their own, that such concepts as the principles of mathematics are inherent in every man's mind, awaiting discovery. But the exact relationship of these ideas to the world of sense perception was the source of strong disagreement between rationalists and empiricists.

In spite of the difficulties inherent in Descartes' system of philosophy, his *Rules for the Direction of Mind* (1628) and his subsequent philosophical works had unparalleled influence on his contemporaries and successors. His works crystallized more than a century of efforts to construct a rational, ordered conception of nature. In applying rational study to the human mind itself, Descartes opened the way for extending the scientific method to other fields of thought. The principles of Cartesian philosophy provided the foundation for the next century of French intellectual inquiry.

Descartes solved the problem of religion by drawing scrupulously orthodox conclusions from his system. He even refrained from publishing one of his works when it appeared that it might be considered heretical. In addition, his writings contain many throwbacks to scholastic theology. Rationalism itself, after all, was as basic to St. Thomas Aquinas as to Descartes. But metaphysical doubt separated Descartes from St. Thomas, as did Descartes' exclusive reliance upon his own mind to distinguish between true and false. Ultimately, the Cartesian universe and the human mind which observed it were not only rational but mathematical in operation; nature was regular, measurable, and intelligible to human reason, if not fallible human perception. For all his Christian orthodoxy, the Cartesian view of nature and the close union of philosophy with science and mathematics marked a radical break with scholasticism and made Descartes the first modern philosopher.

Because of the problematical relationship between the traditional sources of religious belief—divine revelation, Scripture, and traditional authorities— and rationalism, Cartesian philosophy presented profound difficulties for men such as Blaise Pascal (1623—1662), a French adherent of both Jansenism and Cartesianism. The Jansenists emphasized a religious belief based upon the Augustinian and mystical traditions within the Church; and therefore Pascal— himself a scientist—had to make a distinction between faith and reason. He preserved his consistency only by carefully separating his conception of nature from his worship of God. In his scientific work he helped to discover the barometer and to demonstrate that atmospheric pressure works to fill a vacuum. In addition, he invented a calculating machine—the forerunner of the modern computer—which could perform mathematical operations mechanically.

Benedict de Spinoza (1632—1677), a Dutch philosopher of Portuguese- Jewish parentage, went far beyond Descartes. For Spinoza, the universe (infinite, eternal, and perfectly rational) was identical with God. In his pantheistic system, particular aspects of nature were made comprehensible and explicable by ascertaining their relationship to the whole system of the universe. By the same token, particular events appeared to be good or evil only from a limited human perspective. In the long run, as part of an eternal and perfect system, they were inevitably good. With rigorous logic, Spinoza followed the implications of his first premise. He asserted that freedom of the will operates in history only in the sense that men, whose knowledge is limited since he is finite, is forced to choose among alternatives. Man's consciousness of freedom of choice is a psychological fact, but in reality his choice is the result of a series of causes which was not in man's power to alter. At the same time, however, it is possible to speak of good and evil and of better and worse choices. Man's actions are good insofar as they are rational and in accord with his nature.

The primary motive of human behavior, Spinoza claimed, is the natural desire for self-preservation. Spinoza adopted the view that man is a fundamentally egotistical being but that his egotism does not lead him into hedonism or the "war of all against all" that Hobbes had feared. The man who is rational, and therefore good, acts in accord with his long-term interests, submitting to the law because of the advantages which he derives from human association and curbing his passions in favor of reasonable and temperate behavior.

Spinoza is admired by modern philosophers for his very profound insights into human psychology, but in his own day he was denounced by his own Jewish community and by Christians as well. His pantheism and his view of self-interest as the fundamental principle of ethical behavior were considered blasphemous and immoral, and the importance of his work went largely unacknowledged by his contemporaries.

The German philosopher Gottfried Wilhelm von Leibniz (1646—1716) most nearly achieved a philosophical system which incorporated both rationalism and empiricism. One of the greatest mathematical minds of all time, Leibniz invented calculus independently at about the same time as Newton. His other interests included history, jurisprudence, Chinese philosophy, and many other intellectual fields—he was most close to a universal genius that the seventeenth century produced. He was also something of an opportunist, greatly concerned with his reputation in court and salon; he suppressed many of his most important writings when he became aware that they might bring about an unpopular reaction. Some waited a century or more for publication, and many have not yet been published.

Leibniz' fondest dream was to produce a logical universal language to serve as the vehicle for philosophical discourse. He foreshowed modern positivism in his use of logical analysis, especially in his attempts to establish a means of arriving at probabilities when it was impossible to discuss data in terms of laws and prediction.

More than the other rationalists, Leibniz attempted to analyze empirical data in logical terms. His thought reflects the growing debate between Continental rationalism and English empiricism which occupied philosophers in the seventeenth century. The founder of English empiricism, Sir Francis Bacon (1561—1626), was not a seminal thinker like Descartes. He was a gentleman before he was a scientist. For a time Bacon was Lord Chancellor of England under James I. Bacon's questions were more interesting than his answers, which were more often than not incorrect.

Bacon was attracted to the new science because he saw its immense potentialities as a useful field of endeavor. His methodology was radically different from that of Descartes. Bacon believed that the collection of data should be the first step in scientific investigation. To discover the properties of heat, for example, he made lists of hot and cold objects and then tried to establish the basic properties of heat by a process of elimination. He was not successful in this endeavor, and his work on the whole reflected a very imperfect understanding of the usefulness of mathematics in scientific investigation. But Bacon's method of inductive reasoning—building up general principles from the investigation of particular data—made a lasting contribution to English science and philosophy.

Another fundamental element in English empiricism was the belief that human knowledge comes from sense perception. This was at least implicit in Bacon's philosophy, but remained for Thomas Hobbes (1588—1679) to build a philosophical and psychological system upon materialist principles. Hobbes asserted that the problem of human behavior is essentially an extension of the problem of motion in physics. He happily accepted the rational and deductive method of reasoning geometry provides, but he believed that man is actuated by the material universe, that he seeks his physical well-being. Hobbes was not enough of a rationalist to avoid creating a philosophical system replete with contradictions, nor was he a careful enough empiricist to avoid making many factual errors. His contribution to English philosophy rested upon his denial of nonmaterial cause and his subsequent penetration into the principles of human psychology.

It was John Locke (1632—1704) who gave English empiricism its most coherent and persuasive formulation in the seventeenth century. Locke combined Bacon's inductive reasoning with Hobbes' materialism to construct a philosophical system which laid the groundwork for the empiricism of George Berkeley (1685—1753) and David Hume (1711—1776) in the eighteenth century. He began by denying the principle of innate ideas; Locke believed that the human mind is shaped by the gradual accumulation of experience in the world. The sources of knowledge for an individual are his perception of sense data and his awareness of the workings of his own mind. The intersection between the two sources of knowledge is well illustrated by Locke's explanation of man's concept of time. He asserted that man arrived at the concept of duration by observing the succession of his ideas in his mind. The concept of duration was combined with the perception of motion (especially that of the sun and the planets) to produce a means of measuring duration, and the concept of time (measured duration) is thus a combination of man's perception of his own mind and the workings of nature, not an innate idea. Locke called this combined process "reflection" and asserted that it was the source of all knowledge.

Like Descartes, Locke asserted that man knows of his own existence through his perception of himself and that from that perception he can also derive the existence of God. Unlike Descartes, however, Locke insisted that knowledge of the world depend upon sense perception and on our ability to build general principles from particular data. Thus Locke believed that our finitude is an inescapable limit to the establishment of a general and adequate explanation of the universe. Man's investigation of things outside himself is an endless task in which hypotheses and the principles of mathematics are tools to aid in the ordering of data provided by experiment and observation. To Locke, conclusions more often than not are mere probabilities whose measure of veracity reflects the thoroughness with which the data have been tested.

6.3 New Political Theory

Since the sixteenth and seventeenth centuries changed the way man thought about the universe, about science, philosophy, and religion, his view of himself and society could not remain unchanged. Just as the artist and the scientist now functioned as professionals in a predominantly secular environment, so the political theorist began to examine the relations of men in society in a more systematic way, applying the principles and the methodology of the new science and philosophy. Political theory in the sixteenth and seventeenth centuries reflected a new intellectual milieu as well as the growing importance and complexity of the state. Each great crisis in this period, from the Reformation onward, gave rise to a flood of pamphlets which supplied ideological and theoretical positions for all sides in the conflict. The evolution of political thought in the years after the Reformation effectively supplanted the medieval view of society and gave birth to modern political theory.

In politics, as in other fields, the break with the Middle Ages was not sudden. Men in the sixteenth century very often viewed changing conditions through the eyes of their predecessors. The Renaissance and the Reformation were more effective in breaking down the credibility of that hierarchy of authority which had formed the basis of medieval political thought than in building up a new and generally acceptable political theory. The demand that society serve human needs was developed during the Renaissance, partly from the ideas of the conciliar party in the later Middle Ages. Ideas of common consent were not, however, attractive to political theorists of the Reformation.

For both Martin Luther and John Calvin, a godly society could be maintained only with proper authority and discipline. Luther saw a solid foundation for society in the power of the prince, while Calvin believed that an enlightened oligarchy could provide both justice and discipline. The right of resistance became increasingly important to Calvin's successors, however, especially to the Huguenots in France and the Puritans in England. For both parties, resistance could be justified on the grounds that obedience to God took precedence over obedience to the king, with the obvious conclusion that an ungodly king must be resisted as a matter of conscience. Only briefly, in the doctrines of the Levellers in England and a few other radical groups, was kingship challenged on democratic grounds. The resistance of the English constitutional lawyers to the Crown was based on the charge that the king had violated canons of constitutional government handed down from the Middle Ages.

Arguments in favor of the authority of the king were also firmly grounded in the medieval tradition. The theory of the divine right of kings remained a powerful ideological tool in the hands of hereditary monarchy. This idea was of great importance in the development of the French monarchy, receiving one of its most extreme formulations in the attitude of Louis XIV and the writings of his son's tutor, Jacques Bénigne Bossuet (1627—1704). In England, James I exercised his scholarly mind in formulating a defense against the claims of Parliament based upon the divine right of kingship. The basic assertion of such defenders of monarchy was that the hand of the king was in fact the hand of God and that to resist the king was to defy God. The king was responsible only to God for his actions—which were as incomprehensible and inexplicable to men as the will of God Himself.

At the same time, however, the sixteenth century saw a basic transformation in the conception of the nature of political authority. Both the state and the individual were discussed in new terms. In France, the later sixteenth century brought to a climax the long conflict between Protestant and Catholic which threatened the very existence of the monarchy. Protestant victory threatened to dissolve the state, and the Catholic cause depended upon Spanish intervention. Under these conditions arose the politiques—a group dedicated to the survival of the French monarchy. In essence, they proposed to consider the political structure and the religious structure of the country as separate problems and to allow religious toleration as a necessary precondition to the preservation of the state.

The leading theorist of the politiques was Jean Bodin (1530—1596). His *Six Books Concerning the State* first outlined the doctrine of sovereignty in clear terms. Bodin saw the state as an entity distinguished from other forms of association—such as family or church—by its monopoly of the power of physical coercion. The state was unique because it possessed the exclusive power to command obedience, a power established by the law and exercised by the king. For the citizen, all other duties were necessarily subordinated to his duties to the state. The conception of the state as a territorial entity—its right to command obedience was limited only by its constitution and physical boundaries—was essential to seventeenth-century political thought.

The concept of sovereignty was further refined and applied to international relations by Hugo Grotius of the Netherlands (1583—1645). He combined the idea of sovereignty of the individual state with a law of nations to govern their relations in war and peace. Grotius believed that this body of international law would be observed because it was natural and just, not because there could be any authority superior to that of the individual state.

The idea of natural law which played such an important role in Grotius' thought was a matter of virtually universal concern among seventeenth-century political theorists. As the concept of a divinely ordered hierarchy of authority faded into the background, it left the state sovereign but without clear moral justification. The seventeenth century found the answer in human nature. The state was seen as the product of man's own needs and desires, and its authority was therefore justified in terms of both morality and self-interest. Most proponents of such a view agreed that men could not live satisfactorily without the state and that the basis of its authority was the tacit or expressed agreement of men to enter into a society and establish a government. By establishing a sovereign, the individual surrendered a part of his freedom, but he received in return social order and justice in his dealings with other men. Natural law provided the basis for such a society, and a contract between the ruler and the ruled provided the means by which men could enter it.

This view of the state provided the foundation upon which the modern view is based. In itself, however, it could not offer a definitive solution to all political problems, because it was capable of a wide variety of particular applications. In some cases, as in the thought of Samuel von Pufendorf (1632—1694), a German follower of Grotius, the theory was used to support enlightened absolutism. Pufendorf believed that men entered into two contracts. The first contract was their agreement to live together as a society. The second contract was their compact with their ruler, who was sovereign but limited by the demands of reason and justice. The ruler thus received both power and an obligation to use it well, and although Pufendorf did not allow for a right of resistance to an unjust ruler, it is clear that he expected the ruler to be guided by his obligations.

The contract theory of government could be used also to support the most extreme absolutism. In England during the revolutionary era, Thomas Hobbes produced his *Leviathan* as a defense of unlimited state authority. Hobbes did not question the existence of God, but neither did he use the theory of divine right to justify the position of the English king. Instead, he built a theory of human motivation and politics in purely secular terms. His thought can be regarded as a blending of the principles of Machiavelli's the *Prince* with the tradition of natural law.

Hobbes' theory of the state was derived from his view of human psychology. He was pessimistic about human nature, seeing man as a self-seeking and less than rational being, motivated by the desire for power and by its accompaniment, fear of the power of other men. According to Hobbes, the basic equality of men in the state of nature (that is, men living together without a sovereign) allowed no man enough predominance to obtain security and produced an endless "war of all against all". Only fear and reasonable consideration of the advantages of order and security induced men to give up their power to a common sovereign with absolute authority over them.

For Hobbes, the sovereign and the state were identical (in other words, the law was merely an expression of the will of the king) and, by definition, absolute. Without any inherent power, natural law could not limit the state. The sovereign possessed the right of life and death over his subjects, and the right of censorship and indoctrination as well. Religion was beneficial to the state because it was conducive to public order. Disobedience was forbidden under any conditions, and to dissolve the contract with the sovereign was to return society to the ravages of the state of nature. The authority of the sovereign was thus limited only by his ability to impose his will on society. In a successful revolution, the citizen owed absolute obedience to the new sovereign once he had successfully established his power.

Hobbes, like many of his contemporaries, adopted the methodology of the natural sciences and deduced a view of the state from fundamental assumptions about human nature. His countryman John Locke was similarly attracted to the principles of science. Like Hobbes, he began with human nature, then examined man in the state of nature, and finally expounded a view of government based on his judgment of man's needs and desires.

Locke was much more optimistic about human nature than Hobbes, however, and he was also on the opposite side politically. An advocate of the Parliamentary cause in the Puritan Revolution, he wrote his greatest work, *The Second Treatise on Civil Government*, shortly before the Glorious Revolution of 1688. His work became the theoretical defense of the Revolution. Like Hobbes, Locke believed that man was motivated by self-interest, the pursuit of pleasure and avoidance of pain. At the same time, however, Locke asserted that the greed of the wise man was moderated by principles of reasonableness—a man enslaved by his desires was not free. A free man lived according to self-imposed and reasonable rules.

In the state of nature, man is free to do whatever he pleases as long as he does not violate the similar right of others. The right of property is one of man's fundamental liberties, and the individual establishes his right to a particular piece of property through his labor. Every man is free from all restraints other than those of natural law. But because each man is his own judge, the state of nature—lacking any supreme power—is insecure and unstable. It is liable at any moment to erupt into a chaotic war much like that described by Hobbes. Therefore men agree to enter into civil society in order to provide for a common judge. In doing so, each man gives up only that part of his natural liberty which is necessary to the maintenance of a state that can make his life, liberty, and property secure. He is guaranteed legal equality with other men in return for his agreement in advance to follow the law. Except for what is commonly agreed to be necessary to the state, man retains his liberty, and if the government transcends its limitations, the contract is broken and man is absolved of his obedience.

Locke was thus an advocate of government limited by the natural rights of the individual, and he favored constitutional government, with power shared between king and parliament, as the safeguard of such a system. Locke's political ideas were timely and brilliant, and his treatise remained the most important formulation of the principles of English liberalism down to the nineteenth century. In the eighteenth century his influence spread beyond England to the Continent, and Lockean ideas permeate *The Declaration of Independence* and *The Constitution of the United States*, the two most important American documents ever written.

6.4 The Heritage of Seventeenth-century Culture

The scientific revolution can be viewed as part of Baroque culture. The art of the seventeenth century was characterized by expressions of deep personal feelings, by an eclectic reliance upon all kinds of techniques and motifs, and by an unembarrassed grandiosity. The same characteristics can be found in the scientific thinkers: an intense desire to establish the truth, an omnivorous knowledge of every discipline that could be useful to their work, and a bold faith in their powers to understand and explain the universe. Baroque artists spared no effort, neglected no technique, refrained from no excess to achieve the absolute in art; similarly, the scientists of the period exhibited a wonderful restlessness, audacity, and selfless passion in creating a new intellectual system. Baroque artists never worried about their many failures, their lapses into awkwardness and bad taste; they simply tried again in their pursuit of aesthetic perfection. The scientists, too, made error after error and blundered into many wrong answers; but in the Baroque spirit, they never doubted that success was attainable, that the great breakthrough was not far off. They learned their mathematics and developed their instruments and even established their method of inquiry at the same time they were formulating their new view of the universe.

By the early seventeenth century it was apparent that the new philosophy calls all in doubt. At Oxford and the Sorbonne in the fourteenth century and at the University of Pudua in the fifteenth century, the Aristotelian-Ptolemaic view of the universe had been seriously questioned, and fragments of a new system had been postulated. But the probing of these late medieval thinkers was vitiated by inadequate mathematics and a social and cultural milieu that did not encourage further inquiry into natural phenomena. The scientific movement began all over again in 1543 with the publication of Copernicus' work, and in the early seventeenth century Galileo achieved the first real turning point in the scientific revolution. Baconian empiricism and Cartesian mathematical rationalism gave direction to the new movement of thought, and after the immense labor of several great thinkers, the new physics received its definitive formulation with the publication in 1687 of Newton's *Mathematical Principles of Natural Philosophy*.

In Newton's work the new physics broke through to a universal system of mechanics that explained the operation of the material world from the movement of a small object to the movement of the planets and related these movements by a universal law of inertia and gravity. Universal gravitation had been proposed two years earlier by Newton's colleague in the English Royal Society, Robert Hooke (1635—1703), but it was Newton who was able to develop this hypothesis (which he arrived at independently) into a complete scientific theory in which the phenomena of nature were subjected to what he called "the laws of mathematics". Newton's *Principles* established theoretical physics in the form it was to retain until the late nineteenth century.

In the following century it became fully evident that Newton's discovery would lead to European hegemony in the world. The new physics essentially engendered the industrial technology of the eighteenth and nineteenth centuries and thereby elevated Europe to a position of power over other civilizations. Thus Bacon's perception of the social significance of scientific discovery and technological change was fully validated: Human knowledge and human power meet in one. Knowledge is power.

The scientific movement of the seventeenth century aimed at a general theory of the physical universe that could be verified. But Galileo and Descartes believed that more than observation and experimentation was required for verification. They wanted a theory that could be verified mathematically. What the scientific movement, Newton in particular, finally achieved was the quantification of nature: a general theory of both terrestrial and celestial physics that could be expressed in mathematical terms. This quantification of nature separates seventeenth century science from ancient and medieval natural philosophy; it was the quality that distinguishes modern science.

Although science became an extremely abstract pursuit by the late seventeenth century, the true spirit of the scientific revolution was not that of a purely disinterested intellectual quest. The statements of Bacon and Descartes reflect a growing consciousness of the social consequences of science—it leads to "human power" and makes men "the lords and possessors of nature". This attitude has also remained a fundamental principle of modern science: All the labor of experimentation and the immense cerebral effort involved in quantification would not only elevate human understanding but also improve human life. It is this double vision of modern science that most distinguished Western civilization from other cultures in the following two centuries.

Chapter 7   The Enlightenment: Power of Reason

The spirit of intellectual life and opinion in Western Europe during the period from about 1715 to 1789 is aptly characterized by the term *Enlightenment*. The leading thinkers of the time firmly believed that theirs was an age of enlightenment, and that it held great promise for improving man's life on earth through the exercise of human reason.

7.1   The Nature of the Enlightenment

What distinguished the Enlightenment, among others, was its critical spirit, whereby men would rationally examine natural events and solve chronic human problems, that marked the unique climate of eighteenth-century thought. What was the "critical spirit" that the men of the Enlightenment purposefully cultivated and consciously chose as the symbol of their intellectual movement? They believed in man's unlimited ability to analyze and explain every aspect of his own nature and the world about him. The critical spirit went hand in hand with a new faith in the power and efficacy of the human understanding, or reason. It meant an unfettered freedom of inquiry and examination, no matter how sacred the subject or how bold the investigation. "Dare to know" —thus the German philosopher Immanuel Kant (1724—1804), writing toward the end of the eighteenth century, defined the critical spirit.

The exercise of the critical spirit often did require a kind of intellectual bravery, because men who allowed their minds to range freely were inevitably forced to challenge the power of traditional authorities and accepted beliefs, particularly in religion and politics. Not only were nature's works to be studied and explained, but human phenomena as well were to be scrutinized in the light of rational principles and judged by their concordance with the fundamental laws of nature. No longer were men satisfied with the traditional theological justifications for the suffering and injustice of human existence. Man's reward—the good life—would be achieved not in heaven but only on earth. The age-old dogmas of the Church were examined, discredited, and finally rejected.

The legacy of Newton was clear and simple. All nature, it was assumed, was ruled by rational, comprehensible laws. Man had been given reason in order to perceive not the greater glory of God but the natural order of the world—in science, in history, in law, and in all institutions and customs of society. Eighteenth-century morality had a secular emphasis that contrasts dramatically with the older belief in divine Providence and the modern feeling that man's fate is dictated by irrational forces he cannot control.

The critical spirit inspired what the men of the Enlightenment thought of as a new way to philosophize about every area of life and thought. In eighteenth-century discourse, philosophy meant more than the abstract theoretical speculation of the scholastic philosophers; it embraced a vast intellectual movement. No authority was allowed to rest unchallenged. To this day it is a matter of historical debate as to which traditional beliefs remained and which were swept away.

Historians have also argued, and probably always will, about the stature of the Enlightenment thinkers—the philosophes—who believed their main work lay in clearing away the rubbish of outworn ideas and archaic traditions. The inclusive and virtually untranslatable French term philosophe is applied to the man of talent who epitomized the Enlightenment. Although philosophes regarded themselves as an extremely cosmopolitan group, and although the group did include such diverse figures as the Scottish empiricist David Hume, the German metaphysician Kant, and the Italian legal reformer Beccaria, the largest and most articulate group was composed of Frenchmen, or of men who lived in France or whose language was French. Furthermore, the dates commonly accepted as marking the Age of the Enlightenment, 1715 and 1789, are peculiarly French in historical significance. Louis XIV died in 1715. His death weakened rigid authority in French society, marked the beginning of a kind of thaw in French literary life, and opened the way to a new social criticism. The year 1789 saw the outbreak of the French Revolution, the beginning of the upheavals that characterize the modern world.

The prototype of the philosophe formulated ideas and propagated them as well. Strictly speaking, he was neither a philosopher nor a literary man, though he interested himself in the latest philosophical speculation and wrote prolifically and well. His style was simple and pungent, and his published work was usually intended for the general reader. He cultivated many and far-ranging interests; Charles Louis de Secondat, Barón de Montesquieu(1689—1755) tended his vineyards, and Jean-Jacques Rousseau(1712—1778) composed an opera. Although most philosophes were not primarily scientists, they prided themselves on understanding and keeping up with the newest development in theoretical and applied science. Many of them—Diderot, for example, and Benjamin Franklin (1706—1790)—conducted experiments of their own. Others, like Buffon(1707—1788), were scientists who wrote about their own work for the general public. Even Voltaire (1694—1778), who had no particular aptitude for mathematics, published a popular exposition of Newton's theories of light.

The philosophes regarded themselves as an international community of like-minded men engaged in a collective intellectual adventure. They kept up a tremendous stream of correspondence among themselves and were seldom stinting on criticism, praise, or gossip. Their role, they believed, was to be the vanguard of the best, most critical, most rational thought of the age. They intended to bear the torch kindled by the great scientific minds of the seventeenth-century.

The philosophes hoped to accomplish great things. Hostile historians have accused them of indulging in a shallow and self-defeating optimism, but most of them were not so naïve. In the course of the eighteenth century the philosophes embraced with less and less confidence the Newtonian maxim that "Nature is always in harmony with itself". Harmony might be a fundamental law of nature, but human institutions were not ordered according to rational principles. Nor were hate, intolerance, and superstition dissolved by the exercise of reason, for men clung to outworn traditions. Old and unjust authorities—in government and religion—stubbornly resisted change. The stupidity of men proved to be the greatest obstacle to the spread of enlightenment.

Nevertheless, the philosophes' crusade to expose irrationality and ameliorate injustices left its own legacy. By their intense analysis of social and political institutions, the philosophes incidentally developed the methodological tools that serve as the foundation of modern social science. Their assertion of the autonomy of the human mind and spirit, coupled with their special regard for the growth of the individual in society, fostered a belief in the natural equality of all men and gave rise to a new conception of civil rights. Their demands that the critical spirit be freely exercised led to the formulation of principles of freedom of speech, writing, and conscience that have been enshrined as the basic tenets of liberal doctrine. Finally, the philosophes' tender regard for all human beings helped to create a new kind of social consciousness that led eventually to a revolutionary attack on the social order itself.

7.2　Philosophy and Theology

Eighteenth-century philosophers preferred to think themselves as empiricists rather than metaphysicians. Like the Newtonian scientists who rejected scholasticism, they turned against the system-building that characterized the work of the great seventeenth-century philosophers: Descartes, Spinoza, and Leibniz. The Enlightenment philosophers hoped to apply the critical spirit in philosophy instead of arguing over abstract speculation that had little connection with the worldly concerns of active men.

What was the proper subject of philosophy? The philosophers of the Enlightenment, inspired by the great strides the scientists had made in perceiving the principles underlying natural phenomena, believed that they in turn could uncover the principles governing human conduct and guiding ethical behavior. For the first time since the classical era, philosophy was entirely divorced from theology; once again it concerned itself primarily with secular life. Philosophical principles—whether in metaphysics, epistemology, or ethics—were now to be formulated on a scientific basis.

The special province of the new philosophy of the eighteenth century was not the metaphysical order of the universe but the hitherto uncharted terrain of human behavior. Eighteenth-century philosophers were not concerned with theological justification of the world order; they even questioned the utility of the traditional language of philosophy. They attempted to strike out on a fresh track by using the methods of empirical science to examine the workings of the human mind and the operations of human nature.

The eighteenth-century philosophers believed that philosophy, like science, could be the vehicle of Enlightenment. They disparaged metaphysics not only because it was abstruse but because it did not seem to help in answering fundamental questions about man. For Locke, the proper task of philosophy is to establish the limit of human knowledge itself and his suggestion was eagerly grasped by his successors.

Locke aptly sums up the goal of the eighteenth-century philosophers, who almost without exception attempted to make philosophical speculation a useful part of natural philosophy. Man's secular concerns were the proper subjects of philosophy. Philosophy should help man to comprehend his own mind and his emotions and teach him how to guide his dealing with the external world. Thus the main contributions of Enlightenment philosophers were in epistemology, or the philosophy of knowledge, rather than in metaphysics, the philosophy of being and existence.

The focal point of eighteenth-century philosophy was the observation of man himself. The titles of some of the most important philosophical works published during the century reveal the new concern with the operations of the mind and the wellsprings of human behavior. The first great work, of course, was Locke's *An Essay Concerning Human Understanding* (1690), which set the tone that was to prevail throughout most of the Enlightenment period. George Berkeley, an English clergyman who eventually became a bishop, published his *Principles of Human Knowledge* in 1710. In 1749 Denis Diderot (1713—1784) published his *Letter on the Blind*, an essay treating the problem of how sense impressions (or, in the case of blind people, the absence of them) might affect moral judgment. In 1754 Etienne Bonnot de Condillac (1715—1780) published *The Treatise on Sensations*, which closely followed Locke in analyzing all mental functions as a response to sense impressions. The subtitle for David Hume's *A Treatise of Human Nature*, published in 1739, is probably the best description of the new methodology of eighteenth-century philosophy. These thinkers were sketching the outlines of an entirely science, one that we now call psychology. Locke may be thought of as the precursor of modern association psychology, and David Hartley (1705—1757), one of his eighteenth-century disciples, was the first writer to use the term "psychology". Hartley was an early theorist of the association of ideas. If all thoughts and emotions were triggered by sensations impinging on the mind, he said, physical sense impressions would ultimately account for all our ideas, including moral beliefs and judgments. But though the Enlightenment philosophers were confident that morals could be treated scientifically, they were not simple-minded rationalists in their approach to the complexities of the human mind. They did not expect that the science of mind would establish the indisputable principles yielded by other branches of natural science. The operations of the mind would always remain partially obscured, and the intricate patterns of human behavior would never be fully revealed.

The two most important philosophers of the Enlightenment were the Scotsman David Hume and the German Immanuel Kant. Neither was typical of the philosophes, but both made significant contributions to the new philosophy which was based not on revelation but on observation and reason. Kant had a profound influence on nineteenth-century philosophy, but Hume's major influence was not felt until the twentieth century, when his epistemological ideas were rediscovered by Bertrand Russell (1872—1970) and the logical positivists who followed him. Locke, whose theories were modified and improved upon by both Hume and Kant, remained the best-known English philosopher during most of the Enlightenment period.

Hume was undoubtedly the most amiable of the philosophes. He seems to have managed to remain on good terms with his colleagues; in fact, there is no record of his ever being angry with anyone. He was born in Edinburgh to a family of middle gentry, but his father died when he was a child. He was meant to become a lawyer but was soon repelled by the professional legal life of eighteenth-century Scotland. Eventually Hume liberated himself from his narrow Presbyterian upbringing. After emerging from a period of profound depression in late adolescence, he was able to formulate the principles that first appeared in *A Treatise of Human Nature*, which he published anonymously at the age of 27. *A Treatise of Human Nature* fell flat, but during the 1740s Hume began to make a name for himself through his essays on various topics. In 1748 his revised version of *A Treatise of Human Nature* was published as *An Enquiry Concerning Human Understanding*, which at first was hardly more successful than its predecessor.

Hume's philosophy has been labeled skepticism, but his was not the depressing skepticism of some of the ancient Greeks, who believed that real knowledge of anything was impossible. For Hume, to be a skeptic was simply to recognize, without bitterness, those things that are unanswerable.

All our thoughts, Hume believed, are formed in response to sense impressions. It is very difficult to distinguish impressions from thoughts, because impressions always give rise to ideas; and though ideas seem to possess an "unbounded liberty", this is a delusion. The creative powers of the mind are not autonomous; the understanding is capable only of "compounding, augmenting, or diminishing" data from the senses or experience. Thus, while the natural world is palpable, ideas are fragile and elusive.

How are data from the external world translated into ideas? We arrive at all our conclusions about nature, says Hume, solely on the basis of habit and experience. We assume that the sun will rise tomorrow, but we cannot know absolutely that it will, because reason cannot establish an indissoluble link between causes and effects. Men need not—indeed cannot—refrain from drawing conclusions and making future judgments, but they should realize that these are merely statements of probability. Custom and habit teach us that we can gamble on the operations of cause and effect, but we cannot begin to understand the principles of causality. Thus Hume neatly dispenses with theology—the philosophical doctrine that there is a design and final purpose to be found in nature.

The cutting edge of Hume's skepticism is sharpest when he questions the truths of Christianity. Almost all the philosophes gleefully debunked miracles, but Hume derided the notion dear to the hearts of eighteenth-century deists such as Voltaire and Rousseau that religious belief could be founded on reason. Religion, Hume claimed, was a response to man's need to bolster his hopes and placate his fears. The idea of God is a mental invention with which men try to account for the otherwise inexplicable principle of causality. But the existence of God, says Hume, can be neither proved nor refuted. Religious belief, therefore, is nothing more than a very strong feeling of the imagination, a total emotional commitment to one probability.

The philosophy of Hume and other eighteenth-century empiricists has been severely criticized in that its precepts are nothing but a plea for common sense and that its most profound metaphysical and epistemological teachings amount to little more than a bookmaker's analysis of the odds. The first serious attack on this easygoing empiricism came from Immanuel Kant, who may himself be considered a philosophe. Kant's work stands at the pinnacle of

Enlightenment thought even while it repudiates some of the fundamental assumptions of Enlightenment philosophy.

Kant was born in Konigsberg, a town in East Prussia that is now Koliningrad of Russia. He came from a lower-middle-class family; his parents belonged to the Pietists, a Protestant sect whose members resembled Quakers in the plainness of their lives and their concern with conscience. His career was strictly academic: He studied at the University of Konigsberg, served as a tutor in several aristocratic families, became an instructor at the university, and in 1770 was appointed professor of logic and metaphysics. He began to publish his major works when he was entering his sixties: *The Critique of Pure Reason* in 1781, *Prolegomena to Any Future Metaphysics* in 1783, *Fundamental Principles of the Metaphysics of Morals* in 1785, *The Critique of Practical Reason* in 1788. In contrast to the typical philosophe with much travel and the joy of city life, Kant spent his entire life in Konigsberg, a small provincial capital.

Kant belonged to the last, transitional generation of Enlightenment thinkers. These men, whose work dates from the 1760s through the 1780s, were breaking away from the positions held by the older generation of philosophes. Kant's work, for example, is not only an enormous synthesis of Enlightenment ideas; it is also the first of the great eighteenth-century philosophical systems.

Kant wrote for a small, specialized audience. His ideas were first presented in the form of university lectures, and his writing made no concessions to popular taste. His prose is opaque and baffling to the ordinary reader even in the original German; in translation, it is often impenetrable.

Kant believed in the objective reality of *a priori* ideas whose existence is independent of empirical data. Because he described these ideas as concepts of pure—or transcendental—reason, his philosophy is known as transcendentalism. According to Kant, metaphysics is like mathematics—entirely an *a priori* science, an autonomous, rational system based on no data except reason itself. Metaphysics and mathematics alike deal with concepts whose truth or falsity cannot be discovered or confirmed by any experience.

Unlike Descartes, however, Kant did not deny the validity of sense experience or the usefulness of empirical science. Sense perceptions and the results of scientific experimentation were reliable so long as they described appearances. Pure reason alone could formulate concepts, and real knowledge of the world was to be found only in these concepts of the mind. The mind could rise above the indeterminacy of natural events by imposing its own laws of pure reason on the world. Kant reasserted the primacy of human reason. Thus, for Kant, metaphysics was the highest, freest, and most pristine form of rational speculation; and as he divorced metaphysics from empiricism, so his ethical system was also liberated from all ties with experience and common sense.

Kant's ethics is founded on his belief that the rational concepts which formulate laws of nature can dictate laws of ethical behavior as well. Hume had said that morality was essentially a matter of common sense. Earlier eighteenth-century moralists like 3rd Earl of Shaftesbury (1671—1713) and Bernard de Mandeville (1670—1733) had identified virtue with happiness; a good act was simple to know, they said, because it made you feel good. Kant tried to cut morality loose from this easygoing brand of utilitarianism. Experience, he thought, only served to show how men actually do act; it was not sufficient to tell them how they ought to act. Good actions could be justified by their motivations or results. Actions that spring from feelings of love, honor, or affection are devoid of real moral value. Like metaphysical concepts, ethical norms must have a conceptual, objective validity; their truth cannot be tested by any worldly standards. The principles that govern ethical judgment and behavior are known *a priori*. For Kant, the highest principle of morality is duty, and his fundamental ethical precept is "Do your duty".

But how is an individual to know what his duty is in any particular instance? To answer this question, Kant formulates the categorical imperative, a concept of duty which prescribes the law of ethical behavior. The categorical imperative may be seen as a restatement of the golden rule. For Kant, men must act not in accordance with how they might wish others to treat them but rather as if they were legislating for all mankind. For moral actions, like natural phenomena, are ruled by inner principles of reason. These principles cannot be revealed by studying individual cases, nor can they be influenced by worldly considerations. Kant sets up one standard against which all moral acts are to be measured: they must be judged by their congruence with the moral law, whose principles are known *a priori*. The idea of duty impels the individual to act in the light of those rational concepts of universal law which ought to govern all men. Duty and the inviolable precept that ends can never be cited to justify means are the twin pillars of Kant's ethical system.

At bottom, Kant's ethical teaching is extremely simple. The categorical imperative seems, finally, to be nothing but the voice of conscience. The eighteenth-century empiricists had treated the human conscience as a bundle of emotions in which affections, inhibitions, ambitions, and fears were tied together in an ever changing combination. Kant rejected this psychological explanation of human behavior. In any case, he was less interested in what men did than in what they ought to do. He treated conscience as an abstract idea of pure reason.

Whatever one's opinion of Kant's ideas and his way of expressing them, his place in Western philosophy must be acknowledged. He belonged firmly within the tradition of philosophic idealism that stretched back to Plato and forward to the nineteenth-century German, Friedrich Hegel (1770—1831). His ideas had a profound influence on the Romantic movement of the early nineteenth century.

Hume asserted that the existence of God was an unverifiable hypothesis. In the late nineteenth century the term agnosticism was coined to describe this attitude of disbelief, but in the eighteenth century agnosticism was so rare that there was no need for a word for it. Hume's contemporaries often called him an atheist, a term applied to anyone whose religious thought seemed outrageous or impious to respectable members of society. In fact, only a very few Enlightenment figures were outright atheists, and their position, even in the latter part of the eighteenth century, was considered extreme and unworthy of serious consideration. The most commonly held religious belief of the philosophes was deism or, as its proponents often called it, natural religion.

Deism may be seen as a compromise arrived at by men who rejected the centuries-old authority of the Church, the dogma of Christianity, and the claims of sectarianism on the one hand and skepticism and atheism on the other. It provided a comfortable middle ground where common sense prevailed over superstition, tolerance over self-righteousness, and an informal, humanistic morality over the teaching that sin in this life leads to punishment in the next. Deism was congenial with the Newtonian view of the world, in which revelation and miracles were superfluous remnants of a priest-ridden, unscientific age. The Deity Himself was a remote and emerging Supreme

Being, who did not interfere very much with the minute operations of the world or the petty concerns of mankind. The growth and spread of deism was contemporary with the burgeoning Newtonian revolution in science. The movement began in England in the late seventeenth century, reached its peak there early in the eighteenth century, and had somewhat diminished by the 1750s. By that time it had spread to the Continent. The most articulate and persuasive deists on the Continent were philosophes of the stature of Voltaire and Rousseau.

Because deism was a belief without formal content or teaching, even its most fervent adherents found it hard to define. But the fuzzy, flexible character of deism also explains its popularity. Every man was left to gauge the depth and nature of his belief and was granted the ability to judge his own actions according to reason and common sense. Deists sought to strip superstition and mystery from religious devotion and expression. They believed that atheism was an error born of despair but that the authoritarian structure of the Catholic Church and the rigidity and intolerance of its doctrines were even more deplorable. Since all nature was an expression of God's will and spirit, there was no need for the petty, constricting dogmas imposed by a corrupt and self-serving church hierarchy. The worship of God must be sought in the hearts of men; it has nothing to do with ceremony, with formality and empty words.

The essence of deism was its capacity to embrace virtually any form of religious worship, so long as it came from the heart and was free from dogmatism and irrational authority. For the deists among the philosophes, the end of religion, as of all rational thought, was to serve not God but humanity.

7.3   Social Criticism

The philosophes found much to criticize in the social and political institutions of the ancient regime. Their zeal was directed at clearing away the rubble of prejudice, superstition, and irrationality. They meant to liberate the human spirit and lay bare the natural order of things—in government, in religion, in the administration of justice. They envisaged themselves as rational reformers, not revolutionaries. For them, revolution was neither desirable nor necessary.

The philosophes were true conservatives. They spoke much of the "natural" equality of all men, but they stopped far short of advocating real egalitarianism. They raged against the inequalities of an economic system that allowed the poor to starve, a legal system that could not defend justice, but produced the prejudices that inhibited freedom of thought; but they shied away from radical change. However, as the century wore on and the disease of society did not yield to mild treatment, the philosophes grew impatient. The later generation of philosophes prescribed stronger medicine and more drastic cures.

Most of the philosophes belonged to the relatively small, elite group of educated men in eighteenth-century European society. They were cultivated; most of them were men of leisure. Some were wellborn, and all had powerful connections among their friends and patrons, if not in their own families. Yet most of them remained on the fringes of power. They might be asked to advise governments or even to draw up programs of reform, but they were seldom given any real responsibility. Their talents as publicists were always recognized, but except in England and, for a time, in Prussia, they wrote in constant fear of arbitrary, erratic, and inconsistent censorship by government or church. Their only real weapons were their pens and their ability to appeal to the common sense and conscience of their readers, and in this they were remarkably skilled. It is hard to find another era when so many social critics were also accomplished and prolific popular writers, whose books were short and readable and, in spite of censorship, were often available in cheap editions.

The Enlightenment is often called the Age of Voltaire; in a sense his career was a distillation of the style and thought of the whole era. Voltaire was born as Francois Marie Arouet (at the age of 23 he added the more aristocratic sounding "de Voltaire"). His father was a Paris notary, a solid bourgeois citizen who intended that his talented son become a successful lawyer. Voltaire was educated at a fashionable Jesuit college, where he was supposed to acquire social polish and useful connections among the rich and wellborn. But instead he nurtured a passion for poetry and a taste for the heady atmosphere of Parisian salons. At the age of twenty-one, he was imprisoned in the Bastille for a year, on a charge of writing libelous verse about the regent. It was his first encounter with the strict censorship against which he battled for the rest of his life. Literary fame came early in his career; poems and plays which no one but scholars read today were the main source of his reputation. It was only as an old man in the 1760s and 1770s that he built a new reputation as a violent anticlerical crusader and humanitarian reformer.

In 1726 Voltaire was again imprisoned in the Bastille, this time for having insulted a great noble, whose servants summoned him for a dinner party and gave him a public beating. He never forgot the lesson in the realities of power in an aristocratic society. After his release from prison Voltaire spent two years in England and returned to France a devout admirer of English institutions, English science, and English religious toleration. His *Letters on the English*, with its enthusiastic praise of the openness of English life, was published in Paris in 1734 and promptly burned by the public hangman because of its subversive and irreligious nature.

The implied criticism of French society in Voltaire's praise of England caused a furor that led to Voltaire's semi-exile from Paris. He spent most of the next decade at the château of his mistress and intellectual colleague, the Marquise du Chatelet, who encouraged him to work in science and mathematics and started him on *The Age of Louis XIV*, one of the first attempts at social history.

In the 1740s and early 1750s Voltaire was attracted to the orbit of Frederick the Great of Prussia, who fancied himself a philosopher-king. The relationship between Frederick and Voltaire was always difficult. Frederick appointed his pet intellectual a court chamberlain and gave him a handsome pension, but both men were too prickly and self-centered to remain friends. During his association with Frederick, however, Voltaire perfected the literary techniques that made his later works masterpieces of polemic and satirical wit. These were tales, brief dialogues, and sharp jokes. Voltaire's most telling social criticism appeared in these light literary forms, which he manipulated with a skill no other writer in French has ever quite equaled.

In 1758 Voltaire settled down on his lavish estate, conveniently near the Swiss border. For the next twenty years he bombarded the public and the French authorities with his little books. Virtually everything he wrote from this point on was to expose an injustice, to attack an abuse, or to propose a reform. Although he was a hypochondriac throughout his life and was always certain that he was on the verse of death, he lived to be 84. Until the end of his life he wrote with the fervor and energy of a young man.

Voltaire was not a theorist. His mind was always captured by the concrete, just as his style focused on the earthy detail, the picturesque joke or description, the lewd suggestion. He always upheld a few fundamental principles: freedom of person, of speech, of conscience, of religion, and of the press. He never totally renounced his religious beliefs, and he abhorred atheism. He meant to reform the archaisms and injustices which deformed the French Church; he called for secular control of the Church's legal functions and for the taxation of church property by the state; he believed secular authorities should be responsible for establishing the legality of marriage and divorce and for overseeing the censorship of publications. But in spite of his lifelong attack, he believed Catholicism should remain the state religion in France.

Voltaire was an ardent proponent of the abolition of feudal taxes and dues and the outmoded regulations imposed by the guilds, but like most of his contemporaries, he had little sense of the problems of industrial workers and did not perceive the significance of the changes in industrial technology that were occurring in England. He called for a thoroughgoing reform of French criminal law and an overhaul of the judicial system. As he grew older, his crusading zeal intensified, and his efforts on behalf of toleration and civil rights for Protestants eventually allowed him to assume the mantle of a respected elder statesman. In 1764, when Voltaire was 70, one of his most important books appeared. This was the *Philosophical Dictionary*. The first edition was a pocket-size volume of 344 pages containing just 73 entries. It was published anonymously in Geneva, with a false London imprint. Voltaire strenuously denied that he was the author, although it was obvious to everyone that the book was his. Prudence, not modesty, inspired his disclaimers; within a year the book had been ordered and burned by the government of Geneva, the Paris parlement, and The Hague, and had been condemned by the Holy office of the Vatican. But it was widely popular, and new, enlarged editions kept appearing until, by 1769, the *Philosophical Dictionary* comprised 120 articles in two large volumes. The ideas in the *Philosophical Dictionary* were not new or startling, but its style was so captivating that it soon was recognized as one of the most significant vehicles of Enlightenment social criticism.

The topics covered in the *Philosophical Dictionary* include Priest, Love, Great Chain of Being, Circumcision, Divinity of Jesus, Equality, Fanaticism, Institution, Freedom of Thought, Pride, Original Sin, Tyranny, and Virtue.

Techniques vary from subject to subject, but Voltaire leaned heavily on the dialogue, the anecdote, the ironic tale, and—perhaps most successful of all— the matter-of-fact narrative with tongue firmly in cheek. The absurdity of church doctrine, the hypocrisy of the clergy and the magistrates, the inhumanity of men, the irrationality of legal and religious institutions, the wickedness of kings—all these are illustrated in a series of short pungent lessons.

If the *Philosophical Dictionary* was a stimulating introduction to Enlightenment social thought, more and better nourishment could be found in the multivolume encyclopedia published between 1751 and 1772 by Denis Diderot. In 1750 Diderot announced the publication of an encyclopedia that would be the repository of all current knowledge. *L'Encyclopedie* was described as a systematic dictionary of science, art, and crafts. It was undertaken as a commercial venture on the model of a popular English encyclopedia. The French publisher asked Diderot, a free-lance journalist, then known only as a competent translator, to supervise the publication. The choice could not have been better. The French encyclopedia far outstripped its English model. There was nothing else like it in France or in all Europe. Seventeen volumes were published between 1751 and 1772, and by 1780 six more, consisting of agenda, data, and tables, had appeared. The illustrations alone were a vast source of information. They show every aspect of contemporary craftsmanship and are still a magnificent guide to eighteenth-century technology. The encyclopedia was astonishingly popular, considering its price.

Diderot belonged by birth to the class of small craftsmen. He received a traditional Jesuit education and at one time thought of becoming a priest, but he soon embraced deism and later in his life even flirted with atheism. Modern historians have come to see Diderot as one of the most original of all the philosophes. He was a scientist; he wrote moral and philosophical essays; he was the first modern art critic; and in *Rameau's Nephew* he produced an imaginative psychological novel. His most significant contribution in his own day was his role in shaping the encyclopedia and the catalytic influence he appeared to have on his colleagues. His training in science was solid, and he had a more professional understanding of scientific rationalism than such literary figures as Voltaire. The characteristic tone of the encyclopedia—the disavowal of any kind of superstition, the attempt to give a clear, rational account of all natural phenomena—reflects Diderot's own cast of mind.

The presentation of useful knowledge was not the editors' sole aim, however. A good dictionary or encyclopedia, said Diderot, must be able to change "the general way of thinking". The enormous collection of scientific data, he rightly thought, would necessarily encourage readers to cultivate a new, rational attitude toward every aspect of their society. It did not matter that the science in the encyclopedia was soon outmoded; the critical spirit still informed nearly every article.

The implicit ethical teaching of the *Encyclopedie* was utilitarianism. Useful knowledge of nature was more valuable than abstract speculation about God and the universe—by definition, useful knowledge was secular. It was assumed that rational understanding of the scientific world would uplift mankind far more than moral preaching. Although old superstitions were debunked, the men who wrote for the encyclopedia did not attempt to attack the Church explicitly. Religion was undermined simply by being ignored. By their choice of subjects, the editors made it clear that religion was not one of the things men needed to know. There was scarcely any mention of Biblical figures, though many articles dealt with the ethnography of primitive tribes. Subjects like creeds, religious controversies, and church history were dismissed in a few words. The article on the stocking-knitting frame was about ten times as long as the one on cathedral.

How effective was the encyclopedia? Undoubtedly it reflected and reinforced a sense that common and menial pursuits were dignified and important. It may have contributed to the increasing democratic consciousness and self-respect of the small artisans and shopkeepers who were the popular democrats of the French Revolution. The encyclopedia had been described as the Trojan Horse of the ancien regime, and perhaps it did help to subvert the old order from within. Although the editors had set out to teach and instruct, not to destroy, their work was a very successful instrument of propaganda for the new, rational style of thought.

The philosophes, who exercised the critical spirit in examining the economic relations of their society as well as its political, religious, and social institutions, inaugurated a new discipline—political economy. In the 1750s a group known as physiocrats launched a concerted attack on mercantile theory.

This was by no means the first attack on mercantilism, but it was the first one undertaken in a scientific spirit. François Quesnay (1694—1774), the Marquis d'Argenson, and the statesman Anne-Robert-Jacques Turgot (1727—1781) were the leaders of the group. They thought of themselves as "naturalists" whose goal was to discover and implement the natural principles of economic life.

The physiocrats believed that only agriculture was truly productive and that land was the most important source of wealth. France was the major agricultural nation of Europe in the eighteenth century, and the overriding interests of the landholding class were taken for granted. The physiocrats insisted on free trade in agricultural products. There should be no barriers, they said, and no frontiers, monopolies should be abolished, and large government contractors whose operation inhibited a free market should be suppressed. Since the land was primary source of national wealth and land taxes the most reliable form of state revenue, capital should be applied to agriculture to increase the productivity of the land.

The physiocrats' program was a rational, attractive attempt to solve the upsetting fiscal problems facing the French government. Their plan to develop a class of rich, large-scale farmers by diverting the flow of capital from banking and commerce to agriculture appealed to landholders throughout Western Europe. The physiocratic doctrine appeared first in Quesnay's article "Farmers" in the 1756 edition of the *Encyclopedie*, and during the 1760s the group had an important, if short-lived, influence on European economic thought. But despite of its rationality, the vision of a free agricultural market never became a reality. The system was too naïve and simplistic to survive, and by the middle of the 1770s the physiocratic doctrine was supplanted by the teachings of the Scottish political economist Adam Smith.

Adam Smith (1723—1790) was a tough-minded reformer with an austere, middle-class background similar to that of his friend David Hume. He was educated at the University of Glasgow, where he became a professor of moral philosophy. His contacts with the philosophes were frequent, and he was familiar with the doctrines of the physiocrats, which he rejected. Smith believed that any meaningful economic analysis had to focus on commerce and on the means of production. Like many members of the eighteenth-century intellectual community, he was revolted by the militarism and unreasonably restrictive legislation that buttressed the old mercantile system. In 1776 he published *The Wealth of Nations*, probably the most influential book on economics ever written. It was a devastating critique of contemporary economic policy and a demand for immediate reform. Smith presented a vast amount of data in a lucid, elegant fashion, and though there is hardly a statistical table in the entire text, it is still an important source of information about eighteenth-century economic life.

Smith was by no means an apologist for private enterprise, but he was a fierce critic of economic nationalism, and he railed against the restrictions of ancient guilds and obsolete monopolies. Like all the philosophes, he yearned for freedom—in trade as well as in government—and believed that an individual has the right to choose his occupation and gain autonomy over his economic life. Contemporary government was inefficient and unwieldy; any rational program of economic reform was bound to demand an end to governmental interference. Smith never claimed that free trade would function perfectly, but he preferred the natural operations of a free economy to government controls. He did not ascribe any inherent virtues to the profit motive, nor did he believe that businessmen were especially benevolent. While he perceived that psychological motivation was a prime factor in economic development, he knew that the desire for profit must be curbed by moral restraint.

Adam Smith's thought had a far-reaching influence on English commercial legislation of the early nineteenth century. In the course for legal reform, his counterpart was Jeremy Bentham. Smith preached free trade, cheap and efficient government, and the abolition of monopolies; Bentham's formulation of the principle of utility provided an empirical tool for measuring the rationality and effectiveness of legal and political institutions.

Jeremy Bentham (1748—1832) was a precocious child who was sent by his ambitious father to an elite preparatory school, to Queen's College, Oxford, and one of the Inns of Court for legal training. As Bentham immerged himself in the archaic irrationality of the law, he began to search for a principle that would establish a clear path through the maze that was English common law in the eighteenth century. He never did practice law, but he spent his life in attempts to reform it.

The foundations of utilitarianism had been laid down by Locke and Hobbes, and Bentham's fundamental assumption that man is ruled by "two sovereign masters, pain and pleasure" was not new. It was his attempt to back up the doctrine that was significant. Taking Francis Bacon as his model, he hoped to establish the principle of utility as the basis for nothing less than a complete science of human behavior. There was only one standard, he said, for judging institutions: Did they bring about the greatest possible public happiness? This happiness, he believed, could be quantitatively measured by calculating individual sums of pain and pleasure.

In his later years, when he worked out specific calculations in minute detail, Bentham's thought became difficult and his writing baffling. But his early works, *A Fragment on Government* (1776) and *An Introduction to Principles of Morals and Legislation* (1789), are simple and clear; they are read and studied even today. The practical legislative effects of Bentham's crusade became apparent in the early nineteenth century. He created a link between eighteenth-century rationalism and the liberal reform movement in Victorian England.

Montesquieu, perhaps the most profound and original of all the philosophes, was a dispassionate observer of society and its institutions rather than an ardent reformer. He belonged to the magistrate class, and favored the traditional intermediary role of the parlements (which stood for the interests of his class) between the authority of the Crown and the pressures of the people. Montesquieu was born in a château near Bordeaux. As was customary, a passing beggar was made his godfather, to remind the child of his obligations to the poor. He received the usual classical education, with its emphasis on Latin literature and Roman history, and then studied law in Paris. In his early twenties he inherited his lands and wealth and, on the death of an uncle, the family judicial property, the office of president of the Guyenne parlement. The young Montesquieu took his judicial responsibilities very seriously even though they were uncongenial. He consoled himself by cultivating other interests: he studied literature, history, and science and became an active member of the Bordeaux Academy.

Until he was 27, Montesquieu led a respectable, uneventful life. But in 1721 his *Persian Letters*, an incisive attack on French regency society in the guise of an epistolary novel, was published anonymously in Amsterdam and became an instant literary success. Although antecedents could be found in the work of Pierre Bayle in the late seventeenth century, the book inaugurated a new French literary form. In the episodic *Letters*, Montesquieu assumes the personae of two Persians who comment freely and irreverently on the strange customs they encounter in their European travels. The description of French society by these alien and supposedly objective observers is comic, pungent, and devastating. In a lighthearted way, Montesquieu's relativistic treatment of institutions and social values foreshadowed the technique he would develop more thoroughly and systematically in his great treatise on government and law.

Beneath its sparkling surface the book makes a fervent plea for liberty. The playful anecdotes narrated by the Persians reveal the hypocrisies of a society that claims to be rational and just but is, in fact, perverse, authoritarian, and cruel. Montesquieu was deadly serious and evenhanded in his criticism. Implicit throughout the book is his belief that man can recognize and liberate himself from the bonds of prejudice and injustice by exercising his reason.

In style as well as substance, the *Persian Letters* was a significant, liberating work of art. Its racy, free-flowing, almost colloquial language was a marked departure from the formal, heavily Latinized French considered appropriate for serious literature. At once recognized as a masterpiece, the book was so popular that in Paris it "sold like bread".

Soon after the stunning success of the *Persian Letters*, Montesquieu sold his judicial office. He traveled widely in Europe and spent two particular years in England, where he was elected a fellow of the Royal Society. In 1734 he published a history of Rome in which he expounded the theory that societies, like individuals, pass through stages of health and sickness. A whole society decays, he said, when its internal structural principles crumble.

In 1728 Montesquieu began to accumulate data on government and law from all over the world for his most important work—one of the enduring monuments of the Enlightenment thought: *The Spirit of the Laws*. The work, published in 1748, was nothing less than an outline of the fundamental principles that order human government, law, and society. Human institutions are intelligible, Montesquieu believed; they can be reduced to simple principles if they are studied like biological organism and examined according to their natural development. But in his search for scientific principles, he never lost sight of the tenacity of human instincts. The book is informed by one piercing vision—that men do not rationally establish governments or make laws. Rather, these take their shape irrevocably from conditions of society and in response to deep-rooted human needs. Institutions reflect the structure of society and cannot be treated as though they exist in a vacuum. It is a gross error, Montesquieu held, to wish to reduce the sentiments of men to a system.

Nevertheless, in the thirty-one episodic sections that comprise *The Spirit of the Laws*, Montesquieu describes what he calls the "general spirit" as a series of responses to two different factors: moral causes, which include religion, law, and custom, and physical causes—climate, population, geography—which were unalterable. In a country where the morals of the people are sound, it is hardly necessary, he said, to have laws at all. This conception of the functional relationship between the needs and pressures of society and the development of its legal institutions is Montesquieu's unique contribution to what would become the disciplines of social science. The great French social theorists of the nineteenth century, Auguste Comte and Émile Durkheim, claimed him as the precursor of sociology.

What captivated Montesquieu's contemporaries, however, was his simple, elegant prose and some of his more superficial observations. They eagerly grasped his classification of governments under three simple types—monarchy, despotism, and republic. They welcomed his attack on slavery, his condemnation of all forms of tyranny, and his distaste for religious intolerance and harsh penal codes, and they supported his praise of commerce as a vehicle of civilization.

Although he never failed to celebrate the true spirit of liberty in the few places where it seemed to flourish, Montesquieu did not try to formulate any proposals for reform. It was more important, he believed, to analyze, to comprehend, to be aware of differences among peoples and societies, than to rush into rapid changes based on ill-formed principles. He was a fervent advocate of limited constitutional monarchy and pleaded for peace and for the protection of the rule of law against despotism; he believed in gradualism above all. Balance is hard to achieve, easy to disrupt. Sometimes the very imprecision of the law allows for the exercise of liberty.

Montesquieu's concept of evolutionary jurisprudence could be interpreted in two conflicting ways. One was extremely conservative—indeed, as expounded by late eighteenth-century writers like Edmund Burke and some post-Revolutionary legal historians, it sounded very much like reaction. Since laws are the outgrowth of deeply-rooted social and cultural traditions, they are not to be changed by individual men, no matter how rational or well meaning they are. The other view was taken by utilitarian reformers like Jeremy Bentham and by nineteenth-century liberals and is still the doctrine of many legal sociologists. Since laws are not absolute but must be judged in accordance with their social value, they must be changed in response to new social realities.

Less patient philosophes could not accept Montesquieu's cautious attitude toward reforming the legal systems of the ancien regime; its cumbersome, cruel, and irrational procedures were an appalling anachronism in an age when men prided themselves on their humanity and civilization. It was perfectly clear to anyone who looked that the medieval structures no longer functioned properly. The multiplicity of law that fascinated the scholar in Montesqueiu enraged Voltaire. The customary law was rigid and absurd; the relics of the feudal past, utterly nonsensical. What is worse, the burden of the law fell most heavily on the poor and ignorant. Was it too much to ask, Voltaire wondered, that law be in accord with, if not justice, then at least common sense and humanity? The rottenness of the legal system seemed just one more sign of the decadence of the ancien regime.

The philosophes might rail, but they failed to come up with a rational program of legal reform. A short-tract by a Milanese aristocrat, Cesare Bonesana Beccaria (1738—1794), did make some practical suggestions and thereby laid the foundations of modern penal theory. Beccaria was an intelligent but somewhat indolent young man who admired the ideas of the philosophes and joined a reading and discussion group formed by some young Milanese. Everyone in the group was assigned a topic to read up and report on, and Beccaria happened to get criminal law. The result of his study was a brief, simply written book published in 1764, *An Essay on Crimes and Punishments*. Within six months this work by a young man with no legal background and no experience in the administration of criminal justice went through seven editions of a French translation. Voltaire wrote a commentary, which helped to popularize it all over Europe. Catherine the Great invited Beccaria to come to Russia to codify its criminal law. And by the time he was thirty, he was appointed to a professorship in political economy at Milan. He never again produced anything of importance.

Beccaria did not have to preach. Enlightened opinion was ripe for his recommendations. Everyone loathed the confusing and arbitrary procedures that disfigured the European criminal codes, and Baccaria offered sensible remedies in an elegant, concise, and rational manner. One overriding principle, he said, ought to pervade the administration of criminal justice. Rather than satisfying private vengeance, punishment should be meted out according to the good of the greatest number of people. The aim of all punishments is prompt, unambiguous, and certain.

Beccaria's utilitarian analysis was the sharpest stroke of all against the often dishonest legal system of the ancien regime, in which secret accusations, torture, the imposition of harsh statutory penalties for minor offenses against property, imprisonment for debt, and promiscuous recourse to capital punishment were long-established practices. Against this remarkable irrationality, Beccaria set up a viable system of alternatives. Crimes against property were to be punished by fines or, if the criminal was unable to pay, by imprisonment. Political crimes would incur banishment—this being far more healthy for the state than the imprisonment of dissidents. Capital punishment would be abolished outright; the severity of a sentence would be measured by its duration. Beccaria also proposed a reform of the prison system. Prisoners should be classified according to the nature of their offenses and separated according to their categories.

Beccaria's ideas captured the minds of a generation brought up on the writings of the philosophes. However, except for one important achievement—the abolition of torture in most European countries by the end of the eighteenth century—his proposals were honored more in theory than in practice. Even in England, where his influence was felt most strongly, his ideas were not implemented until the first part of the nineteenth century.

The critical spirit which led the philosophes to probe the nature of men in society also gave rise to a new attitude toward the writing of history. In scholarship alone, the eighteenth-century historians never matched the seventeenth-century clerics whose collections of documents and compilations of charters they eagerly used. But they were liberated from the theological framework that limited the historical vision of their predecessors even while it intensified their scholarly dedication. The Enlightenment historians no longer had to account, as the seventeenth-century writers had been obliged to do, for the unfolding of God's plan for the destiny of men and nations.

History in the eighteenth century was rapidly becoming a popular form of literature. The works of Voltaire, Montesquieu, and the Scottish school represented by Hume and his meticulous colleagues William Robertson (1721—1793) sold extremely well. The average layman read much more history than he does today and no doubt enjoyed it more. These writers had a new confidence both in their own mastery of their material and in the receptivity of their audiences. The greatest historian of the century was Edward Gibbon (1737—1794), an Englishman who undertook a lifetime of work on his *The Decline and Fall of the Roman Empire* (1776—1788), a continuous narrative from 200 to the fall of Constantinople in 1453.

Descartes had dismissed history as a tissue of gossip. While it was possible to comprehend nature rationally, he believed, human nature and the development of human institutions were irrational, refractory, and beyond the knowledge of men. It was exactly the perplexing tangle of human motives, actions, and accidental events that fascinated the historical writers of the eighteenth century. True history, they said, must delve beneath the surface network of contradictory events. They discarded the Renaissance assumption that history is shaped by the action and character of great men, recognizing that the causes of events must be sought, as Montesquieu believed, in the whole structure of a society. Events may seem accidental, but they are shaped by unseen forces. This fundamental canon of modern historiography was a new and fresh concept in the eighteenth century.

With the exception of Gibbon's study of the decline of the Roman Empire, the histories that were the product of Enlightenment culture are virtually unread today. Contemporary scholars are far more interested in the work of the Neapolitan scholar Giovanni Battista Vico (1668—1744), who wrote in almost total obscurity during his lifetime. Vico, the son of a bookseller, was poor and largely self-educated. His first interest was law, but when he failed to win a competition for a university chair in civil law, he turned to historical studies. Eventually he did receive a professorship—in rhetoric. His researches in philology, jurisprudence, and ancient history were undertaken in solitude and carried on without renown. Not until his works were rediscovered in the nineteenth century by the French historian Jules Michelet (1798—1874) and in the twentieth by scholars and critics interested in philosophy was Vico recognized as an important historical theorist.

The philosophes, with their confident belief in the linear progress of history, did not share Vico's concern with the function of the unconscious in historical development. Nor were they interested in Vico's concept of the cycle through which all societies passed in their evolution from primitive to organized civilization. The theory was presented in Vico's one great book, the *New Science*, first published in 1725. The *New Science* drew on such divergent sources as Homer, Plato, Tacitus, Bacon, and the jurist Grotius. Vico, reacting against what he saw as the aridity of Cartesian rationalism, coined a counter slogan—"we know only what we do".

The *New Science* was to be nothing less than the history of human consciousness. Vico examined primitive language, song, and myth—the Homeric legends in particular—for clues to the imagination and thought of men in the early stage of civilization. There were three main cycles, he believed, through which each civilization had to pass. First came a primitive, preliterate age, where "men first feel without observing". Then came the heroic age, the era of epic poetry—"then they observe with a troubled and agitated spirit". The last stage of the cycle was represented by Western European civilization, in which language and institutions were developed to a high degree—"finally they reflect with a clear mind". When they reached this last stage, societies were bound to decay from within, although Vico did not predict precisely how or when this would happen.

Vico's work was fragmentary, often obscure, and sometimes based on specious evidence. The *New Science* is not a widely-read book even though Vico's visionary grasp of the evolution of whole civilizations and his concern for the history of the inarticulate and the irrational assure his reputation today.

7.4 Emotion and Unreason

Beneath the reasoned clarity of Enlightenment thought ran a dark stream of emotion, unreason, and anti-intellectualism. It emerged full-blown in three astonishing books published by Jacques Rousseau in the early 1760s, but it existed throughout the era and could be discerned earlier in the century in literature and in religion.

The most successful and enduring popular religion found a good expression in the teachings of John Wesley (1703—1791). As a student at Oxford, Wesley decided that the dry platitudes of the Church of England provided no food for the soul. Other men who sought an emotional experience and an opportunity for communion with God in religious worship also rejected the bland and worldly style of the established Church, but few of them were imbued with Wesley's messianic spirit. Wesley focused on preaching, exhortation, and a new "method" of spiritual devotion. After experiencing a mystical conversion at the age of 35, he devoted the rest of his life to teaching through the Methodist society that all men, despite their inherent sinfulness, could also achieve salvation.

Wesley's "method" combined moral Puritanism with uncontrolled emotional abandon. The response he evoked was, literally, wild. In his diary Wesley notes that his preaching led to many cases of what we would call hysterical reaction, manifested by trembling, groaning, weeping, and even convulsions. This was the "enthusiasm" that the philosophes found so baffling and disgusting.

The great revival movement of the eighteenth century spread through Western Europe and the United States, where the impact of the camp meetings led by the powerful preacher George Whitefield (1714—1770) is well documented. In Germany the form of evangelicalism known as Pietism flourished. Although the movement went underground to some extent after 1740, the Pietist strain reappeared toward the end of the century and fed the mysticism of Romantic writers. In America, where a large proportion of German immigrants belonged to Pietist sects like the Moravian Brethren, evangelicalism was a significant religious current throughout the eighteenth century. The religious revival even touched Eastern Europe. In Poland, a small sect of Jews—the Hasidim—turned away from the traditional authority and book-learning that had been the preserve of the rabbinate. The Hasidim encouraged dancing and singing as the expression of religious mysticism and joy. Indeed, music played an important role throughout the religious revival. Wesley's hymns were strong, simple, and very moving, and some of the simple religious poems set to music by the Moravian Brethren are small masterpieces, similar in spirit to the work of Bach.

The vein of anti-intellectualism implicit in evangelical religion went relatively unnoticed, since the new emotional piety was generally restricted to the poor and ill-educated, people who were not expected to read books or indulge in rational thought. But when expounded by Rousseau, the cult of emotion and the explicit mistrust of civilized reason could no longer be disregarded. The immediate response of the intellectual community to this neurotic, rude man, who wrote in praise of undisciplined nature as persuasively as the great philosophes had of cool rationality, was shock and dismay. Just as Wesley and his followers, who sought spiritual satisfaction in communion with God, were alienated from the established denominations, so was Rousseau, who yearned to bring men back in touch with the wellsprings of nature and their own instincts, alienated, if not from the literary culture of his day, at least from the worldly life style of the philosophes.

Rousseau was born in Geneva. His mother died at his birth, and the child was rejected by his father. According to his own account, the boy who tortured himself with guilt for his mother's death became a man whose relationships with women were always abnormal and frustrating. Although he was the apostle of the loving education of children, he allowed his own offspring, whom he fathered with a servant girl, to be brought up in an orphanage. His battles with society, with life, and with himself were never resolved. As contrasted with the amusing eccentricity that marked the conduct of so many of the philosophes, Rousseau's behavior—often pathological—reveals the torments of a seriously disturbed psyche. He was always difficult to deal with, even at his best, and at his worst he was subject to fits of paranoia.

Rousseau's education was haphazard, his early career aimless and unsuccessful. His first interest was music, but his new system of notation was a complete failure, and in 1749 he entered an essay contest sponsored by the Dijon Academy on the question: Have scientific advances improved morals? He won the prize by asserting that progress had, in fact, corrupted morality. It was the first enunciation of his favorite theme: that civilization oppressed, degraded and finally destroyed the natural values of mankind. In the late 1750s he cloistered himself at the country retreat of one of his patronesses, where he proceeded to turn out the works that established his fame or notoriety. His sentimental novel of lost virtue, *La Nouvella Heloise*, his treatise on education, *Émile*, and his political manifesto, *The Social Contract*, appeared between 1760 and 1762. *Heloise* was tremendously popular; *The Social*

Contract was a theoretical blueprint for the French Revolution and the authoritarianism of the modern state; but *Émile* was one of the most explosive works on education ever to appear in the Western world. It was condemned in both France and Geneva, and for a time Rousseau was forced into hiding. Not until the 1780s, when the seeds of Romanticism were taking root, were Rousseau's ideas widely accepted. But *Émile* so enchanted Kant that he is reported to have broken the habit of a lifetime by forgoing his afternoon walk to pore over the book. Kant hailed Rousseau as "the restorer of the rights of humanity" and called him the "Newton of the moral world".

What did Rousseau preach in *Émile* to stir such controversy? He went much further than the philosophes, who managed to enjoy the pleasures of life under the ancien regime even while they criticized its irrational institutions. Rousseau rejected the hierarchical society of aristocrats, merchants, and citizens, claiming that the good life was possible only for men who liberated themselves from all its bonds. The unequal society of eighteenth-century Europe was corrupt and degrading. In *The Social Contract* Rousseau sought to guard the individual against the tyranny of the state; *Émile* is a guide for man to obtain his emotional freedom and spiritual autonomy in the face of the overwhelming tyranny of the social order. Just as authentic freedom is the goal of Rousseau's ideal state, so the liberation of the individual is the aim of the educational program he lays down for his pliant pupil.

Émile's education from birth to marriage is thoroughly described in the book, which blends the novel and the memoir. The adult Émile is nothing less than the model for the good citizen of the state Rousseau envisions in *The Social Contract*—a state where men, subject only to the collective authority of the general will, are able to live according to the pure dictates of nature. Émile leads a carefree, healthful existence out in the country away from the immoral influence of society. He plays (always with his tutor), roams through the woods, and learns the principles of science through his own simple experiments (although these are elaborately organized by the tutor). He learned about the sanctity of property the hard way, when his own little garden is uprooted.

Émile has no formal lessons, since the only real teachers are "experience and feeling". His natural instincts are always the right ones, and they must be left untouched. He is taught a trade—carpentry—because manual labor is the closest approximation to what man does in the state of nature. He is not bothered by lessons in literature or philosophy. Rousseau despised Locke's dictum that children should be reasoned with. Reasoning, Rousseau believes, comes after education. When he reaches adulthood Émile is, no doubt, a well-adjusted individual—but he is also a bit of a dolt. He may be liberated from society, but his dependence on his tutor lingers—though this does not seem to bother Rousseau. Émile escapes corruption by the simple expedient of having been brought up in total ignorance of society.

Émile can be viewed as Rousseau's own fantasy of wish-fulfillment, a compensation for his terrible childhood. Many of his ideas have been incorporated into the fundamental canons of progressive education, though Freudian psychology has called into question Rousseau's belief in the pristine goodness and purity of all childish instinct. Rousseau's revulsion at the inhibiting effects of traditional child-rearing and his impassioned plea for a return to nature stunned his first readers, but his ideas were embraced, at times to an exaggerated degree, during the ensuing Romantic era.

In his fear of the influence of society on natural man and his obsession with the unbridled expression of natural emotions, Rousseau anticipated Romanticism. By refusing to recognize the benevolence of reason, he turned against a cherished pillar of Enlightenment thought. Nevertheless, while Rousseau hated society as it existed—the ancient hierarchy of church, class, and state that distorted natural man—he did believe that it could be shaped by human reason to serve man, and thus he shared in the Enlightenment spirit. Like his contemporaries, he hoped to transform society to fit human nature and human needs, but his emphasis was unlike theirs. To Rousseau, nature could not be ordered and tamed; it must be worshiped as a wild and uncontrollable force.

7.5 The Heritage of the Enlightenment

The eighteenth-century cultural movement was many-sided, and its contribution to the development of Western civilization was extremely complex. It is true that the *experiences* of modern industrial society and the knowledge gained from post-eighteenth-century science have given us insights into human nature that the philosophes lacked. But demonstrations of the limits of Enlightenment thought do not detract from the essential role of eighteenth century in Western civilization: the Enlightenment represents the great turning point at which the assumptions about man, society, and nature that had prevailed since ancient times were at last consciously rejected and a new set of attitudes came to prevail.

The philosophes emphasized the most radical implications of Renaissance humanism, of Baconian meliorism, of Lockean empiricism, and of Newtonian science. The Enlightenment brought to fruition the secular attitude implicit in the Renaissance. The fifteenth-century humanists had delighted in man's experience and potential, but they could not refrain from integrating this secular spirit within a traditional Christian framework. The philosophes boldly concentrated on human experience and achievement and refused to compromise their secular approach. They regarded Locke's thesis that understanding is the product of experience—the impress of environment upon the individual mind— as a liberating doctrine: men were not limited by a cast of mind or set of ideas they had been born with, so claimed by Plato and Descartes. Men could know anything and be conditioned in any direction by the circumstances of environment, education, and experience. Consequently, there was nothing inevitable about the ideas and institutions that currently prevailed—these ideas and institutions could, and should be superseded. Man's future was unlimited. The philosophes believed that Newton's discovery of the laws of physics had at once demonstrated the infinite capacity of the human mind, given men the key to the mastery of nature, and opened up the possibility of applying natural laws to the functioning of society and politics, thereby greatly improving the circumstances of social and individual life.

The radical philosophy of the Enlightenment represented the first clear and self-conscious attack upon the doctrine of the great chain of being, of the fixed, immutable hierarchy of the universe, that had been the dominant world view in Europe from the fifth century BC and that still gave intellectual respectability to the ancien regime in the seventeenth century. God, King, Church, Lord, and People were held to be the fixed order of the world; the ideas in the human mind were regarded as innate, needing only to be discovered, and there was no alternative system of government. Voltaire saw, with astonishing insight, that the empirical movement in philosophy, begun with Locke, had inaugurated a direct challenge to the old order, opening up the possibility of an intellectual revolution. Hume's analysis of the nature of human understanding stands at the opposite epistemological pole from Platonic idealism. Far from expressing a lack of faith in the power of the human intellect, Hume celebrated the unlimited grandeur of human thought: None could predict its achievement; none would question its potential to rise above the best ideas of the past.

The epistemological revolution of the eighteenth century paralleled, and in part inspired, the greatest change in the fundamentals of political thought in three thousand years. This new doctrine asserted that political and social institutions were no more inflexible and eternal than the ideas of the human mind. Just as human understanding is molded by the impress of experience, so should forms of government be related to human need. The laws of a society are not to be derived from a heavenly pattern; they are to be adapted functionally to environmental and social conditions. Montesquieu's *The Spirit of the Laws* decisively affirmed radical functionalism in political theory. From the new functionalist political theory, Rousseau extrapolated revolutionary implications. There is nothing natural and inevitable, he argued in *The Social Contract*, about prevailing political institutions which foment inequality and injustice; they are artificial constructs which can and should be changed.

Enlightenment thinkers did more than formulate a new set of assumptions for political and social thought. They accorded the economic aspects of social life a distinct set of operative rules, free from traditional theoretical and moral claims. Adam Smith developed a theory of the right ordering of economic life, which would add to the general welfare of mankind. Following Locke's denial of external authority and in imitation of the laws of the physical universe that Newton had discovered, Smith advocated that each man be free to pursue his self-interest in the economic market. This individual self-interest would coincide, as by the actions of an "invisible hand", with what was most agreeable to society.

It was characteristic of Enlightenment culture that the attack upon the old order was not left on an abstract, theoretical plane. The standards of rationality and humanity were applied to just about every aspect of political, social, economic, and legal life. This spirit of social criticism and political protest turned out to be the most persistent and pervasive aspect of the Enlightenment heritage. The essential message of the philosophes was: We shall bring everything and everyone to account before the tribunal of reason and humanity. This remains the fundamental progressive creed in the Western world.

Chapter 8   The French Revolution and the Industrial Revolution: Political and Economic Transformation

The Enlightenment, which was centered in France but made itself felt in virtually every part of Europe, reached its climax with the important writings of Voltaire and Rousseau. It had taken upon itself the task of examining critically almost all aspects of the human condition. But it remained to be seen whether this kind of Enlightenment could be translated into significant and lasting political reform. The answer was not long in coming.

8.1   The French Revolution

In Paris, on July 14, 1789, a furious crowd stormed the Bastille, a fortress prison that symbolized royal oppression. This uprising marked the beginning of the French Revolution, a violent decade during which thousands lost their lives at the guillotine. The Revolution was the violent result of a combination of old inequalities and injustices, new ideas about freedom and the limits of government, and internal economic problems.

At first the revolutionaries formed a National Assembly to rectify injustices and draw up a constitution. However, while moderates worked toward a constitutional monarchy, radical groups like the Jacobins demanded a republic. Eventually, in 1792, the radicals seized power and beheaded King Louis XIV. A strongly centralized republic was created under Robespierre and Danton, and with it a powerful Committee of Public Safety to watch over internal security. Thus began the Reign of Terror, during which many people had their heads cut off at the guillotine simply because they were suspected of disloyalty. After Robespierre himself was beheaded in 1794, reaction set in. Political clubs were disbanded, riots were suppressed, and a conservative regime framed a new constitution providing for a republican government headed by a Directory.

Amid this turmoil, an obscure corporal from Corsica named Napoleon Bonaparte(1769—1821) had risen in the ranks of the French Army and in public opinion. Armies under his command conquered Italy and Austria. Returning to Paris, he boldly took control in a brief, bloodless coup. He abolished the Directory and made himself first consul. "The little corporal" became a dictator.

Napoleon strengthened the central administration, set up the Bank of France, reorganized the education system, and founded the Imperial University. His Napoleonic Code remains the basis of French Law. Moreover, by 1812 his empire in Europe reached from Norway to southern Italy, from Austria to Spain.

Yet Emperor Napoleon sought to expand farther. In 1812 he raised an army of 600,000 and marched toward Russia. Russia at this time was ruled by Czar Alexander I, once Napoleon's ally and a shrewd and powerful leader. When Napoleon arrived at the gates of Moscow, he found the city silent and deserted. Those who remained set fire to the city, and Napoleon soon stood among ruins. He had no choice but to return to France through the bitter Russian winter. As the frost-bitten, half-starved troops trudged homeward, swarms of Russian Cossacks cut the French flanks to ribbons. Of the original 600,000 soldiers in Napoleon's Grand Army, over 500,000 died, were captured, or deserted.

Several more years of political maneuvering and military defeats forced Napoleon's abdication. He retired to the island of Elba, near Italy, but less than a year later, he raised one more army, only to meet final defeat near the Belgian town of Waterloo at the hands of the British Duke of Wellington. Exiled to the barren island of St. Helena, Napoleon died in 1821.

8.2   The Heritage of the French Revolution

The basic idea of the French Revolution, as stated in the *Declaration of the Rights of Man and of the Citizen* of August 27, 1789, was that government did not belong to privileged, hereditary, or self-selective elites and power groups in a society but to the people—that is, to the governed. The democratic ideal of 1789 regarded the citizens of a state not as disparate individuals and groups subject to the will of the government but rather as "the nation", a collective entity in which sovereignty resided. Consequently, the concept of political equality had as its corollary a powerful impetus toward nationalism, the feeling that a people are bound together in an indissoluble community with a life of its own apart from the institutions of a centralized government. In France, the long war against the enemies of the Republic after 1793 greatly increased the intensity of this national feeling. The fraternity of the people as a collective entity became as central to the revolutionary ideal as the liberty and equality of individual citizens.

Thus, from the moment of triumph of the first great democratic movement in Western civilization, a fundamental tension was apparent—the tension between the right of the individual to freedom and equality and the responsibility of the individual to the needs and will of the nation. Democratic equality emancipated citizens from the tyranny of absolute monarchy and aristocratic privilege, but it did not inevitably imply greater freedom for the individual. On the contrary, the democratic state, rationally organized, could make and enforce demands upon the individual far greater than the ancien regime was usually capable of implementing.

The democratic movement of the late eighteenth century proclaimed the principle of popular sovereignty. Beyond this principle, however, its heritage to the modern world was complex and even ambiguous. On the one hand, that heritage asserted the liberal belief that the state should allow individuals to pursue their private interests. On the other hand, it asserted that the private interests of individuals had to be subordinated to the common good, and it gave government the power to see that this was done. Thus the conflict between collectivity and individuality that had existed in ancient and medieval societies was by no means prevented by the implementation of the egalitarian ideal but greatly intensified. It has remained a persistent issue in modern political life.

In the thought of the radical wing of the French Revolution there was a cognate motif that became central in Western civilization: the idea of revolution itself. In Jacobin theory, revolution became a rejuvenating force in society, an entity that had its own style. In the Jacobin mind, revolution became not a mere vehicle for political change but a way of life in itself. The revolution in France, however, was not confined in France. Democratic revolution was regarded as a universal movement which would inaugurate a new era everywhere in Europe.

All twentieth-century worldwide revolutionary movements have perpetuated the Jacobin ethic and aesthetic of revolution: apocalyptic, universal, and beautifully and morally violent. In the modern world, this revolutionary ethic and aesthetic has competed with and challenged Christianity as the prime millennial faith. Like evangelical Christianity, the Jacobin revolutionary ethos offered not merely a program for social reform but a life style, a culture, and an outlet for love and hatred.

It was precisely because the revolution in France became a collective entity with a style and culture of its own that after 1793 it could not be satisfactorily identified with a particular set of constitutional forms or a specific program. When the Revolution became an all-encompassing social force, it was best comprehended by association with one man, or at most a small group of men, rather than with a specific list of demands and expectations. The tendency of the French Revolution—and of all subsequent revolutions—was for the leadership to be taken over by steadily smaller groups and finally to be usurped by an authoritarian figure who proclaimed himself the embodiment of the movement. This was what Napoleon and the like had done.

The egalitarianism of the French Revolution, except for the assertions of a minute extremist group, stopped far short of socialism. In this sense, it is true that the Revolution served the interests of what might be called the middle class; it did not greatly help the industrial worker and the urban and rural poor. But, due to its democratic assumptions and attitude, the Revolution did open the way for the socialist movements of the nineteenth century.

The era of the French Revolution was the great turning point in the development of modern French government and society, and it profoundly affected the political and social structure of nearly every other European country. It also witnessed Britain's rise to a position of leadership in Europe and world affairs and the emergence of a new era of national consciousness. Most important of all, though somewhat obscured by the upheavals of the years 1789—1815, Europe—and especially Britain—had begun to experience an even more radical and permanent transformation—the Industrial Revolution.

8.3 The Industrial Revolution

From 1830 to 1870, the effects of the Industrial Revolution began to be felt in Europe. People were generally healthier, more vigorous, and—because of the manufactured clothing that had become available—better dressed. Pottery, made more efficiently, aided sanitation. Medical advances reduced disease.

However, the introduction of the factory system and the leap in urban population brought about new poverty and hardship. Children were sent to work in thousands of factories; housing grew cramped; and gloomy factory sites darkened city skylines. In political and social terms, the "working class" became a well-defined division of society.

Yet the Industrial Revolution also led to new methods of transportation, communication, and production. Inventions and improvements drew Europe closer together. By 1830 the steamboat was a familiar sight on European rivers. Railway lines were laid in France in 1830, in Germany in 1832, and in Russia in 1860. By 1900 most ships on the seas were steamships.

As early as 1816, underground cables carried telegraphic messages short distances; cables reaching long distances under water were perfected in the 1850s, when England and France, and then Ireland and Newfoundland were linked. Experiments with the telephone began in the United States around 1837, and European inventors continued to try to develop a commercially successful telephone in the following decades. It was not until 1874, however, that the American Alexander Graham Bell found the answer. By 1877 in Germany, eight hundred villages were linked by telephone.

After 1870 steel and steam became the kings of industrial and economic growth. Steel girders permitted the construction of high buildings, and steam eased transportation and increased factory power. In 1880 Thomas Edison put a practical incandescent lamp on the market, and by the 1890s electric power had become feasible. As the nineteenth century drew to a close, Europe, like metropolitan England, began to become what it is today: A land that in addition to its natural beauty is characterized by cosmopolitan and multifaceted cities—among them Paris, Rome, and Moscow.

8.4　The Impact of the Industrial Revolution

From an agency of social change in various parts of Europe, the Industrial Revolution became synonymous in the later nineteenth century with the common experience of Western civilization; from a torrent that threatened the old agricultural and hierarchical order, industrialization became a vast ocean that engulfed the Western world and then significantly penetrated traditional societies in the non-Western world.

In 1815 England was still overwhelmingly rural, with London as its preeminent urban center. But in the north factories were rapidly converting insignificant villages into expanding industrial towns. The pattern of modern industrial society, with all its dynamic economic power and all its ecological and social problems, had emerged in Manchester, Birmingham, and Sheffield. By 1815 the thrust of industrialization and urbanization was transforming the English environment with each passing year, eating away more and more of the old England of rural stability and village community.

The extensive employment of women and children, chronic conditions of overcrowding, dreadfully inadequate sanitation, crime, and epidemics gained for the new industrial towns a very bad reputation among contemporaries and among later historians and social theorists. By and large this reputation was deserved. But the conditions in the towns of the early machine age must be considered in the perspective of two important facts. First, the workers themselves were not entirely convinced that they had passed from a rural heaven to an urban hell. Unemployed farm laborers and Irish peasant immigrants were willing to endure bad housing and the other grim aspects of Manchester because they could get jobs in such factory towns. In many instances, the industrial laboring families enjoyed a higher standard of living than had been available to them in the picturesque villages of aristocratic rural England. Second, the abysmally inadequate control of the new urban environment was in part the consequence of the failings of the pre-industrial old regime itself—its negligent and hostile attitude toward the poor, its chaotic system of local government, its inexperience in dealing with social welfare and public health.

The factory system required a tremendous adjustment in the psychology and daily habits of the working class. Industrial workers had to be taught to subject their daily lives to the authority of the bells that announced the beginning and end of the work shift. The difficulty of teaching workers accustomed to the greater freedom possible in agricultural labor to adjust to industrial schedules was one reason why early factory managers liked to use women and children, who were psychologically more malleable.

Industrial workers also had to learn to change the glut-and-famine attitude traditional in rural society. In the old economy, many workers—not only on farms but in cottage industry—were accustomed to labor only until they had earned enough to tide them over for a few weeks or months and then to withdraw and apply themselves to the pleasure of consumption, to drink and leisure. The early entrepreneurs had to educate workers in the advantages of long-term saving and teach them to work for a better future for themselves and their families.

Workers also had to be educated to regard new industrial processes as opportunities to be exploited rather than as threats to be resisted. Many of those who suffered most from unemployment during the early decades of the Industrial Revolution in Britain were engaged in technologically obsolete industries, such as handloom weaving. The natural response of workers faced with competition from new machinery was to riot and destroy the machines— machine-breaking by "Luddites" was common in Britain's embryonic industrial society. As late as the 1830s, violence was a common working-class response to industrial change, and it was not until the 1850s and 1860s that British workers were generally convinced that industrialization could benefit them, given the help and protection of trade union organization.

The Industrial Revolution had another consequence for the workers; it gave them a class consciousness, made them into a community, and induced them to organize. In the early decades of the Industrial Revolution, the formation of labor unions was bitterly fought by employers, resisted by the government, and condemned as illegal by the courts.

The landed class also had to make a painful adjustment to industrialization and urbanization. Although some lords had invested in the new technology— particularly in transportation and mining—it was only very slowly that the aristocracy recognized the great advantages to national wealth and power that the factories represented. Most lords simply ignored the tremendous economic upheaval in the new towns; many regarded the environmental change as a dreadful departure from the beauty of rural England, and this emphasis on the ugliness of the new society was also a favorite theme of intellectuals and artists. Even more painful for the aristocracy was the recognition of industrial capitalists as political equals; in 1815 the new industrial towns and the entrepreneurs still had no representation in the House of Commons. Acceptance of the lords of industry as social equals by the landed aristocracy was quite unthinkable. That acceptance came slowly and grudgingly in the second half of the century.

The Industrial Revolution thus inaugurated the most profound transformation in social attitudes that had occurred in many centuries. Partly in response to working-class resistance and aristocratic hostility, the new industrialists developed a distinct ideology that was to have a great influence. This ideology has been variously called "economic liberalism", "laissez-faire philosophy", and "the Manchester school of economics". Since the second half of the nineteenth century it has been generally viewed as a conservative social theory designed to serve the selfish interests of grasping capitalists, but when it was developed, between 1800 and 1820, it was regarded by its proponents as a liberating, indeed radical theory, drawing upon the ideals of the Enlightenment and conducive to the welfare of mankind.

With the rapid industrial expansion in the new towns, this laissez-faire policy was given a meliorist tone—free enterprise would produce harmony and peace among the nations of the world. David Ricardo (1772—1823), a retired London stockbroker and the author of *Principles of Political Economy* (1817), became the founder of modern economic science. Among his discoveries were the principle of comparative advantages (that countries can benefit by specializing in goods they produce efficiently and trading internationally to buy others), and the law of diminishing returns (that continued increments of capital and labor applied to a given quantity of land will eventually show a declining rate of increase in output).

According to the new economic theory the wages and employment of the working class were also subject to the operation of the free market and inflexible economic laws. Thomas Malthus (1766—1834), in 1798, had claimed that when workers are paid more, they produce more children, thereby glutting the labor supply, driving wages down, and causing unemployment. Therefore the workers "are themselves the cause of their own poverty". It is not fair to see Malthus and Ricardo as mere ideological spokesmen for the

Manchester capitalists. They were independent and brilliant social theorists, convinced that the Industrial Revolution had brought with it grave economic and social problems.

Britain thus took the lead both in the area of new economic theory and in technological and social transformation. Modern industry developed first in Britain because all the necessary conditions existed there: a surplus food supply, capital for investment, an ample and fluid labor force, and a suitable intellectual climate. While in some areas the Napoleon Wars contributed significantly to economic and social progress, on the whole they tended to distract the attention of European statesmen and politicians who might otherwise have made a start at tackling the gigantic problems created by the incipient technological revolution.

The technology that we have learned to take for granted is a product of the late nineteenth century, and it is not easy for us to realize how much the material things it produced altered the quality of social and personal life. Not the least of the consequences of the revolution in transport and communication was the advent of democratic politics on a national scale. Politicians went out from their capitals to address huge crowds in every corner of the nation, and the populace was informed—or misinformed—about current events and issues by papers that printed news of yesterday's happenings from telegraphic reports. By 1900 a global economy, and also a global politics, was emerging. The integration of the world greatly increased the probability that international incidents in Asia and Africa would engender confrontations in Europe and that struggles among European powers would precipitate global warfare.

The life style and daily expectations of the common man were transformed. It was not until the later nineteenth century that a sick person stood a better chance of survival within a hospital than outside it. The advent of the gas-light, and then the electric light, altered the quality of life in all cities; no longer did nightfall plunge the world into terrifying darkness. Proliferation of the forms of mass entertainment—the popular press, theatres and music halls, spectator sports, and then motion pictures—enormously increased the variety of leisure enjoyment available to the common man, who was now educated in state-supported schools. By competing with religion for the workingman's free time, politics, labor union activity, and popular entertainment contributed to the decline of church attendance, particularly in Protestant countries.

Chapter 9   Romanticism: Fresh Insight into Human Experience

During the last decade of the eighteenth century and the first half of the nineteenth century, political revolution and economic change were paralleled by great transformations in art, literature, and philosophy. To cultural historians the period between 1790 and 1850 is known as the Age of Romanticism. During these years, artists and intellectuals made a frontal attack on the ordered, rational universe of Locke, Newton, and Voltaire. They proclaimed their rejection of the teachings and style of the Enlightenment, developing new canons for art, morality, and political thought.

9.1   The Romantic Movement

Romanticism was a revolution in human sensibility and self-consciousness, and it affected every major European country. Romantic writers embarked on a strange, wondrous, and often fearful voyage of discovery. The subject of their explorations was the human personality itself, everywhere breaking free of the intellectual straitjacket of classical thought. The Romantic eye was attentive to those aspects of personality that the eighteenth century had scorned, ignored, or branded as illegitimate vestiges from barbaric ages. Like Napoleon, whose super-mortal myth dominated the age, the Romantics seemed at times to respect no limits and no laws. They were intoxicated with power—the power of man to create, to conquer, to transcend, to discover, and to experience his unique self. Romanticism was a creative response to a world in which all the old certainties had vanished, a world in which the received wisdom of centuries suddenly seemed no more than a collection of threadbare clichés.

The Romantics were men seeking to build a new world on the ruins of the old. Severed from the certainties of the Enlightenment and the fixed political and social order of the ancien regime, they became rebels, though sometimes quite ridiculous rebels. Prometheus, Don Juan, Faust were all Romantic heroes because they dared to defy the very gods. Yet denying the gods was no easy matter and was certainly not conducive to serenity. When the Romantics were not exulting in their mission, they were racked with doubts, anxiety, and self-recrimination. They suffered from a sense of their own impotence and inadequacy. With passion and self-pity, Romantic writers recorded both their misery and their triumphs.

To the eighteenth century, nature had been the source of stability and law. The nineteenth century rediscovered the wild, capricious side of nature. The eighteenth century had fixed its gaze on celestial bodies traveling in their prescribed orbits. The nineteenth century discovered nature awesome, tempestuous, and beautiful. Not planets but mountains, hurricanes, and daffodils thrilled the souls of the Romantics.

To apprehend the lawful, orderly universe, eighteenth-century illuminati had relied on reason as the highest faculty of man. But the world of the Romantics was a world of change, of growth and decay, of flowering and festering; and to confront this new universe, they found reason static, cold, and generally bankrupt. The Romantics welcomed back into the universe ghosts, spirits, dreams, gods, and beautiful yearnings. Peasants, children, and physical and moral outcasts became fit subjects for literature and painting. The Romantics were not interested, or claimed not to be interested, in mankind in the abstract sense. They were interested in unique, individual, particular men. Men were not uniforms; each had his own aspirations, talents, and needs. All men were not suited to live under the same social system, designed by Parisian philosopher-gentlemen, for no single system suited all cultures and all circumstances.

The men of the Romantic era lived through wars and revolutions, which toppled government once thought to be holy and respectable and which redrew maps and boundaries a dozen times in the space of two decades. They were intensely conscious of mutability in human affairs. Whereas the eighteenth century had enjoyed positing absolute laws to govern humans as well as cosmic affairs, the nineteenth century was, of necessity, profoundly relativistic in outlook. Biology came to replace physics as the source of metaphors, concepts, and analogies. Whereas physics emphasized symmetry, balance, and mathematical certitude, biology emphasized process and organic development, mirroring a dynamic rather than a static world.

The powerful minds of the Romantic Age, however, continued to hold fast to the Enlightenment creed. Classical liberal economics, for example, and Bentham's utilitarian philosophy remained immune from Romantic attack. But such thinking was anathema to the Romantics. As a generation, they mistrusted formulas which laid claim to universal validity. They were haunted by the specter of the French Revolution. They had seen "the Rights of Man" lead to unspeakable carnage and suffering. In the name of an abstraction called Liberty, they had seen armies ruthlessly impose the will of a despot on people who simply wanted to be left alone to till their fields. The French Revolution and Napoleon had set about ruthlessly destroying the past. Everywhere laws, constitutions, and social institutions had been standardized, codified, and rationalized. The brutality of this operation made the Romantics feel a new reverence for variety—for the unique, the idiosyncratic, and the mysterious in individual personalities as well as in states.

In England some of the major writers of the neoclassical period had placed a new value on emotion. Laurence Sterne (1713—1768) had written in praise of "dear sensibility"; his novel, *A Sentimental Journey*, published in 1768, had demonstrated that tears and laughter could enrich experience and permit the world to be viewed with fresh eyes. And the eighteenth century produced at least one writer—Jean-Jacques Rousseau—who was to become to the next generation the personification of Romantic Man. The Romantics regarded Rousseau's *Émile* as the proclamation of a new philosophy and his *Confessions* as a realistic rendering of their own inner lives. Rousseau had sensed that all men would be moved by impulse and emotion and sometimes by perverse desire, and he had been willing to present his own life as a case history. For this, he had been condemned in his own time. But the Romantics found in him the archetypal modern man.

In 1774 Johann Gottfried Herder (1774—1803), the pastor in the tiny German principality of Schaumburg-Lippe, published a book with an awkward title, *Still Another Philosophy of History*. It was a direct attack on the historical thought of Voltaire and an indirect challenge to the French-dominated "cosmopolitan" culture of Europe. Herder questioned the classicists' dream of reviving the glories of Greece and Rome. All cultures, he maintained, are unique and inimitable, and all are capable of producing beautiful works of art. It is not the philosopher's task to judge past eras, ranking them in some absurd hierarchy of greater or lesser civilization. To understand a people or an era, the first requirement is sympathy on the part of the observer.

The discovery of oral tradition among various "primitive" European peoples was not the work of Herder alone. It was going on throughout much of Europe in the middle decades of the eighteenth century. And the ballads, myths, and folk tales unearthed in these years were to play an important role in the evolution of Romanticism. It was discovered that poetry, universally recognized as one of the supreme arts, could be produced by peasants as well as academicians. In 1756 James Macpherson (1736—1796), a Scot, had published his *Fragments of Ancient Poetry Collected in the Highlands of Scotland*. The poetry in this volume Macpherson falsely attributed to the pre-Christian Celtic bard, Ossian, who became a Romantic hero, depicted in innumerable paintings of the early nineteenth century. Alongside the discovery of pseudo-Celtic folklore, there came publication of the mythology of Scandinavia and Germany, introducing the heroes of Valhalla. The epic grandeur of these sagas forced a reevaluation of the "low" literature of the common people.

There was also a reevaluation of two of the titans of Western literature, Homer and Shakespeare. Scholars were beginning to reach the astounding conclusion that Homer himself had been a primitive, recounting his tales in a pre-literature society, and that his songs had attained their heroic grandeur not because he had triumphed over his impoverished environment but because he had mirrored it. Herder and other young Germans were pointing out that Shakespeare, the greatest master of drama, had been unashamedly a "popular" writer; so much was evident from the language of the plays, which was earthy as often as it was noble. Language, announced the Shakespeare enthusiasts, had impoverished since the sixteenth century, and this was the fault of the cultural tyranny exercised by Versailles. In the name of noble simplicity, the idiomatic, the colorful, and the quaint had been expurgated. A monotonous uniformity had replaced rich variety. The popular and provincial in vocabulary and usage had been banished, and, similarly, human experience had been stifled, cramped, and distorted.

Struck by the fact that the Bible itself seemed to be the work of a primitive people, Herder looked upon the Book of Genesis not only as superb poetry but as an early attempt of man to explain the origin of the world. Such attempts, he argued, must be treated with wonder and admiration, not with contempt. The theology, or the myths of the primitive, non-Christian people, were monuments from which historians and philosophers might learn much. He was grappling his way toward what was eventually to become comparative anthropology. By the time he published his historical works, he had come to believe that the poetry, philosophy, science, and theology of a people had to be understood as a synthetic whole: a common spirit permeated all expressions of a culture. The past was better approached by and more accessible to those who retained the reverent wonder and curiosity of a child than those who belittled, categorized, and depersonalized experience.

The year 1774 was important in German letters. Besides the publication of Herder's first historical writing, it saw the appearance of a slim novella by Johann Wolfgang von Goethe (1749—1832), a young Frankfurt lawyer. This work, *The Sorrows of the Young Werther*, was to capture the imagination of an entire generation of Geothe's countrymen. Superficially, it is a simple, even a trite story of frustrated, disappointed love, ending with the tragic suicide of the hero. But overnight this hero became the idol and in not a few cases the model of smitten, pining lovers throughout Europe. Emulation of Geothe's fictional Werther produced a fad of blue frock coats and yellow waistcoat as dreamy, unhappy young men set off to wander around the countryside, a sketchbook in one hand, and a copy of "Ossian's" poems in the other. In Leipzig and Copenhagen the novella had been banned, as "Werther-fever" propelled young men out of windows or put pistols to their heads. Geothe himself came to deplore the reception of his little book. He had meant Werther to be a tragic symptom, a walking neurosis, not a hero and prophet for his time.

Geothe produced Werther in four weeks' time, weaving into it his own grief at an unhappy love affair. The young hero, talented, well-educated, and handsome, with excellent worldly prospects, combines in his person all the characteristics prized by the rebels from the mainstream of eighteenth-century culture. The story of the young man's advance toward extinction takes on the quality of a great psychological drama. His own sensibilities, which he cares to cultivate, at last render him wholly unfit for the mundane world. In gradually severing his ties to that world, he finds solace in the violent grandeur of nature, which renders insignificant and paltry all the petty loves and strivings of man. In the end, his grasp on the world is totally loosened, his will to live completely sapped.

Werther thus became the first victim of the enigmatic disease that would plague so many nineteenth-century figures in literature. In the Romantic era his peculiar psychological state became a sign of membership in the spiritual elite, the mark of an artist and sufferer.

9.2 Romantic Literature

To speak of Romantic literature is to speak both of variety and abundance. All over Europe, but especially in the most remote and primitive corners, the Romantic ideology led to the collection of works that no one till then had bothered to notice. Myths, ballads, legends, and all folk songs were transcribed and anthologized. Furthermore, the ideas derived from Herder created a new consciousness of the importance of "national" literature.

Countries which had been quiet so far as literature was concerned suddenly produced poets, and some of them were very fine indeed. A Russian literature of international stature developed within a few decades as Alexander Pushkin (1799—1837) and Nikolai Gogol (1809—1852) burst upon the world. Hungary produced Sándor Petőfi (1823—1849), who is still regarded as the national poet of the country. In Poland appeared Adam Mickiewicz (1798—1855), probably the finest poet of that nation. Hans Christian Anderson (1805—1875) was writing in Denmark, Thomas Moore (1779—1852) in Ireland, Robert Burns (1759—1796) in Scotland. The American Romantic flowering came much later than in Europe—in the 1840s and 1850s.

The three distinctive thought patterns of Romanticism were created in Germany, Britain, and France. Romanticism in German literature began with the storm and stress movement of the late eighteenth century, which emphasized the Promethean, demonic qualities of humanity. Its monument was Goethe's *Werther*, and it also influenced the great poet and dramatist Friedrich Schiller (1759—1805). Both Goethe and Schiller, in their more mature work, moved in the direction of classicism and away from the sentimentality and personal intensity of Romanticism. But they remained loyal to central doctrines of the Romantic ethos. In Goethe's *Faust* the hero pursues an endless quest for self-realization, while Mephistopheles represents false and dangerous satisfaction with what has already been achieved in life and culture. Schiller's finest drama, *Wallenstein*, explores the tensions and crises of a transcendent personality within the context of the Greek tragic tradition. His last work, *William Tell*, issues a call for national liberation.

The central figure in German Romantic poetry was Heinrich Heine (1797—1856). His personality, his philosophy, and his mastery of the lyric form all placed him in the front rank of the writers of the Romantic era. Scion of a wealthy German Jewish family, he spent half his life in France, a failure by the standards of bourgeois society. His goal was the union of Hellenic beauty and Judaic-Christian morality, which would combine spiritual and personal love. Along with this personal quest for God, beauty, and love, Heine was very much involved in the political and social issues of his day and invariably took the radical side. He was enemy of tyranny in all forms and became a socialist in his later years. The sufferings of the workers seemed to him the shame and disgrace of Germany and even of Western culture in general.

Except for Heine himself, the leading minds of German Romanticism in his generation expressed their ideas not through belletristic literature but through social and political theory, philosophy, and history. Heine was deeply disappointed at this development. He pointed to the lack of integration of philosophy and art with social and political life in Germany—a split of pure intellect from practical affairs which, he prophesied, would have catastrophic implications for the culture of the Fatherland.

It is generally agreed that 1798 was the year when fully self-conscious Romantic poetry first appeared in England. That year saw the publication of the *Lyrical Ballads* of William Wordsworth (1770—1750) and Samuel Taylor Coleridge (1772—1834), the two key figures of the first generation of English Romanticism. The preface to the *Lyrical Ballads* was the first and most influential manifesto of the new literature in Britain. The poems took their subject matter from the incidents and situations of humble and rustic life. The poet, Wordsworth asserted, is a man like all others, but with a difference. He has a special sensibility, a deeper knowledge of human nature, a heart more tender, more moved by enthusiasm and passion. Poetry is both sublime and immortal. Its object is truth itself—not the remote and impersonal truths of science but intimate, affective truths of the human heart.

Bitter disillusionment with course of events in revolutionary France had moved Wordsworth to a profound reconsideration of what constituted the good society and the good life, and indirectly this reconsideration had led him to a new view of poetry. Returning from a year in France, he had looked back on his childhood in the beautiful Lake District of north-western England, and the wisdom of the country folk there seemed to him superior to the wisdom of the ideologues of the French National Assembly.

In confronting nature, Wordsworth believed, we confront ourselves. Nature is a catalyst for the human mind: A sudden encounter with a natural phenomenon—a mountain stream, a field of waving flowers—reveals harmonies and discords in our own souls to which we have long been oblivious. The process of self-discovery recorded in Wordsworth's greatest poem, *The Prelude*, comes about when the imagination, stirred by nature, becomes fruitful. From the meeting of the reflective mind and the sensuous world, there ensues creation. The separation between man and the natural world is erased; each becomes the measure and mirror of the other.

Unlike Wordsworth, who painted the inner significance of common scenes, Samuel Taylor Coleridge in his best-known poems, *The Rime of the Ancient Mariner* and *Kubla Khan*, evoked exotic, surreal realms—symbolic rather than naturalistic worlds. *The Ancient Mariner*, a parable of guilt and regeneration, was written in imitation of the folk ballads collected by antiquarians of the mid-eighteenth century. Coleridge insisted that his poetry was not allegorical, that no single key would unlock its secrets. For him, poetry was a dynamic figment of the imagination, whole in and of itself, not reducible to paraphrase or moral. Coleridge was conscious of the magical properties of words: His *Kubla Khan* has been described as the most musical poem in the English language.

Although Coleridge's poetic output is small, he is also a philosopher and social critic and one of the seminal minds of nineteenth-century Britain. Instinctively distrusting the new world of finance and industry, he made sensitive comment on the brutal competitiveness of early industrial Great Britain. No rights existed, he asserted, without duties and responsibilities, else the communal principle would be lost and the world would be ruled by egoism gone wild. In practice, the emphasis on duties and responsibilities placed Coleridge on the side of institutional authorities.

Unlike Coleridge and Wordsworth, the second generation of English Romantic poets—particularly Percy Bysshe Shelley (1792—1822) and George Gordon, Lord Byron (1788—1824) —was defiantly radical. Shelley was variously a proponent of women's emancipation, nudity, vegetarianism, atheism, and democracy, and Byron was vilified and ostracized by the Tory establishment as a traitor to the political and private morality of his aristocratic social milieu. His death in 1824 in the Greek war for liberation made him a hero and martyr to nationalist movements across all of Western Europe. Whereas Wordsworth and Coleridge had favored duty and authority, Byron and Shelley sang in praise of liberty—intellectual, moral, and political.

Alone among the major English Romantics, John Keats (1795—1821) stayed aloof from political and social questions in his poetry. Though he tried all his life to work out some satisfactory relationship between art and life, it was to art itself that his mind constantly reverted: It is the highest reality, the only claim man could make to immortality. His belief in the absolute primacy of art made him a forerunner of the later nineteenth-century aesthetes who enshrined the doctrine of "Art for Art's sake". Perhaps because he sensed the fragility of his own health, Keats was painfully and ecstatically aware that all sensuous beauty will perish. He wrote poetry that combined acute passion with exquisite delicacy of detail, seeking to capture in art the quintessence of life. To Keats, sensation and thought became, at least in art, equivalent; his poetry is meditation on the significance of beauty.

By temperament an anarchist, Shelley loathed institutional authority as a drag on the soul. He shared with the Enlightenment a passionate belief in the goodness of human nature and a vision of a golden age yet to come when mankind would be happy, prosperous, and fully emancipated. His greatest literary creation is *Prometheus Unbound*, a lyrical drama based on the story of the god in the Greek pantheon who has loved mankind so much that he defies Zeus in order to bring the gift of fire to men. For this, Prometheus has been consigned to chains, but the chains are destined one day to be broken, for Prometheus' love for man and for liberty is no impotent yearning. He could endure struggle forever, and his ultimate triumph is assured.

In Shelley's *Ode to the West Wind*, destruction and ruin are but a prelude to regeneration and new life, not only for the poet but for all men. Yet poetry had a special mission: It alone could animate men's hearts to those altruistic impulses which would usher in the golden age to come. Art could lift man from the pit of the egotistical self to sympathy with all humanity and all beauty of thought and action. The imagination of the artist thus became the chief agent of moral good in the universe. It was the artist who built toward the reign of love that man was destined one day to achieve, despite tyrants and the inhibitions created by society.

While Shelley never lost touch with the practical steps by which the new world was to be built, Lord Byron quickly abandoned politics after making a few speeches in the House of Lords. Following an incestuous love affair with his half-sister and an unhappy marriage, he abandoned England as well, to spend the last eight years of his life as a wandering exile and a living legend. Byron's heroes—Childe Harold, Manfred, Cain, Don Juan—are, like him, arch-rebels, isolated from both nature and man. Damned and tormented, they are also irresistibly attractive pilgrims and soldiers of liberty, standing outside society and its constraints. Although their transgressions—particularly of sexual taboos—eventually bring about their ruin, they are men who hurl themselves against all barriers, willing to pay the price of extinction in order to realize personal freedom. Byron himself tried to escape from the nihilistic implications of his heroes' lives, but he could find no faith, no anchor. Unlike Wordsworth, he found no solace in nature. He could not, like Keats, posit art as the highest reality and the great reconciler of all contradictions, and he was not blessed with the surging optimism of Shelley. The contradictions between what men desired and what society and nature permitted seemed to him irreconcilable.

The world inhabited by the English Romantics was changing with unprecedented speed. Their lifetimes coincide with the first Herculean stages of the Industrial Revolution, which permanently altered the material and social basis of life for all time to come. Even as Wordsworth idealized the self-sufficient, isolated, rural communities of England, these communities were vanishing forever. The growth of factories and large urban conglomerates was radically altering the most elemental relationships of human life. Traditional class and family structure were breaking down to be replaced by—no one knew precisely what.

All the English Romantics agreed in idealizing the artist and in exalting his special faculty, the imagination, as a vehicle of personal and social regeneration. It was a creative response to the advent of the modern world but also an ambiguous and sometimes pitiful one. Even as they wrote, the advent of industrial mass society, of which they were so acutely conscious, was utterly transforming the social role of the artist. They were living on the threshold of an era in which art and ideas were to become commodities to be sold in the open marketplace, when, for the first time in history, artists were in danger of becoming lost in the crowd. When "art" and "culture" seemed threatened, when the artists' social function was no longer clear, literature and art were exalted as a special, higher branch of ethics.

The complacent bourgeois, as well as the wage slave whom he had brought into being, was feared and detested by the Romantic artist, who saw in the routinization and mechanization of society his own nemesis. Byron felt that he had better die young, or else he would surely settle into conformity and respectability. To escape this fate before dying, he discovered and dramatized alienation as the special plight and badge of distinction of the artist. The violent, satanic rebelliousness of the Byronic hero is, psychologically speaking, the bravado of the individual haunted by the fear that he is doomed to be homeless and superfluous in mass industrial society.

The tremendous impact Byron had on the European Romantic movement is matched by one other British writer, Sir Walter Scott (1771—1832), who is virtually the creator of a new literary genre called historical novel. Already an established poet, in 1814 with the publication of his first novel he achieved high popularity with the middle-class reading public. And in his lifetime his influence on the writing of history was as important as his influence on the novel. In Scott's fiction, the ideas of Herder are given flesh and blood. Through sympathetic imagination, he brought to life societies long dead and depicted their customs, their dreams, their speech, and their manners as unique and wondrous. Reading Scott, one feels and sees what a medieval abbot or a seventeenth-century Scottish laird will be like.

Scott's wide appeal is a significant indication that Romanticism was not the special preserve of creative, first-class minds. Scott satisfied on a popular level the desire to feel and experience a life wholly different from one's own. Exoticism had been a strain of the Romantic Movement since the eighteenth century; it was part of the appeal of the old ballads that had been collected and anthologized. Scott made it respectable as literature as well as a plea for the preservation of old mores and institutions, confident that the heart of man would find room to accommodate them.

Continuing in the same vein, English Romanticism tended increasingly in the direction of emotionalism and sentimentality. In the novels of the Brontë sisters—particularly Charlotte Brontë's *Jane Eyre* and Emily Brontë's *Wuthering Heights*—this tendency was combined with great dramatic power and skill in the portrayal of turbulent passions. Popular Romanticism was skillfully exploited by Charles Dickens (1812—1870), who loaded his novels with weepy scenes of beaten, neglected, and brutalized orphans. The 1840s saw a rash of novels decrying the new industrial system, levying many of the same charges that Coleridge had made many years earlier. Novels such as *Sybil*, by Benjamin Disraeli (1804—1881), the future prime minister, described the "two nations" of rich and poor, living side by side in mutual misunderstanding, and caused many a tear to be shed over the plight of poor but honest factory hands. This popular Romanticism significantly shaped the ambience of nineteenth-century England. Pity and compassion became respectable and permeated mid-nineteenth-century British life. Sentimentality, one of the prime offshoots of Romanticism, mobilized many of those who passed the first factory acts, fought to abolish the slave trade and slavery, and founded schools for the instruction of the poor.

Charles Dickens, with his passion for social justice and his sentimental evocations of the goodness of the suffering poor, won an enormous audience. But these are not the qualities that place his finest work—such as *David Copperfield* and *Great Expectations*—in the front work of Western literature. Dickens's greatness lay in his delineation of character, his ability to capture the facets of human personality. The characters in his novels are recognizable social types, but at the same time they are real individuals whom we can never forget. From the experiences of a miserable childhood and youth and a hectic early career as a journalist, Dickens was able to create, with loving care and unsurpassed skill, a gallery of early nineteenth-century humanity.

The Romantic Movement in American literature originated in the Boston area in the late 1830s as a direct offshoot of English Romantic thought. Ralph Waldo Emerson (1803—1882) was very influential in disseminating transcendental, individualistic, and anti-mechanistic doctrines. But the development of American Romanticism was shaped by the ambition of native, particularly New England writers to gain a place in world literature, by a humanistic and evangelical reaction against the early stages of industrialization, by a radical democratic faith in the virtue of the common, and by a grandiose sense of the capacity of individuals, as exemplified in the phenomenal achievements of America's western expansion. Emerson, a rhetorician of some power, is only a second-rate philosopher. More important as an original thinker is Henry David Thoreau (1817—1862), whose *Walden* is one of the most sensitive and persuasive statements of the Romantic belief that the individual can live without mechanistic civilization and can realize the union of self and nature. A Romantic but no transcendentalist, Edgar Allan Poe (1809—1849) explored the occult and the beauty of terror in his poems and tales.

The flowering of the American Romantic sensibility came in the 1850s in the novels of Nathaniel Hawthorne (1804—1864) and Herman Melville (1819—1891) and the poetry of Walt Whitman (1819—1892). Hawthorne made excellent use of the seventeenth-century historical setting to explore, with unusual psychological insight, problems of guilt and mental anguish. Melville's *Moby Dick*, although not widely appreciated until the twentieth century, is now recognized as one of the greatest works of Romantic literature, an enormously powerful and intricate examination of the individual in conflict, and at the same time in symbiotic union, with nature and fate. Walter Whitman's poems expound a rampant democratic individualism at the same time that they communicate, in free verse, an entirely personal vision.

The full flowering of Romanticism in France, the home of neoclassicism and the Enlightenment, was not achieved until the 1830s and 1840s, by which time it was already a spent force in England. It first appeared on the extreme Right, flourishing as a kind of diseased sentimentality among ruined aristocrats and unregenerate royalists. Francois-René vicomte de Chateaubriand (1768—1848), was the first French Romantic writer of note to appear in the nineteenth century. Chateaubriand came from an old provincial aristocratic family whose life had been completely overturned by the Revolution. While exiled in England, he was beset by poverty and loneliness, which, coupled with a naturally melancholic temperament, produced a sudden, mystical religious experience—a common phenomenon among the exiled, demoralized nobility whose world was all chaos and confusion. In the eighteenth century French aristocrats had been notoriously atheistic, cynical, and worldly, and the disasters that befell them in the 1790s seemed to be divine punishment for their former frivolities. By 1800, when Napoleon had consolidated his position and many émigré noblemen were returning, France was ripe for a religious revival.

In 1802 Chateaubriand, who had been appointed to a diplomatic position by Napoleon, published *The Genius of Christianity*, subtitled *Poetic and Moral Beauties of the Christian Religion*. Two sections of this work, *Atala* and *Rene*, became widely celebrated. Set in a fantastic American landscape of green serpents, pink flamingos, tulips, pines, and magnolias, *Atala* is the bittersweet love story of two ill-fated Indian lovers who attain not each other but the ecstatic solace of a kind of primitive Christianity. *Rene* is the tale of the progressive dissolution of another dreamy, listless, insatiably dissatisfied Werther, who had the misfortune of being consumed by a hopeless—though highly spiritual—love for his sister. Chateaubriand's kind of sentimental Christianity was an avenue to God particularly suited to aristocratic sensibilities, and it remained important through the entire nineteenth century, capturing several egotistical and rebellious intellects.

The first generation of French Romanticism appeared to be firmly wed to reaction. Alfred de Vigny (1797—1863), Victor Hugo (1802—1885), Alphonse de Lamartine (1790—1869)—young poets who first made their impact in the 1820s—were all inclined toward monarchy. Delicately lyrical, painting soft, muted word-picture, sensuous and religious at the same time, the new poetry provoked both puzzlement and irritation among the still strongly entrenched academicians, who were neoclassicists fighting a grand last-ditch battle to preserve the culture of Pierre Corneille (1606—1684) and Jean Baptiste Racine (1639—1699). Excluded from the major literary organs, the young writers gathered in small, informal groups to propagate the new artistic ideas. One of the bibles of the new movement was *De l'Allemagne*, an appreciation of the literature of Germany written by Madame de Staël (1766—1817), the formidable daughter of an ill-starred minister of finance of the old regime. A salon patroness of considerable talent, she wrote several influential works calling for a new literature, which was to be national, popular, and Christian. Sir Walter Scott was also producing an impact: The 1820s and 1830s saw the publication of a spate of historical novels, of which the swashbuckling adventure tales of Alexandre Dumas (1802—1870) were the most popular.

At first young writers pleaded only cultural tolerance—freedom in arts and letters—but as the restrictions on civil liberties and freedom of the press were multiplied, the battle became politicized, and French Romanticism underwent a complete ideological turnabout. In 1830 Victor Hugo, who was fast emerging as the leader of the new movement, published a manifesto that identified Romanticism with liberalism and advocated the double goal of freedom in art and freedom in society. A great many French Romantics became intoxicated with a fervent, naïve love for "the people". Both Hugo and Lamartine saw themselves as writers who had a special rapport with the working class of Paris. It was their divine mission to lead the people, whose instincts were good but whose education was unsound, to a love of art and poetry, just as the people would in their turn infuse the poet's art with their own vitality and fresh vision. The Romantics envisioned the people, simple and good, in huge, surging crowds, manning the barricades that toppled the Bourbons, singing "The Marseillaise", moved by a divine spark of freedom. Lamartine enjoyed standing on Parisian balconies exhorting the people to take up the torch of Liberty.

This alliance of liberalism and Romanticism was a generous, impulsive, exultant creed that aimed at nothing less than the regeneration of all mankind, the emancipation of oppressed peoples such as Poles and Italians by a new triumphant march of French armies, the striking down and confounding the censors, police spies, and princes everywhere. Moreover, this idealistic espousal of "the people" was not confined to France alone. Throughout Europe it affected young writers who, while remaining ignorant of actual class interests and aspirations, championed and extolled the eternal, suffering people who would one day rise like a great ocean wave and sweep away tyranny and oppression.

Perhaps the greatest literary monument of this discovery of the Parisian proletariat is Victor Hugo's *Les Miserables* (1862), a kind of literary symphony to the eternally oppressed but unvanquished people. *Les Miserables* is a voyage through sewers, prisons, and hovels of the great metropolis, filled with passion, crime, evil, faith, and unsuspected sublimity. In Hugo's masterpiece of subterranean Paris, beauty and redemption are found in misery and squalor.

Hugo remained a democrat for the rest of his life, but democracy as an ideal and as a social reality was receiving a negative reaction among many Romantics unable to share his optimistic, messianic faith in redemption through suffering. The trouble was that democracy was inexorably bound up with the ascendancy of the middle class, and toward the middle class the later French Romantics almost without exception felt the most profound disgust, fear, and loathing. The Romantics, particularly in France, turned to be the first generation of artists to perceive that the bourgeois had already become the measure of man. The new culture became their culture, and writers such as Stendhal (1783—1842), Honoré de Balzac (1799—1850), and Charles Baudelaire (1821—1867) found it appalling. The philistine bourgeois obsessed the late Romantics; to subvert and finally destroy his commodity-ridden world was their dearest wish. The rest of mankind, including the aristocracy and "the people", was surrendering to the soulless materialism of the bourgeois, the implacable enemy of all talent and sensitivity. The artist alone was left as custodian of the higher values. It was his sacred duty to wage unremitting war against modernity, which he equated with machinery, technology, material progress, the profit motive, and spiritual paralysis.

The social reaction to the ubiquitous bourgeois was the creation of "bohemia" as a separate community wherein the artist dwelt. Paris in the middle years of the nineteenth century was the first city to develop the artists' quarter—today a feature of most metropolises—as a distinct, ongoing oasis for those who chose to live outside the respectable society. Here the Left Bank developed as a refuge for real and would-be painters, writers, and students. And as Parisian bohemianism developed, it elaborated its own dress codes and styles of behavior. Young France in the 1840s lived in garrets and cultivated outlandish hairdos and foppish dress to distinguish itself from the ordinary denizens of the city.

Behind the garish ostentation there was a method and a rationale. Young Romantics were carving out of their own empire in the midst of a hostile society. The values they chose to cultivate and display were those perceived to be inimical and threatening to the bourgeois. The bohemians developed the cult of youth as a virtue and a style. Youth and creativity, youth and originality, youth and courageous flamboyance became ideals because bourgeois society collectively was a kind of geriatric ward of the dying in spirit. Similarly, the cult of joblessness—while in part, of course, a cruel necessity—was also a point of pride, since pursuit of a career and a well-paid job was held to be deadening to all instincts but the acquisitive, the grasping, the social-climbing. Along with a career, it was felt, came a household, an establishment, and a routinization of life which was fatal to the imagination. Thus marriage—which, of course, entailed the necessity of a career—was often treated rather like funeral.

The most significant artistic response to the unfriendly environment encountered by the artist was the formation of the aesthetic ideal summarized as "Art for Art's sake". Vastly influential in the dissemination of this philosophy was the poet Theophile Gautier (1811—1872), who sported red waistcoat and acted as a kind of spiritual mentor to Parisian intellectuals of the 1830s and 1840s. Gautier saw it as his task to rescue young writers from a misguided meddling in political and social problems. Art serves neither freedom nor liberalism, nor morality; it serves only itself. The present world is to be rejected outright on the grounds that it is aesthetically and morally repulsive and beyond salvation. In these circumstances the artist has to look out for himself alone, lest he and his work as well become contaminated by the general poison. The doctrine of "Art for Art's sake" led inevitably to the creation of poetry that could be appreciated only by the artists themselves. This trend was a complete about-face from the position of the early Romantics, who had pleaded for a popularization and democratization of literature.

Gautier's most famous pupil was the poet Charles Baudelaire (1821—1867), who displayed most of the chief characteristics of late, embittered, disillusioned Romanticism. Baudelaire created in his person the dandy as the spiritual aristocrat pitted against all the grossness of the modern age. His dress, his walk, his habits of eating and conversation all had to be sculpted with elaborate self-control. The ideal of the traditional bohemian had been the natural play of instincts and impulsive spontaneity, but Baudelaire scorned this lack of restraint and artistry. He aimed at total mastery of the self—the perfectly composed outward manner as a reflection of exacting internal standards of behavior and thought. This self-imposed discipline gave the dandy a heroic dimension. He was a sojourner in this vile world, but he was not of it; it did not touch him.

Baudelaire was much taken with the aesthetic possibilities of depravity, partly because depravity was so useful a means of shocking the dull and dozy bourgeois. He entitled his great collection of poems published in 1857 *The Flowers of Evil*. The artistic point of this magnificent collection was that beauty could be made out of any material whatever, even the most sordid and ugly. Thus he wrote about prostitutes, beggars, criminals, lesbians, and other social lepers, constructing nevertheless the most delicate, lyrical tone poems imaginable from this unlikely subject matter. By resting his case on the moral depravity of man, Baudelaire made another radical departure from early Romantics like Wordsworth and Shelley, who retained faith in the natural goodness of man. But it was not horror as such that attracted Baudelaire; it was the beauty that could be extracted even from horror despite the conspiracy of the social and natural order to destroy it.

Two great French novelists—Stendhal and Balzac—shared many of Baudelaire's antipathies. Stendhal (1783—1842) set out to study the problem of how best to survive in an epoch he considered almost wholly damned. The world depicted in *The Red and the Black* (1830) is turned into mutually hostile classes, within which individuals wage a relentless battle of one-upmanship. But it is also littered with ambitious young men like Julien Sorel, who are rootless outsiders, compulsively on the make. The grandeur of the Napoleonic era is past. The Revolution has reached a state of total exhaustion; all combatants have been discredited; society is in a kind of paralysis. Julien Sorel, consumed by drives which once could have been expressed in great political deeds, is doomed to war against an era that oppresses him by its mean dimensions. The clever Sorel is forced to assume the role of bandit, operating by stealth and ruse to outwit a society that is instinctively hostile to talent, ambition, and intelligence. He is the perpetual opportunist caught in his own game and finally destroyed.

Stendhal shared Sorel's hunger for an age when heroes were not automatically outcasts. He idealized the classical world, the ancien regime, Renaissance Italy—any era, in fact, which allowed unbridled energy to master human events and human destinies. Having despaired of substance, he staked all on style. He had an abounding ambition for splendid gestures. Thus revolutions pleased him aesthetically, for they occasioned grand outbursts of passion, magnificent spectacles which dispelled for a moment the triviality and boredom of the daily round. Stendhal was an unashamed worshipper of the great man—like Napoleon—who alone could give drama to the mundane and petty which made up modern life.

The same disenchantment with post-revolutionary bourgeois society is reflected in the novels of Honoré de Balzac. He was obsessed with depicting every aspect of contemporary France, with subjecting every class and every occupation to pitiless scrutiny. His masterpiece, *The Human Comedy*, was to consist of some one hundred and twenty separate novels. He worked with such energy or monomania that more than ninety were actually completed at the time of his death in 1850. Balzac was much influenced by Sir Walter Scott, but whereas Scott had labored to bring the past to life, Balzac turned his attention to the present. Scott had the sensibilities of a historian; Balzac, those of a sociologist. He sought to observe and record every detail in the lives of his protagonists, down to the special jargon of their jobs.

With Balzac, and to a certain extent even with Stendhal, we begin to move away from the great Romantic tradition. These writers did not seek to transfigure reality; this was all too plainly beyond the artist's capabilities. Their task was to document, to report the facts. It was the beginning of the shift to realism and the science of society.

9.3 The Romantic Social and Political Thought

The Romantic reconstruction was not confined to literature and the arts; it affected every area of human thought and experience and none more profoundly than social and political theory. The Church and the monarchy were the chief victims of the Republic of Reason. It was only natural that after the Revolution had done its worst, the old order should mount an intellectual as well as a political counteroffensive. But Romantic political thought was not merely propaganda for the old order. The disruption wrought by the French Revolution had been so traumatic that thoughtful men everywhere were led to reexamine not only the principles of stable and just government but the fabric of society within which governments operated. The relationship of government to society, family, and Church received new attention. Continuity was discovered as one of the first principles of a sane society. The violent rupture with the past which the French Revolution had attempted produced a new respect, even a reverence, for a different kind of change—the change accomplished by slow growth and maturation, the imperceptible modifications that habits and customs make on institutions. Edmund Burke(1729—1797) found in this principle the glory and longevity of the British constitution. A generation later, Alexis de Tocqueville (1805—1859) discovered that continuity persisted beneath the most destructive upheavals and that the ancien regime and the revolutionary Republic had had more in common than the revolutionaries had realized. Not only was it undesirable to wipe out the old and the past; it was not even possible.

The violent, destructive side of the French Revolution made men wonder how far history and the tide of human events were amenable to management and direction by individuals. Was national destiny shaped by men, or was it the product of vast, blind, impersonal forces? If the latter, what was the nature of these forces? The answers offered were various. Race and nationality were put forth as anterior to political development, as great animating powers that conditioned or even determined the march of historical events. The early socialists saw economic and technological revolutions as antecedent and primary, politics as no more than superstructure. The German philosopher Hegel suggested that history is governed by the inner logic of its own, a dialectic which assures that each stage of historical development would be a unique higher synthesis of the thesis and antithesis of previous eras. Hegel, as well as the English philosopher and historian Thomas Carlyle, focused on Napoleon and decided that individual men could on occasion rise to the level of vast impersonal forces and become "world historical individuals" beyond the understanding or judgment of ordinary mortals. The power of crowds in the French Revolution left an indelible impression on sensitive minds of the post-revolutionary generation. The French historian Jules Michelet was the first to suspect that the anonymous multitudes which the ancient world and the eighteenth century had treated only as "rabble" might themselves be one of those great, mysterious forces that moved the world.

Reflecting on and analyzing of the French Revolution enlarged historical consciousness throughout Europe. Men could not help but see that they were living in a new era, one such as mankind had never before experienced. The probing of the past was undertaken from a variety of motives; it might provide a guide to present action, a justification for this or that political regime, but it also provided consolation—reassurance that the old order and the old certainties had not been utterly destroyed. The historical past was an anchor which enabled men to ride out present tempests.

The dethronement of reason after the French Revolution, coupled with the personal agonies men experienced in a world in which stability seemed permanently undermined, pushed some of the most sensitive to a new exploration of the meaning of religious truth. The early nineteenth century is generally cited as the period during which the mass of Europeans became firmly secular in their outlook. But this was also the period when the search for God became for many a personal hunger. By and large, the new departures in religious thought came from outside the established churches and had very little concern for dogma or theology. Chateaubriand, Schleiermacher, Kierkegaard rested their case for religion on their own emotional, aesthetic, and psychological needs. The new mass movements—Methodism, Evangelicalism, Pietism—were similarly based on direct, personal appeal to the intimate demands of the heart.

Burke has long been called the father of modern conservative thought—a somewhat bizarre title to bestow on a man who championed the American Revolution and was part of a progressive, reformist faction in his own country. Burke's *Reflections on the Revolution in France* was published in 1790, well before the French Revolution entered its bloodiest phase. It soon became the catechism for all those to whom the revolutionary doctrines were anathema. The book was endlessly praised and elaborated on by publicists in émigré circles in France and Germany, striving to protect absolutism. It was translated into German by Friedrich Gentz, personal advisor of Metternich, the conservative Austrian statesman. Gentz went on to produce a comparison of the American Revolution and French Revolution that found the two great upheavals entirely dissimilar—the one preserving, while the other destroying liberty. In France after 1815, Count Joseph de Maistre (1754—1821) drew on Burke's inspiration to rehabilitate and vindicate entirely the government of pre-Revolutionary France. Maistre who was witty and incisive, became the mouthpiece of intransigence, stating baldly that social order was based on Providence and that to tamper with constitutions or with sovereignty in the name of reform was to tamper with the ordinances of God. Maistre's argument was a great support to the pre-revolutionary alliance of Church, monarchy, and aristocracy.

Burke's *Reflections on the Revolution in France* is far more profound and searching. Burke took his stand against those who, talking about social contracts and inalienable rights, thought that constitutions could be fashioned by a flourish of the pen. The essence of his argument lay in the assertion that governments are not fortuitous constructs but part and parcel of a social fabric which includes customs, habits, other forms of association, religious sympathies, and all manner of prejudices. Governments represent the habits and wisdom a people accumulated over centuries. All "rights" are historic rights, products of the circumstances that have called them forth. Burke asserted the priority of the community over the form of government. No political system, he felt, could be severed from the community that had produced it.

In Burke's organic view of society, men are creatures whose sympathies extended naturally from their families to their neighborhoods, to their towns, and finally and last to their governments. To jostle one set of loyalties and affections is to disturb them all. A constitution, like a tree, springs up differently in different soils; it is nourished and watered naturally by the community, and it grows and changes eternally. Burke's view, unlike those of Gentz and Maistre, is profoundly relativistic. Reform and conservation of the past are not opposites but complementary processes, going on all the time spontaneously and often unconsciously. As a conservative, not a reactionary, Burke saw in the French Revolution the ruinous dissolution of all specific, traditional loyalties, and he feared an atomized society. The separation of the individual from the community, estate, town, guild, family, and class into which he had been born was inimical to the Romantic conservatives' idea of freedom, for freedom is inconceivable without variety and individual peculiarity. All leveling and equalizing doctrines tend toward despotism.

Burke was essentially a practical man, whose political philosophy never lost touch with actual conditions in England. It was in Germany that his ideas received their most extreme expression. The German Romantics did not always understand Burke, but they made a cult of worshiping him. Adam Miller (1779—1829), the chief German philosopher of political Romanticism, transferred Burke's theory into mysticism. His lectures, delivered at a period when Germany was politically prostrate before the armies of Napoleon and later published as *The Elements of Politics*, had a profound effect on the development of German political thought. For Miller, the state represents "the totality of all human concerns". Adulation of the Middle Ages led him to advocate that the nobility should be entrusted with the direction of the state and also to subordinate the values of the present to those of the past. Present human happiness and welfare count but little against the immortal community. Individual life has no meaning apart from the state, which alone put paltry men in touch with eternity.

Miller was led by his theories to a new discovery of the virtues of war. War is preferable to peace because the tears, the shared grief it produced made the state in time of war a powerful emotional reality, while in times of peace and prosperity men tended to take the state for granted. Later in the century Karl Marx (1818—1883) commented that Germany had experienced and reacted to the French Revolution on a purely philosophical plane—hence the extremism of the German response.

In Great Britain, where the Industrial Revolution had advanced further and faster than elsewhere, the vitality of Romantic thought was rapidly channeled into an attack on industrialism and the resulting mechanization of the human spirit. Thomas Carlyle (1795—1881), essayist, historian, and impassioned social critic, expressed the frustration that many of the most sensitive mid-century minds felt in confronting the new society. Along with Samuel Taylor Coleridge, he was the chief disseminator of German Romantic thought in Britain. It was Carlyle who first spoke of the industrial age as the era when "the cash-nexus" supplanted all other relationships and values. Carlyle, in fact, was lamenting the same dissolution of the social ties of family and community that Burke before him and Marx after him saw as the chief characteristic of the new age.

The industrial epoch, wrote Carlyle in *Signs of the Times*, an essay published in 1829, was not a heroic, devotional, moral, or philosophical age but "the Mechanical Age". And the mechanization of life was not confined to external and physical phenomena—men were becoming mechanized in thought and feeling. Carlyle detested the liberal utilitarians, who, he felt, were attempting to comprehend and manage life and experience by the computing principle. He showed himself a true disciple of Burke by lashing out against those who sought to cure social and spiritual ills by tinkering with mere political arrangements. The Romantic bent of Carlyle's thought is obvious in his stress on the primacy of inward experience, ethics, and spirit.

Carlyle was not content merely to denounce. He wanted regeneration. He struggled all the time with the problem of how to combat spiritual emptiness. In *Past and Present* he held up a glorious (if unreal) picture of medieval

England as a society that had not lost its veneration for spiritual values. Modern laissez-faire government he loathed for its "Donothingism", which he saw simply as an abdication of social responsibility, a symptom of the drying up of compassion and fellow-feeling. He sought frantically for a class of men to free society from the moral atrophy in which it was sunk. For a time he pinned his hopes on the great new industrialists themselves, the captains of industry who might be educated to their social responsibilities; but as he grew older, he turned more and more to the veneration of great men—heroes—as the saviors of men's souls. He wrote biographies of Cromwell and Frederick the Great and a set of essays on heroes and hero worship. It was a familiar pitfall for disillusioned Romantics. Beset by a sense of impotence in the face of the relentless impersonal forces of the age, they put their hopes on charisma, on some mighty personage who would transfigure the world by his personal example. But this hope more often than not led to bitter disappointment.

The changing nature of political power, of which the French Revolution had provided such an unforgettable example, haunted nineteenth-century Europeans. It was gradually becoming clear that power was passing to new classes of men—to the much despised bourgeois and perhaps ultimately to the mob. Tocqueville, the French political analyst, was one of the first European thinkers to set out to study with scientific detachment the transformation of political and social life under the impact of democracy. He chose for his case study the United States, the country where democracy had achieved its fullest development. *Democracy in America*, published in 1835, still stands as one of the pioneering works of sociology as well as an immensely incisive analysis of the character of American life. For Tocqueville, America was the land of equality, which had been achieved by the erasure of those distinctions of rank and status that characterized traditional societies. He regarded the drive for equality as the great tendency of the modern age. He saw it operating in the monarchies of the ancien regime long before the coming of the French Revolution.

Tocqueville is the first modern political analyst to perceive clearly that liberty and equality, far from being essentially the same thing, might in fact be inimical and incompatible. No governments, he said, were as powerful or despotic as democratic ones. Democracy, by dissolving time-honored social identities, leads to a greater and greater reliance on government; all authority now devolves on the state, which the people have no reason to mistrust since it represents them and is shaped in their own image. As each man becomes more and more the replica of his neighbor, his individuality is lost.

On the whole, Tocqueville feared popular despotism less than the permanent degradation of culture, which seemed to him sadly but inevitably bound up with the progress of democracy. Equality distrusted and was frightfully jealous of all distinction; it was the implacable enemy of distinguished talent, intelligence, wealth, and social privilege. Tocqueville saw much that was admirable and exciting in American life, but he feared that the progress of democracy—particular its advent in Europe—would turn mankind into "a flock of industrious animals, of which the government is the shepherd". He decided that, emancipated from the fetters of class and tradition, the individual, far from coming into his own, was impoverished, diminished, and circumscribed. Coleridge, Burke, and Carlyle had all had foreboding of this fundamental modern dilemma.

If Tocqueville surveyed the future with apprehension, the greatest German philosopher of the age, Georg Wilhelm Friedrich Hegel, must be classed with the optimists. Perhaps Hegel is the last nineteenth-century thinker to attempt to include all the contradictions that rent modern philosophy in a single, coherent, all-embracing system. The world, Hegel believed, embodies God's rationality, and human history must therefore be similarly rational. History is purposeful and amenable to human understanding. It is, moreover, progressive, continuously moving to higher stages of development. But in human affairs progress is not tranquil and linear. The universe is dynamic and organic. All is in a state of flux, strife, and contradiction.

Hegel capitalized, so to speak, on chaos, by making conflict and the clash of ideas and cultures the very mechanism of progress. This is the heart of his famous dialectic. Consciousness comes about through the seeing of opposites, then through their integration. This, in turn, leads to the seeing of new opposites. The dialectic led Hegel to the conclusion that there is no finality in any structures, be they moral, metaphysical, or social. Truths of one age are superseded by the new-found knowledge of the next, though the old is always conserved in the new synthesis. Since the resolution of one conflict automatically engenders another, the world is constantly evolving.

Like his fellow Germans and like most Romantics, Hegel made the community rather than the individual his starting point. He recognized that men everywhere are nurtured and determined as cultural and moral beings by their societies. Man finds his fullest expression in products of communal life— art, religion, philosophy, and the state. The discords that beset human life can ultimately be resolved only within a community. The great antithesis between freedom and necessity, for example—the discussion and debate of philosophers and theologians since time began—can be reconciled only in the state. Hegel's choice of the state as the center of his moral universe, itself an actual embodiment of the highest morality attained in any age, was to have enormous consequences in the future development of all German political thought and quite likely, in the actions of the men who shaped modern German history. Not all states, of course, are equally rational or free. Like ideas, states are in constant competition. The highest development of "the world historical spirit" is found in different peoples in different historical epochs. As one nation's mission is fulfilled, it yields the center of the state to another. The dynamic creativity passes to another people, another land.

If Hegel impressed anything on his followers, it is that history moves according to a grand, providential design, that it obeys laws and follows patterns that can be discerned, at least in retrospect. But if societies are shaped by the unavoidable working-out of great ideas, then it follows that individual actions and volitions do not count for very much. In fact, Hegel's grand conceptual scheme renders the role of the individual highly precarious and problematic. Individual responsibility for controlling political events becomes illusionary or at any rate dubious. Immanuel Kant's great concern for the individual as moral agent is abandoned. In the Hegelian view, individuals can attain significance only if they are moving with the trend of the times, only if they conform to the prevailing world-spirit. To talk of opposing history is nonsense. Insofar as men try to do so, they are relegated to insignificance— moral as well as historical.

The state embodies the highest development of morality at any given time, and every stage of historical development is necessary. These two propositions, when combined, reduce all too easily to the assumption that whatever is, is necessary and is therefore as it ought to be—that "Whatever is, is right". In the next century this vulgarized interpretation of Hegel became the rationalization for acquiescence to some of the greatest tyrannies the world has ever seen.

In Hegel, one of the paradoxes that threads its way through so many aspects of Romantic thought—the painful opposition between man perceived as petty, wretched, and impotent and man perceived as heroic, magnificent, and godlike—finds a curious resolution. Caught in the ebb and backwash of history, man is utterly insignificant. On the other hand, a man or a nation marching in turn with the spirit of the age is invincible. In rare instances such a man may even become a "world historical figure", advancing the destiny of mankind—an Alexander, a Caesar, a Napoleon. Hegel remained a fan of Napoleon to the end of his days, even after Bonaparte's armies had vanquished the philosopher's homeland. World historical figures are exempt from ordinary standards of moral judgment. They could be selfish adventurers or scoundrels satisfying their own whims so long as these private pleasures served history. The heroes of Carlyle, Byron, and Stendhal had retained certain recognizable ethical dimensions. For Hegel, these ceased to matter.

While Hegel was reshaping the foundation of the philosophy of history, Western Europe was experiencing an epidemic of books that laid the foundations for history as a formal academic discipline. The influence of Herder and Scott and the need to understand the French Revolution led to a great spate of historic studies in the early decades of the nineteenth century. Of the many tomes that were produced, the works of a German, Leopold von Ranke (1795—1886), and a Frenchman, Jules Michelet, established new standards for historical research, a new sense of how the past should be approached and understood.

The year 1824, when Renke published his first book (he was to produce dozens over a period of 60 years), is generally regarded as the beginning of the critical, scientific study of the past. Ranke announced in his preface that he intended simply to "show how things really were", leaving it to others to draw lessons from history. This seemingly modest pronouncement was to reverberate down the halls of academia for generations. It was the debut of allegedly value-free history: the facts, all the facts, and nothing but the facts. History was no longer to be a great morality play or a statesman's manual of conduct. Ranke said that he wanted history to be objective, to be science. His influence was vast: In the decades that followed, dozens of his students were appointed to university chairs throughout Germany. Yet Ranke was more influenced by Hegel than he cared to admit, or perhaps realized, for he tended to see history as a series of epochs, each one carrying to fruition the germ of some great idea—for example, Protestantism. For Ranke as well as for Hegel, history came to be the inevitable working-out of great ideas in no particular ethical context.

Michelet's work is utterly different. His multivolume *History of France*, produced over a period of more than 30 years, was everywhere with values. Deeply influenced by Vico, the eighteenth-century philosopher who first suggested that civilization is the collective product of humanity, Michelet saw humanity as the great inarticulate multitudes, the anonymous peasantry, the riotous urban crowds; he wanted to become the tribune of the voiceless people who had been cheated of access to history by illiteracy, poverty, and servitude. In his *History of the French Revolution*, the people are the only hero. *History of France* is the story of the progressive development of the masses to ever greater self-consciousness and self-assertiveness.

Michelet was moved to tell the story of "the people" by his own passionately democratic temperament. His political prejudice led him to a view of history that was ultimately much richer and deeper than that of Ranke, his conservative German peer. Frustrated in his attempts to find the voice of the common man in diplomatic charters and government records, he looked elsewhere—to medieval cathedrals, oral traditions, and other monuments of the collective mind of each epoch. Michelet had read Herder and, with him, believed that all knowledge is one: Human culture can and must be understood as a totality. This Romantic desire to apprehend and encompass all facets of human experience, to embrace together man, God, and nature, inspired the enormous creativity of the first half of the nineteenth century.

The social and psychological dislocation produced by the tempests of the French Revolution, combined with evangelical and pietistic subversion of the comfortable, commonsensical deism of the eighteenth century, produced a sudden quest for faith. Homeless and estranged from the bewildered new social order, men sought new grounds for certainty, for a new basis for conduct, an explanation for their despair and loneliness. Chateaubriand was typical of the sizable group of aristocrats who sought solace in a return to the Catholic Church. Ultraconservative Catholicism became something of an affectation among the European aristocracy following the French Revolution.

A more serious manifestation of the prevailing mood of repentance was the sudden flowering of High Church Anglicanism in England after a century and a half of easygoing latitudinarianism. Because the movement centered round a group of Oxford University intellectuals, it came to be called the Oxford movement. It produced at least one great theologian in the person of John Henry Newman (1801—1890). The Oxford movement was a return to the doctrinal conservatism of Anglicanism as it had existed in the seventeenth century under Archbishop Laud. Its leaders brought a new austerity and solemnity to the established Church and, by emphasizing the importance of ritual, liturgy, music, and prayer, satisfied the new taste for awe and beauty. Some of its adherents, notably Newman, were led the whole way back to the Catholic Church. The 1830s marked the beginning of periodic outbursts of conversion to Rome, which continued in England well into the twentieth century. While some of these were certainly the fashionable affectations of young aesthetes, many others must be seen as symptoms of the new need for authority and mystery which developed in an increasingly secular world.

In Germany, the longing for the lost unity and harmony of universal Christendom found its highest expression in the poetry and prose of Novalis (1772—1801). Like many Europeans in his day, Novalis saw the Protestant Reformation as the birth of Europe's nemesis, the intellectual seedbed of the social and political anarchy that led straight to the disaster of the French Revolution. His writing mingled aspirations for a new European oneness with a mystical faith in the special destiny of Germany as the vehicle of mankind's deliverance. But he conceived of Germany as an ethos rather than a political construct. The state was a divine work of art, a poetic creation.

On Religion: Speeches to Its Cultural Despairs, by celebrated preacher Friedrich Schleiermacher (1768—1834), is far more important in the development of religious thought than lyrical outpourings of Navalis. Deeply affected by Rousseau, Schleiermacher saw religious faith as one of the primary instincts and impulses of man. For him, religion and piety has nothing to do with dogma and theology—these are products of the reflective critical intellect that transcribes (and falsifies) the religious experience, which is intimate, personal, and not communicable in words. Piety alone, said Schleiermacher, could restore to man a sense of his own wholeness; without it, he is a creature torn by antagonistic faculties and desires.

Schleiermacher made the individual personality the point of departure for all religious sentiment. Everything men experienced as holy *was* holy. Religion is both the supreme expression and fulfillment of the human personality and the means by which the individual is united with the natural order, attaining extinction of the private self in the great mystery of the One and the All. Grounded in psychology, in the primitive instincts of man, it could not be undermined by logic or reason; it became inviolate to all onslaughts of modern skepticism.

It was only a few steps from the pious affirmation of Scheiermacher to the bitterness of Soren Kierkeggard (1813—1855), the Dane who is generally regarded as the founder of modern existentialism. Whereas Schleiermacher had made faith independent of reason, Kierkeggard insisted that faith exists only when reason is defied and violated. The test and sign of faith is the ability to believe with perfect serenity that which is a paradox, ridiculous and absurd. Kierkeggard was an isolated figure in his own day, and it is difficult to find characteristically Romantic elements in his thought. He shared with his age only an acute apprehension of the wretchedness of the human being severed from all traditional authority, compelled to strike out on his own in a lonely, terrifying voyage of discovery. His influence was to come much later.

Other religious explorers began in profound pessimism and ended in triumphant affirmation. Such a man was Hugues Félicité Robert de Lamennais (1782—1854), a priest who became an embarrassment to the Church by gradually reviving the long dormant Christian social gospel. Christianity, he reminded the world, had once been the religion of the poor and the oppressed. He wanted the clergy to become missionaries in the modern world, getting their hands dirty in the slums and hovels of Paris. Lamennais advocated the solidarity of all the lowly against the tyrants and usurpers of liberty and the parasites who fed on their fellowmen. It was an old message but one which neither the conservative French Church nor the papacy was particularly anxious to hear expounded. His views were condemned by a Papal encyclical. He became more and more mistrustful of authority and, after the publication of *Words of a Believer* in 1830, broke with the Church entirely and became the apostle of a humanistic, radical Christianity. Lamennais was one of a small group of Catholic intellectuals who tried to push the Church toward a creative confrontation with the new industrial urban masses. He feared that popular atheism would be the inevitable result of the perpetuation of the alliance between the Church and political reactionaries.

The philosophical justification for the demythologizing of Christianity was provided by Ludwig Feuerbach (1804—1872), a disciple of Hegel. In *The Essence of Christianity*, published in 1841, Feuerbach announced that God had been created by man and that it was the very time for mankind to reclaim its own. Mankind, he argued, had taken its highest nature, its most sublime aspirations and ethical ideas, and set them up as a transcendental autonomous power. Actually the sublime is human. The Divine Being is nothing more than a symbol of man's own highest potentials; while no individual possesses these magnificent capacities, the human species does. But having created God, man had impoverished himself and denied his own latent perfections. When he set God as his antithesis, he split his own personality. The Christian God—or any other god—is an anthropological construct. Once understood as such, He would lose his mystery, and man would become truly free. Until such time, Christian ethical precepts must always seem coercive—the impositions of an alien being. A turning point in history would come when man recognized that consciousness of God was nothing more than consciousness of the human species.

Feuerbach's fusion of anthropological and psychological arguments to explain the origins of religion had a great influence on the development of ethical and religious thought. Karl Marx was profoundly impressed by his work. The idea that man had at some time in the distant past alienated a part of himself for the benefit of some phantom or illegitimate master was applied by Marx not to morality but to labor. The plea to expropriate the usurper and thus become fully human and free remained the same.

9.4 The Heritage of Romanticism

While the modern world derived the essentials of its liberal, meliorist credo from Enlightenment culture, the contribution of the Romantic era to modern thought was no less important. Through their exploration of the relationship between self and nature and between self and society, Romantic philosophy, literature, and art opened up new perspectives on the meaning of individual experience. All subsequent explorations of how the individual relates to the external world have been extrapolations from the revolution of the human spirit that Romanticism proclaimed. From Romanticism, later nineteenth-and twentieth-century culture derived the doctrines, assumptions, and attitudes that created modern sensibility and that fundamentally conditioned the way in which Western civilization has understood human experience.

The Romantic heritage inculcated a set of values that still inspires both individual and communal action and a distinctive life style that remains extremely attractive, particularly to intellectuals, artists, and the young. The implications of the Romantic ethos for political and social theory tended in several directions, some mutually contradictory. But all who wish to act in society today must continually work within the context of the Romantic heritage—to perpetuate, to modify, or to oppose it.

The Enlightenment had established the belief that the authority of government resided in the consent of the governed. But in eighteenth-century thought "the people" was still a lifeless abstraction. The Romantics gave it life and individuality. Rejecting the elitism of eighteenth-century culture, the Romantics attributed the value of purity, wisdom, and beauty to the thoughts and mores of the common man with an intensity that went far beyond the democratic statements of any previous era. Romantics relished the idea that the honest laborer—particularly the rural laborer—was the bearer of the primordial wisdom and sense of justice of mankind.

In general, the Romantics adored those who were excluded from power in society—not only the workers and the poor, but also women, old men, and children. As most powerless and defenseless, children and youth were accorded a special value in the Romantic vision and invested with the most profound wisdom.

The adoration of childhood and youth as a time of pure vision and uncontaminated integrity has been a recurring theme in modern thought, with mixed social consequences. The Romantics arrived at this perception partly out of their antiestablishment bias and partly out of sheer sentimentality. But the youth creed was also a corollary of the main philosophical movement of the Romantic era, usually called idealism or transcendentalism. This philosophy claimed to find in each man an innate intellectual power and life force that transcended the physical world and imposed on it whatever order, beauty, and justice it contained. An adherent of transcendental philosophy could well believe that human creativity and virtue exist in children in a particularly pure and uncorrupted form.

In the perspective of the long-range development of Western thought, Romantic transcendentalism marked a revolt against eighteenth-century empiricism. Immanuel Kant showed the Romantic thinkers the road back to philosophical idealism. Kant concluded that the human mind could never penetrate to knowledge of the ultimate reality—the noumenon, or thing-in-itself. Instead, the mind imposes order and coherence on the phenomenal world of experience by applying its own categories of space, time, and causality. Although Kant's metaphysics still fell within the Enlightenment tradition, his German disciples used his theory as the starting point for a philosophy of transcendental idealism.

One of the more effective exponents of this extremely influential intellectual movement was Arthur Schopenhauer (1788—1860). He took the simple but audacious step of effacing the distinction between Kant's phenomenal world of human experience and the noumenal world of ultimate reality. By so doing, Schopenhauer reached the conclusion that human thought and feeling give value and meaning to all reality and that the world is the product of the human mind. Romantic transcendentalism thus abolished the dichotomy between self and nature, between the individual mind and the external world. Since the mind imposes order and beauty on the world, self and reality are one.

German idealism got a very mixed reception from succeeding generations of philosophers. It had many adherents until the end of the nineteenth century and very few after that time: The trend of twentieth-century philosophy has been decidedly away from metaphysics. But as Schopenhauer clearly perceived, Romantic transcendentalism had great significance for the arts; nearly all of the painting, literature, and music of the twentieth century, insofar as it professes a theory, assume the validity of the artist's imposition of meaning on experience.

A leading aspect of the Romantic heritage in Western culture is the belief that history is extremely important and that historical writing is one of the major art form. This concern with history is in part simply another manifestation of Romantic devotion to truth in art—the past was another area of experience that could be given coherence and beauty by the artist. At its most abstract level, the Romantic devotion to history is a product of the idealist philosophy. For if reality is to be found in the meaning that mind imposes on phenomena, the history of all experience, of all phenomena—world history—should reveal a pattern of the ultimate reality. This is the starting point for Hegel's philosophy. In the total experience of the past we can discern an objective, rational pattern that reveals the form of Reason, of Spirit —the Absolute, the truth about reality.

In the twentieth century both rightwing and leftwing disciples of Hegel have claimed universal truth for their reading of the Spirit of History and have sought to impose their vision of the "necessary course" of the World-Spirit on unbelievers. Hegel and his disciples transformed the Romantic fascination with history into the historicist worship of history as the only source of objective truth. Whatever terror and torment this philosophy has left in its wake, Hegel must be given his due as the preeminent philosopher of history in Western civilization.

Romanticism not only stimulated new insight into both individual and social experience which are still vital in the culture of the world today; it propounded a philosophy of life that evolved into a distinctive life style. Romanticism put the greatest value on action; it taught that ideals must be lived from day to day and that freedom and redemption lie in the experience of struggle itself.

The transcendental heroism embodied by Faust or Byron led to admiration for the activists of history, for the self-sustaining, self-fulfilling heroes. Carlyle adored Oliver Cromwell and Frederick the Great, and Stendhal admired Napoleon. It also inspired Romantic enthusiasm for revolution—not only to liberate the poor and overthrow despotism, but also to provide a true revolutionary's life style: to risk life for freedom and to direct the vital force of humanity at the moment of crisis. The Faustian-Byronic Romantic heroes have been ever-recurring types in Western culture and society—assuredly, as much as statesmen and entrepreneurs, the makers of the modern world.

Chapter 10   Socialism: Faith in Human Progress

The disintegration of the Romantic Movement, the failure of the revolution of 1848, and the steady pace of industrialization and urbanization all contributed to a significant change in higher culture and thought in the years between 1848 and 1870. The period was characterized by a widespread enthusiasm for the methods and the accomplishment of science, technology, mechanics, and organized research. The leading European thinkers of the 1850s and 1860s abandoned the Romantic quest for the absolute in favor of critical analysis and scientism.

10.1   Science and Technology

Scientism can be defined as the desire or the effort to apply the techniques used in the natural sciences to all aspects of life. Since scientists had been remarkably successful in discovering the physical laws of the natural universe and predicting the behavior of natural phenomena, Europeans at mid-century asked why scientific methods could not be applied to the study of man in order to achieve a "realistic" understanding of his biological and psychological nature, his society, and his economic and political systems.

Science was firmly joined to technology in the second half of the nineteenth century, and the fruits of the union were everywhere apparent: Railroads were stretching across Europe and North America, iron and steel were replacing wood and brick, and complicated machines were enriching their owners and producing a variety of new and exciting products for consumption by the affluent, growing middle class. The Suez Canal, built between 1856 and 1869, was more than a political and commercial achievement; it was a feat of engineering that would not have been possible fifty years before. In the Victorian age (1837—1901) it was difficult not to believe that hard work and scientific techniques could solve all problems, human as well as material.

The Crystal Palace, a towering structure of iron and glass built for the Great Exhibition of 1851, seemed to represent the very spirit of the Victorian age, for here the common elements of earth were translated, by human ingenuity, into a monument to science and prosperity. It was built, within a few short months, of prefabricated, interchangeable parts. Its chief designer, Sir Joseph Paxton, had once been a gardener. His rise to eminence through intelligence and hard work made him the very prototype of the middle-class hero, the self-made man.

The Palace was the focal point of the Great Exhibition, which was intended to bring together the finest examples of scientific and manufacturing achievement. This it accomplished, leaving little doubt that Britain led the world in material progress. More than six million people visited the exhibition, including large numbers of British workingmen, but it remained a peaceful festival at which capitalist and worker alike could congratulate themselves on their accomplishments and speculate on the glorious future.

The exhibition had the enthusiastic support of the royal family and this relationship was entirely appropriate, for the dominant industrial bourgeois class found its natural leaders in Victoria and Albert, whose court was an upper-middle-class household on a royal scale. The virtues of the royal couple were those most admired by the middle class—decency, hard work, and devotion to duty. Neither aristocratic idlers nor wild-eyed radicals were encouraged by the queen, and the prince's deep attachment to learning and science was entirely characteristic of the educated bourgeois.

The accomplishments of science between 1848 and 1870 amply justified its public image. Both the theoretical advances and their application to industrial and human problems were so notable that the period has been described as a second scientific revolution, comparable to that of the seventeenth century. The intellectual process by which natural science had been divided into several distinct disciplines—such as physics, chemistry, biology, and geology—was intensified in the first half of the nineteenth century. But now advances in one science influenced others; international exchange of information was extensive, thanks to the growth of scientific journals and the rapid communication for which science itself was responsible. Improvements in instruments and techniques kept pace with progress in ideas, and in Germany, at least, the development of the universities provided scientists with professional training as well as with laboratories and equipment.

In physics and mechanics, nineteenth-century scientists took a giant step away from the Newtonian system, and in these same fields they formed the most fruitful alliance with industry. In England, experiments by Michael Faraday (1791—1867) established the concept of lines of magnetic force and proved that electricity and magnetism are convertible into each other. James Clerk Maxwell (1831—1879) built on Faraday's experiments to provide the theoretical basis for the electromagnetic theory of light and accounted for the attraction and repulsion of magnetic bodies in terms of forces produced by the action of a field, departing from the hard, massy particles of Newton's universe. Maxwell did not attempt to say what electricity is; he described how it worked, using physical and mathematical analogy.

The basic principles of thermodynamics had been established in the 1830s, but scientists of the 1850s and 1860s were able to make significant advances in the field. Newly discovered laws governing the relationship between heat energy and mechanical energy were basic to modern physics and engineering and crucial to the provision of power for industry and engines for transportation and manufacture. The study of organic chemistry was also particularly well suited to a materialistic era. Scientists' attempts to separate matter into its chemical components resulted in the development of such new products as artificial fertilizers, dyes, rubber, and explosives. Biochemistry was developed as a scientific specialty during these years, while biology itself became the revolutionary science of the century with the work of Charles Darwin(1809—1882). Even before Darwin, biology and geology had captured the attention of the educated public—amateur naturalists and fossil hunters were fascinated by speculation about the age of the earth and the development of plant, animal, and human life.

Louis Pasteur (1822—1895), the French chemist, did most of his important work in the third quarter of the century, even though some of his basic principles were not accepted until later. Studying yeasts, he traced the process of fermentation to the presence of microscopic "germs" and went on to prove experimentally that these same microorganisms are present in ordinary air as well. The English surgeon Joseph Lister (1827—1912) carried Pasteur's principles into the operating room when he insisted upon antiseptic surgical procedures, with dramatic implications for medical practice and hospital mortality rates. Pasteur rescued the French silk industry by isolating the bacilli of various diseases of the silkworm and then joined his efforts to those of Robert Koch (1843—1910) of Germany to isolate the anthrax bacilli and produce a workable vaccine against the disease. Pasteur's work on rabies and the first successful inoculation of a child who had been infected by a rabid dog assured the acceptance of the germ theory of disease, with incalculable results for human life expectancy.

The mid-nineteenth century was the great age of university organization. Though the major impulse for this movement came from science, scholarship in every branch of knowledge benefited. Old universities were expanded and reformed, and new kinds of schools and new fields of study began to develop.

In science, particularly on the Continent, the gifted amateur was giving way to the trained professional. As scientific apparatus became more sophisticated and more expensive, as research techniques were developed and the body of existing knowledge expanded, it was no longer possible for a gentleman to become a scientist through self-education at home in his leisure time; formal instruction and well-equipped laboratories were essential. In addition, industry required trained technicians to understand its new machines, as well as skilled workmen to operate them.

Germany was preeminent in providing education to meet the needs of science. There, eminent scientists and scholars were almost always attached to universities, and university teaching was improved by the development of the seminar system. Due in part to the intimate involvement of the state in the educational process at every level, German libraries and laboratories were the best in the world. New universities—particularly in the United States—were modeled on the German universities, and German became the language of scientific and scholarly communication. Between the 1840s and the 1870s, Germany rose to the top rank in industry and manufacture primarily through the excellence of its technical education.

In Great Britain the government stayed out of education until after 1870, and only a few iconoclasts like the prince consort (a German) challenged the traditional preeminence of classical education. The objective of the best British education remained the training of cultural gentlemen. In the 1850s the British civil service was reformed, and admission to the bureaucracy began to be determined by competitive examination, but the nature of the examinations was such that the best preparation for them was the classical and philosophical training provided by Oxford and Cambridge. Thus the formal education of the men who governed the British Empire remained focused on Plato and Cicero. France had an uneven educational system, with a few outstanding schools; overall, it was in no way comparable to the German system.

Germany led the world in scholarship of all kinds, not in science alone. This period, for example, saw the founding of the great German schools of Biblical history and criticism. In the so-called higher criticism of the 1850s scholars applied the "scientific" methods of philological and textual criticism to the Scriptures, assuming in the spirit of the age that theological questions could be answered by extensive research and a scientific approach. Earlier, in 1835, David Friedrich Strauss (1808—1874) had analyzed the various Gospels as if the Bible were any ancient text, and the popular furor that his work aroused was echoed in 1863 with the publication of *Life of Jesus* by Ernest Rénan (1823—1892). Although much less scholarly, Rénan's work was widely read and attracted public attention to the school of higher criticism.

Biblical studies and textual criticism helped stimulate the expansion in historical scholarship in the 1850s. An increasing interest in modern history produced discussion among historians as to the definition of historical periods, particularly the dividing line between the medieval period and the modern. The concept of the Renaissance was first fully expressed in 1860 by the Swiss historian Jacob Burckhardt (1818—1897) in his *Civilization of the Renaissance in Italy*. This was no dry collection of data but an exciting, interpretative work which defined the Renaissance as a political, social, and cultural phenomenon that began in Italy during the fourteenth century. Through such studies in the past, nineteenth-century scholars hoped to find the sources of their remarkable present.

The search for a usable past was conducted by scholars armed with the critical methods developed by the early nineteenth-century German school of historians; it was supported by governments wishing to foster national sentiment. In Britain, France, and Germany, government subsidized scholars who edited medieval documents, and chairs were founded in the universities to reward and maintain historians who would write imposing accounts of the national past and train young scholars in scientific methods and nationalist interpretations. In Germany a host of historians expounded the glories of the medieval Holy Roman Empire and, going further back, analyzed the institutions of the barbarian German tribes. Since many of these historians were middle-class liberals, their discovery that the inhabitants of the primeval German forests were freemen who made communal decisions in pristine parliaments is not surprising. The greatest of the French scholars, Fustel de Coulanges (1830—1889), demonstrated to the satisfaction of his countrymen that the origins of French institutions lay in the late Roman Empire, rather than in Germany. At Oxford, William Stubbs (1825—1901) propounded a Germanic origin for cherished English institutions. In a magisterial three-volume work, he portrayed the whole constitutional development of medieval England. Thomas Macaulay (1800—1859), a liberal civil servant and man of letters, described in colorful manner the struggle for liberty against Stuart despotism in the late seventeenth century, and George Bancroft (1800—1891) similarly recounted the rise of freedom in the United States. Never before, and perhaps never since, did the work of historians have such a wide audience as in the 1850s and 1860s. In leading Western countries, historians gave to nationalist and liberal dogma an impressive and apparently secure scientific foundation in the experience of the past.

10.2 Social Sciences

The general term *positivism* can be used to describe any philosophy that concerns itself with observable phenomena rather than metaphysical speculation. Since the laws of physical nature can be ascertained by research and rational thought, some men reasoned, these methods should be effective in determining the laws that govern human nature, psychological or social. The founder of the special doctrine of positivism, in the sense of a specific philosophy, was Auguste Comte (1798—1857), a French philosopher. Once the laws of human association had been established, Comte believed, it would be possible to adjust social, political, and economic systems to conform to human capabilities and requirements. Comte himself aspired to participate in the adjustment.

Although Comte relied heavily on the work of earlier thinkers, including his mentor Saint-Simon, he is known as the founder of sociology and gave the discipline its name. His special contributions were his law of three stages and his classification of the sciences. He believed that all human societies develop through three stages: The theological based on primitive anthropomorphism, the philosophical based on metaphysical abstraction, and the scientific based on natural laws. The sciences can be classified from the simplest and most general to the most complex—mathematics, astronomy, physics, chemistry, biology, and sociology. Western man, having attained mastery of the first four, had reached the scientific stage of biology in the mid-nineteenth century. Comte believed that he himself had appeared just in time to initiate the last of the sciences—sociology. Despite endless quarrels over his more extreme ideas, Comte exerted a significant influence on contemporary philosophy. His eagerness to apply the scientific method to social problems appealed to many thinkers of the 1850s.

One of Comte's adherents was Herbert Spencer (1820—1903), an outstanding champion of the individual over society and of science over religion. Spencer accepted theories of the early nineteenth-century French naturalist Jean Baptiste Lamarck (1744—1829), who claimed that organisms adapt to environmental changes. Spencer's *Principles of Psychology* (1855) expressed the belief that human psychology is part of evolutionary biology and that the human nervous system has developed in response to environmental pressures. Spencer began as a railroad engineer, and his sociological opinions reflect the practical approach. In the tradition of Bentham and the British utilitarians, he believed that social institutions exist to be useful to man and that a government that interferes with the liberty of its citizens is worse than no government at all. He also thought that a society became increasingly complex and diverse as it progressed, and he welcomed the professional and scientific specialization that eventually would make careers like his own (from engineer to philosopher) improbable or impossible.

The thought and writings of John Stuart Mill (1806—1873) can be described as positivist in a general sense, but the label is inadequate. Son of the utilitarian James Mill, an influential philosophical radical who struggled against the tide of Romanticism in his own time, John Stuart Mill had a sound classical education before he was twelve and went on to study history, political economy, and utilitarian philosophy. He shared the contemporary passion for system and science; whether he wrote on philosophy, economics, or politics, he strove to achieve a synthesis of human knowledge and to offer scientific proof of social and moral theories.

A great logician, economist, and political theorist, Mill played an important role in most of the reform movements of his era, but he is remembered best for the essay *On Liberty* (1859), a lucid exposition of the doctrine of individual freedom. He believed that progress is always accomplished by individuals rather than groups and that man must be free to experiment with progressive ideas if society is to move forward. The free competition of ideas is as essential to a healthy society as the free competition of goods to a healthy economy. Having inherited classical economic theory and utilitarian radicalism from his father's generation, Mill turned them to account in a passionate defense of the rights of individuals and minorities. Fearing the tyranny of the majority, he believed that variety gave life its meaning. Yet Mill could not accept the logical extension of his own position—if man is to be free, he must be free to do evil—and he has been criticized for inconsistency. Mill departed significantly from the principles of utilitarianism and classical economics in his later works. He introduced qualitative and moral considerations into utilitarian philosophy, and favored state action to improve social conditions.

The French historian, critic, and philosopher Hippolyte Adolphe Taine (1823—1893) attempted to apply the strict methods of the natural sciences to historical, psychological, artistic, and metaphysical studies. In the introduction to his *History of English Literature* (1886), Taine emphasized the search for the abstract psychological causes that make history more than a series of events and that should be as accessible to the historian as chemical components are to the chemist. Taine focused on the qualities produced by the specific circumstances of race, environment, and time, which could be computed for any group of people at any point in history. Given sufficient knowledge of these factors, the behavior of a people could be predicted.

In art and literature as in history, Taine believed, race, time, and environment encourage certain styles and discourage others. The artistic forms of an industrial, democratic society must differ from those of a Christian, feudal society, because an artist expresses the spirit of his own age. A founder of historical school of the art criticism, Taine supported his views with studies of the art of Renaissance Italy, of the early modern Netherlands, and of classical Greece, pointing out the distinctive features produced by physical and psychological circumstances. Pessimistic about the nature of man but hopeful for the future of science, Taine had enormous influence on contemporaries and on later historians and art critics.

Walter Bagehot (1826—1877), an English economist, did not attempt to formulate laws or create a vast system, but he was a careful observer, and his philosophical and political theories grew out of his perceptions of existing social and political circumstances. In one of his major works, *The English Constitution* (1867), Bagehot emphasized the "deference"—the quiet recognition of social differences—that made the English system work. Like Mill, he prized individual liberty as the only hope for constructive change. Profoundly influenced by Darwin's theories of evolution, Bagehot attempted in *Physics and Politics* (1875) to apply the theory of natural selection to human history, arguing that primitive societies were strengthened by imposed unity and strict law and advanced societies by free competition.

Like Bagehot, Henry Thomas Buckle (1821—1862) believed that English civilization was the finest flower of human history. In the *History of Civilization in England* (1861), he tried to demonstrate that human progress is governed by principles as regular as those that underlie the physical universe, principles he hoped to establish by inductive reasoning. Buckle equated the progress of civilization with scientific advance. He died too soon to incorporate Darwin's theories of evolution, and his work was soon cast aside for more up-to-date interpretations.

10.3 Marxism

All the social, economic, and political theorists of the 1850s and 1860s appear as minor thinkers in comparison with Karl Marx, the German philosopher and economist who became the master system-builder of the scientific age. After the *Communist Manifesto* by Marx and Friedrich Engels (1820—1895) appeared in 1848, Marx was expelled from Brussels, where he had been living since 1845. He visited Paris and Germany during the abortive revolutions of that year and witnessed the defeat of the radical idealists. Realizing that the intellectual elite of the revolution had failed to attract and hold mass support, he focused his attention more closely on the education and indoctrination of the working class. After the collapse of the revolution, Marx found refuge in England and stayed there for the rest of his life, in poverty and relative obscurity.

The ideas of the early nineteenth-century utopian socialists were denounced by Marx, but many of them survive in Marxist doctrine. Saint-Simon (1760—1825) had perceived that a society can be defined by its economic forms; he anticipated Comte's belief that society can be studied with the intellectual tools of science and Marx's concept of class war. Marx's contemporaries and associates in Paris like Louis Auguste Blanqui (1805—1881) advocated violent revolution and the abolition of private property, and their ideas were very influential during the years just before 1848, when the *Communist Manifesto* was taking shape. Equally influential was Ludwig Feuerbach, whose writings on religion hold the materialistic view of human thought that is intrinsic to Marxist doctrines. Marx was also greatly indebted to British economic theorists—particularly David Ricardo, who had stressed the conflict between the interests of landlords, capitalists, and labor. Marx's system incorporated many of the prevailing ideas of his century.

Toward the end of his life, Marx became well known in European socialist circles. He was active in the First International Workingmen's Association, or First International, founded in 1864, and saw it come to grief through internal philosophical and political dissension. Marx died before Marxists achieved a position of power in any country. He spent the latter part of his life arguing against earlier forms of socialism, anarchism, and political opportunism within the workers' movement. His ideas are among the most dynamic in Western intellectual history.

Marx departed radically from romantic or utopian socialism in many respects but most particularly in the assertion that human history is determined by economic development. He regarded himself as the first "scientific" socialist; like several other social thinkers of the period, he believed that philosophical ideas and social structures are governed by natural laws as regular and inexorable as those of the physical universe. The social, political, and ethical institutions and values of a society are determined by the changing relationship of its members to the means of production and distribution. Out of that relationship arise all the complex institutions and creeds that make a society what it is.

Unlike earlier socialists, Marx—in his mature years—did not urge reform out of humanitarianism or democratic idealism. He appealed instead to reason. Through the study of social and economic forces, he believed, one could predict the future and a reasonable man would cast in his lot with history because (in Hegelian fashion) its course is inevitable. Detesting sentiment and democratic idealism, Marx cast aside the doctrine of the natural rights of man as merely a philosophical disguise for the class interest of the rising bourgeoisie in removing the legal obstacles to its power. He avoided moral argument in his writings after 1848. Instead of appealing to man's better nature or conscience, he sought proof in the objective facts of economics and history. Marx was convinced that the economic interests of the various social groups are incompatible, and he considered the belief that well-intentioned men of different classes may agree a harmful delusion.

To Marx, history reveals the pattern of class conflict: One class gains control and exploits others; in time, oppressed groups rise up and take possession on the basis of new techniques of production and distribution. Just as the capitalistic bourgeoisie displaced the feudal aristocracy, the communistic industrial proletariat will displace the bourgeoisie. When the proletariat achieves full control and imposes its will on the rest of society, a new era of history will begin—in a classless society. The transition from the dictatorship of the proletariat to the classless society was not clearly described by Marx, who was more interested in the achievement of the last but one stage— socialism, and it remains a source of ambiguity and dissension in Communist thought. What is essential to Marxist theory is the doctrine of inevitability: The class war has followed and will follow its prescribed course, and all a man can do is to develop proletarian class-consciousness, the indispensable preliminary to the proletarian revolution.

Although Marx attacked the industrial bourgeoisie and laissez-faire capitalism at the very height of their power, he thought that he could perceive the potential weakness of the capitalist system. Capital accumulates and concentrates, he believed, until society is completely and intolerably polarized. Like fallen systems of the past, capitalism holds the seeds of its own destruction. From Hegelian philosophy, Marx derived an underlying idea of violent, creative change through continual conflict. To Hegel, the nation, or the national idea, operated as the creative force in history; to Marx, creative forces are entirely material; the sources of conflict and change should be sought in economic relationships. Marx was convinced that his study of social data proved that capitalism would inevitably collapse as a result of economic forces already at work. Conflict between employers and workers would increase with the growth of capital, as would the relative number of workers, who would explode capitalism at its apogee by expropriating their expropriators, collectively seizing the means of production and distribution.

The first volume of Marx's major work, *Capital*, appeared in 1867. He made extensive notes for the remainder, and these were edited and completed by Engels and others after his death. Marx wrote *Capital* to provide the factual basis for his economic and social theories. Throughout his life he emphasized study, research, and learning; his passion for fact made him a true representative of his time. Accurate information about the actual working of economic laws in society is essential to Marxist doctrine, which is not romantic speculation but a scientific exposition of things as they were. According to Marx, earlier economists had assumed that economic laws, like physical laws, remain the same in all circumstances. Marx perceived that economic laws evolve with the state of technology and the mode of production at any given moment in history. In *Capital*, he focused on the economic and social conditions produced by the Industrial Revolution, which had created new economic relationships and new classes to engage in the inevitable class war. He stressed the connection between the development of technological means of production and the appearance of the proletariat, and he discussed in detail the periodic economic crises of capitalism—inevitable forerunners of the self-destruction of the system.

Marx's basic economic theories build upon those of classical economists such as David Ricardo and Adam Smith. He accepted their labor theory of value, which states that the commercial value of any commodity is established by the number of man hours required to produce it. Under capitalism, the worker himself becomes a commodity; he—that is, his productive capacity—can be bought and sold like any material object. The political and religious institutions of capitalist society are organized to permit the capitalist class to profit from the surplus created by the workers, and this legalized exploitation of labor is the foundation—the root relationship—of contemporary industrial society.

Various elements of Marxist theory have provided generations of communists and socialists with the stuff of debate and argument. Marx was not always clear, nor did he prove to be right about the subsequent development of industrial society. The Communist revolution finally came in 1917, not in the most advanced capitalist society, but in underdeveloped czarist Russia, a country Marx considered helplessly backward. Nevertheless, *Capital* is a watershed in the history of economic and social thought.

10.4 Darwinism

While Marx was working out his monumental analysis of capitalism in the British Museum, not far away Charles Darwin was formulating the most important new theory in natural science since the Newtonian era. Marx and Darwin were the two great system-makers who laid the foundation for the intellectual history of the later nineteenth century. While Marxism did not command wide attention until the 1880s, Darwin achieved enormous renown immediately upon the publication of his major work.

Charles Darwin was born to a middle-class English family of agnostic and Nonconforming intelligentsia. His grandfather, Erasmus Darwin, had been a well-known physician with a profound interest in biology and in theories of evolution. Charles grew up in the atmosphere of free thought and scientific curiosity that was fairly common in prosperous middle-class households in the early nineteenth century. He was sent first to Edinburgh to be trained in medicine—for which he had neither aptitude nor enthusiasm—and then to Cambridge to prepare for the ministry, which was considered a suitable career for a young man without special talent or ambition. In both universities he attached himself to groups of students and professors who shared the intense interest in geology and fossil hunting that was a current fad among affluent amateur scientists.

Before Darwin could settle down in a country parsonage, as he planned to do, he was invited to attach himself as an unpaid naturalist to a round-the-world scientific expedition on H. M. S. Beagle. The voyage, from 1831 to 1836, transformed an enthusiastic amateur into a scientist and laid the factual groundwork for the theory of natural selection. The young naturalist observed the differences and similarities of related plant and animal forms in different latitudes; he witnessed an earthquake and its dramatic effect on the crust of the earth; he visited the Galapagos Islands and found the indigenous fauna dominated by reptile forms distinct from yet related to mainland forms and to reptile forms to other islands in the Pacific. He collected fossils wherever he went, but it was not until he got them home and identified them that he began to relate them to living animals.

When Darwin returned to England in 1836, he prepared his extensive notes and journals for publication and won the attention and assistance of the English scientific community. He became the secretary of the Geological Society and a close friend of Sir Charles Lyell (1797—1875), the leading geologist of the period, who had delineated a theory of the evolution of the earth. With notebooks crammed with objective data and a mind filled with wonder at the variety of life, and with the benefit of hypotheses propounded by Lyell and by his grandfather, Darwin began to work his material into a scientific theory. He did so primarily by study and discussion with practical men—gardeners and animal breeders whose business was selection and alternation in plant and animal species.

In 1838 Darwin read *An Essay on the Principle of Population* written by Malthus and was struck by its description of the "struggle for existence" that controlled potentially explosive human populations. Within the next few years, he transformed Malthusian struggle into a great systematic natural law that explained both the similarity and the diversity of plant and animal species. The concept of evolution itself was widely accepted in scientific circles long before Darwin. Geology revealed the development of species as well as the age of the earth. But it did not explain how or why changes occurred. Jean Baptiste Lamarck, the French naturalist, among others, had defied the traditional religious view of fixed species (created once and for all by the Lord when the earth began), but Lamarck had believed that animal species changed—almost purposely—in direct response to environmental conditions and transmitted the changes to their offspring. Darwin did not object to this inheritance of acquired characteristics, but he saw that purposive adaptation to environmental change was not sufficient to explain variation of species, particularly in plants.

By 1842 Darwin had made a sketch or outline of his theory of evolution through natural selection. He was in no hurry to publish it. Plagued by poor health, he spent the next sixteenth years gathering and studying facts to support and fill out his hypothesis. He trained himself in zoology, anatomy, botany, and animal breeding. In 1858 he received a manuscript from a young naturalist then on an expedition to Malays. The author, Alfred Russel Wallace (1823—1913), had arrived independently at the theory of natural selection. Honorably, Darwin forwarded the manuscript to the Linnaean Society, where it was read together with an abstract of Darwin's 1842 outline. The joint reading attracted little attention, but Darwin was spurred to finish his book. In November 1859 he published *On the Origin of Species by Means of Natural Selection, or the Preservation of Favored Races in the Struggle for Life.*

Since evolutionary theories were well accepted before Darwin wrote, what is the significance of his work? Natural selection is the key. In Darwin's theory, favorable variations that arise at random in plant or animal forms tend to be preserved because they confer on their owners an advantage in the struggle for existence—the continual competition within a species for substance and survival. Lamarck had claimed that a giraffe elongated its neck by stretching to reach the leaves at the top of the tree and passed on that acquired characteristic to its offspring; Darwin believed that those giraffes which had longer necks than their fellows tended to survive and thus to reproduce that characteristic in their offspring. Less-favored strains tended to die out, and thus competition shaped a species. Darwin borrowed from Herbert Spencer the phrase "survival for the fittest" to characterize the process.

Darwin perceived that the struggle which forms a species takes place primarily within that species—its members in competition with one another. While Lamarck believed that adaptation is a function of response to environment, Darwin made competition the forming agent. This seemed to answer the question posed by the existence of similar forms in very different environments and different forms in very similar environments—for example, animal forms isolated on separate islands. Darwin had observed what growers and breeders could do with domestic plants and animals by artificial selection for one chosen (favored) characteristic. Natural selection does the same thing on a much larger scale, and it has almost all of geologic time in which to work.

Darwin's view of the process of inheritance did not go much beyond that of Lamarck. Like most of his contemporaries, he believed that characteristics are inherited through "blending"—for example, a tall parent and a short parent produce a medium-size offspring. Knowing nothing of mutation, he made no attempt to explain why variations arise in the first place, leaving an enormous gap in his theory. (Religious fundamentalists often filled it by asserting divine interference.) Although Darwin never knew it, the problem of heredity was solved in his own lifetime. While the fight over natural selection raged in England, an Austrian monk named Gregor Johann Mendel (1822—1884) was performing experiments with garden peas that eventually became the basis of modern genetics. Mendel discovered the basic principles of heredity on which evolution depends, refuting the theory of the " blending " of parental characteristics. He realized that discrete characteristics are inherited in units (now known as genes) and that this process occurs according to mathematically describable laws. Although the results of Mendel's experiments were published in 1865, they attracted no attention until the beginning of the twentieth century.

The first edition of *On the Origin of Species by Means of Natural Selection* sold out at once, and it soon became obvious that its publication was a major scientific and philosophical event. It was a solid, well-reasoned work that appealed to the growing educated class, many of them amateur scientists. Yet Darwin did not have it all his own way. A tremendous protest arose along with the applause. Even though the book itself deals with plant and animal species and not with men, Darwin's supporters and adversaries alike applied the theory at once to human evolution. The opposition to Darwin was of two quite different varieties, but both were concerned with the evolution of man.

Official and unofficial representatives of organized religion, particularly those of the Protestant faith, opposed Darwin singly and collectively. Many believing Christians feared the loss of man's unique position on the earth as profoundly as their counterparts in the sixteenth century had feared the loss of earth's unique position in the heavens. Notable among the religious opponents of Darwinism was Samuel Wilberforce, bishop of Oxford, whose scathing review of *The Origin of Species* provoked the biologist T. H. Huxley, Darwin's self-appointed defender, to reply in a famous debate. With supposedly crushing sarcasm, Wilberforce asked Huxley whether it was through his grandfather or his grandmother that he was descended from monkeys, and this attitude survived in many parts of the world after natural selection was accepted by the scientific community.

Despite its vehemence and persistence, the fundamentalist opposition to

Darwin was intellectually and philosophically less significant than the opposition that arose among those who resisted what they considered to be the degradation of man. Romantics and philosophical idealists resented the denial of man's unique soul. Within the scientific community, Darwinism became a kind of generation symbol, with younger men acclaiming the new theory and older men skeptical of its novelty and concerned about the security of entrenched ideas. Whatever the opposition, however, natural selection was widely accepted within one decade. After all, there was little to challenge it. No other scientific theory approached *The Origin of Species* in scope, factual backing, or reasoned argument.

Most of the arguments over natural selection turned on the origin of homo sapiens, although no theory of human evolution was put forward in *On the Origin of Species by Means of Natural Selection*. Darwin's adherents took up the subject because that was the issue raised by the Church, by representatives of the intellectual community, and by the general public. Huxley and Wallace propounded theories of human evolution, concentrating at first on man's body rather than his mind. Huxley wrote of the "missing link" between man and his distant ancestors that he hoped to establish. Wallace declared that man's development had been controlled by natural selection until his brain reached a certain critical size, at which time he was freed by reason to take charge of his own progress; physical change ended when natural selection ceased to operate. The "most favored races", he felt, assured human progress by competing successfully with the weaker and less fit.

Darwin joined the argument in 1871 with the publication of *Decent of Man and Selection in Relation to Sex*. The new book was less forceful than *The Origin of Species*, not as thoroughly documented and well reasoned. Darwin hoped to put social science on a biological basis, but he wrote very cautiously in order to avoid offending religious believers. Darwin believed that human morality had developed through social institutions favorable to survival. Characteristics like loyalty and altruism helped a tribe or a community to maintain its existence in the face of competition. Darwin assumed that moral and cultural progress has always accompanied the advance of technology and always would—that the race will grow better as it grows more sophisticated. He never gave up his belief in progress. He did not accept Wallace's ideas of racial superiority, but he could not shake off the vision of Syndey Harbor in

Australia—a bustling, progressive port in a continent peopled with dying aborigines. Darwin perceived a danger in removing through social progress the spur of competition that had made Western man such a complex and successful creature.

In Darwin's later works the concept of sexual selection played an increasingly important role. He explained the apparently useless tail feathers of certain male birds as variations that tended to attract the female and thus assure reproduction, and he extended his concept to human and racial differentiation. He began to rely more and more on Lamarck's ideas of adaptation through use, departing considerably from the theory of natural selection—but by then that theory had permeated almost every field of scientific and social philosophy.

Although Darwin's theory of evolution clearly confronted theologians and religious leaders with a new problem, it would be a mistake to imagine that widespread conflict between science and religion racked the Western world. The cataclysmic effect *On the Origin of Species by Means of Natural Selection* is supposed to have had on Christianity was much exaggerated by late nineteenth-century controversialists and early twentieth-century historians. Once the initial shock wave had passed, many believers—theologians and clergy as well as layman of most Protestant denominations—sought to reconcile Darwinism and religion wherever they appeared to collide. Some found the theory of evolution a marvelous confirmation of the glory of God manifest in nature, and many were willing to accept a Divinity who had created a few simple forms and left them to evolve into an incredible variety of complex species. Men who still wanted to believe could look for God in natural laws instead of in unnatural miracles. Although some of its spokesmen initially launched vigorous attacks on the new science, the Church of England came to realize that there was no irreconcilable conflict between Darwinism and Christianity, and Darwin was buried in Westminster Abbey.

The relationship between Darwinism and Christianity must be understood in a broad context. From the early decades of the nineteenth century, all traditional religious groups were threatened by the spread of liberal, secular culture. An even greater challenge than Darwinian science had been posed by the historical criticism of the Bible, which called into question the historicity of the Old and New Testaments. Furthermore, the advance of industrialization and urbanization had so expanded the possibilities for material accomplishment and enjoyment that many people had simply lost interest in a life directed by traditional dogma. In both Europe and America a significant decline in the churches' influence had occurred by the 1860s. At the same time, various religious groups were beginning to disagree about the response believers should make to the new liberal, scientific culture.

The Church of England and most Protestant groups slowly but steadily accommodated themselves to intellectual and social change. But there were exceptions: A small group in the Church of England, taking its inspiration from the Oxford movement of the 1830s, continued to express hostility toward contemporary scientific and secularized culture, and the Baptists and some Methodists and Lutherans remained fundamentalist, rejecting both the higher criticism of the Bible and the new science in favor of a simple faith in the liberal text of the Bible. In Western Europe and the United States, a split gradually developed between Orthodox Judaism and Liberal or Reform Judaism, which eagerly accommodated itself to new social and scientific ideas. Significantly, Liberal Judaism gained its adherents among wealthy Jews who felt emancipated from ghetto culture and moved freely in society.

It was in the Roman Catholic Church that the issue of the relationship between modern thought and traditional faith became most crucial. In the post-Napoleonic period, the Church had tended to ally itself with the forces of reaction. In 1832 the Papacy condemned liberty of conscience, freedom of the press, and revolution against authority. Early in the pontificate of Pius IX (1846—1878), it appeared that the Roman Church was moving toward an accommodation with the new political and intellectual trends. But Pius was driven from Rome in 1848 by republican radicals, and in the 1860s the Papal States were lost to the newly united Italian state. Following these indignities, Pius became extremely hostile to the whole thrust of European political and intellectual life. Not only Darwinism but nearly every other aspect of modern liberal and rational thought was condemned by the Pope's *Syllabus of Errors* in 1864. At the same time, the papacy sought to harden belief in medieval Catholic tradition as a bulwark against the growing secularism of the age. The Immaculate Conception of the Virgin Mary was made a dogma in 1854, and papal infallibility became an absolute article of faith by ruling of the Vatican Council in 1870. This latter decision was designed to remove any doubt that the pope could legislate for every Catholic on moral, social, and political issues.

This extremely conservative stance of the papacy was by no means universally favored by Catholics. Especially in Britain and Germany, many liberal Catholic intellectuals—such as the eminent historian Lord Acton— fought vigorously against the reactionary policies and particularly the doctrine of papal infallibility. Pius IX 's intransigent hostility to liberalism and science greatly enhanced the influence of ultramontane groups within the Church in each country. The ultramontanes were invariably political reactionaries, often monarchists and intellectual obscurantists. Thus the Roman Church not only cut itself off from modern thought and science but came to appear to liberals everywhere as their implacable enemy. In Germany and Austria, papal support of the ultramontanes encouraged Catholics who flirted with racist myths and anti-Semitic doctrines in the late nineteenth century.

For the Darwinists who believed that the support of revealed religion had been removed from traditional morality, there was a real problem. How could they justify traditional ethics without Christian revelation? Herbert Spencer's solution was utilitarian: He declared that morality is useful, that right behavior brings individuals happiness and public good. Man will behave better as society progresses—as it inevitably will, since evolution and progress are identical. Most of Darwinists, including Darwin himself, were strictly conventional in their standards of public and private morality. Vice and social disorganization—crime, prostitution, alcoholism—caused misery and suffering here and now; a wise man is good and therefore happy.

But Darwinism had ethical implications that could not be resolved by utilitarian morality. Even Huxley, as he grew older, realized that nature is not a suitable model for human behavior, that the savage struggle for existence is unacceptable to a civilized man. He advocated religious education and grew to appreciate the value of the Church in the battle against the natural man. It became increasingly obvious that natural selection in human society had little connection with the ethical system of the Sermon on the Mount. Although a Darwinist might appreciate the beauty of humanitarian ideals, he would have to admit that they were of little value—and might even be damaging—to the evolutionary progress of the human race.

Darwinism had social and political implications of which its amiable founder never dreamed. The term "social Darwinism" has been used to explain or justify an amazingly diverse collection of theories. In Germany, social Darwinists tended to be democrats and socialists; in England, social Darwinists were likely to be conservatives. Social Darwinism was offered by nationalists as a justification for a strong state and by individualists as a justification for a weak one. In the United States social Darwinism was used to justify the depredation of industrial robber barons. It was claimed as a basis for both militarism and pacifism, for socialism and capitalism, for racism, Pan-Slavism, and abolitionism. Although Darwinism itself was certainly distorted, in most of these "isms" there was some thread of connection with natural selection.

A major connecting link in the varieties of social Darwinism is the idea of progress through struggle. This was particularly evident in the ideas of those who believed in a superman or a superstate that would demonstrate, or create, superiority through competition and war. Some Darwinists disliked violence but acknowledged its place in progressive evolution; others—in the latter part of the nineteenth century, a great many others—glorified war. Violence and war were the mechanisms by which the fittest were enabled to survive and superior men and superior races to dominate their inferiors.

The concept of struggle figured prominently in the ideas of economic Darwinians. Those who favored laissez-faire argued that since the "natural order" tended to bring the best to the top, businesses or businessmen should be left alone to flourish or fail. If a large business swallows up smaller ones, if weak or incompetent workmen lose their jobs, starve and die, it might be unfortunate, but it is an inescapable aspect of progress. Social and economic reforms interfere with nature by protecting the weak at the cost of impeding the strong. Weak plants and animals could not appeal to ideals of equality and brotherhood to defend themselves against predators, and the weaker members of society should not be protected by government interference, which might result in the weakening of all of society.

Scientific socialists, too, appreciated the unsentimental view of life reflected in *On the Origin of Species by Means of Natural Selection*. In Marxism as in Darwinism, history progressed by means of natural, inevitable laws which were not subject to divine or human interference. Marx believed in struggle and progressive evolution. In Darwinism, the inevitable struggle takes place between individuals in the same species, while Marx envisioned the development of proletarian solidarity to replace intra-class proletarian rivalry. Like other social Darwinists, Marx took what he needed from the theory and ignored the rest.

Not all socialists appreciated social Darwinism. Many emphasized cooperation rather than struggle and refused to accept the ruling class in human society as the "fittest" simply because it ruled. These socialists were dedicated to progress through reform. They wanted the state to interfere actively to improve man by improving his environment.

In order to give their theories the appearance of scientific legitimacy, many late nineteenth-century writers used the terminology of social Darwinism, including those of racist myths and totalitarian ideologies. Certainly Darwin cannot be held responsible for all the inferences drawn from his theories. He is not a social philosopher but a scientist, and his main contribution to science is an orderly, lucid scheme of evolution—the greatest achievement of science in the nineteenth century. In evolution through natural selection, the mid-Victorians had a system to satisfy their urge to understand themselves and the world. Its flaws appeared later on. For the moment, it supplied yet another reason to worship science and keep faith in human progress.

10.5 The Middle-class Moral Attidudes

In the 1850s and 1860s the middle class fully came into its own, emerging as the dominant class in Western civilization. This fulfillment of the potential of the political and economic revolution of the late eighteenth century shaped all aspects of European life. Although in most countries the aristocracy still provided leadership in government, the middle class gained a substantial share of power, and the main course of political development followed the bourgeois ideals of liberalism and nationalism. Economic growth was now almost entirely the consequence of middle-class enterprise. Most pervasive of all, the culture and ethic of Western civilization became essentially bourgeois. By the 1860s, the thought, feeling, and style of life in Western Europe were determined by the middle-class ethos. Very little was left of the monarchical and aristocratic ideals and attitudes of previous eras. The bourgeois revolution, which had been launched economically by the advent of steam power and the factory system and politically by the French Revolution, had now reached the decisive state in which middle-class mores, ideals, and expectations were the hallmarks of Western civilization.

The term *middle class* covered all members of European society who were neither landed aristocracies nor peasants and industrial workers. The size of the middle class, which had increased rapidly through the first half of the nineteenth century, varied markedly from country to country; it was twenty to thirty percent of the population in Britain and France and not more than five percent in Russia. Within the middle class, there was enormous variation in wealth. At mid-century the bourgeoisie could be divided into five distinct groups: the shopkeepers and small tradesmen; the professionals, such as lawyers, physicians and civil servants; the prosperous, independent farmers; the intellectuals, students, and artists; the industrial, mercantile, and financial magnates. The last group, the capitalist entrepreneurs, was regarded as the bourgeoisie proper because the great wealth of its members gave them power and influence over society as a whole.

The first category of middle class value was somewhat naïve, quite materialistic, but nevertheless dedicated rationality. The bourgeoisie could be extremely sentimental about personal and family matters, but they were clear-headed pragmatists about making a living and "getting on" in the world—about economic enterprise. They were not prepared to allow tradition and sentiment to stand in the way of business success and social progress. They believed in a realistic appraisal of the economic market and a shrewd analysis of what was necessary for commercial success. For the middle class, knowledge was a functional instrument for personal gain and social improvement.

In the middle-class ethos, this harsh realism, this vulgarized Baconian attitude toward knowledge, was put at the service of the second and most basic bourgeois tenet, the gospel of work. Unceasing labor in one's business, profession, or craft was more than the road to personal and social advancement. Work was virtually identified with human happiness itself; it was man's highest good.

To some extent, the gospel of work was important to the middle-class ethos because it goes against aristocratic and clerical privilege. The bourgeoisie claimed that a man should be given his due for what he achieved; he should earn material reward, not receive it as a gift through noble birth or clerical status. Thus the gospel of work was inextricably bound up with economic liberalism, the laissez-faire doctrine of the free market, and with the radical individualism of the early nineteenth century.

The middle-class doctrine of work and self-help has so often been condemned as a mere façade for greed that it is necessary to stress that the nineteenth-century middle class did work hard, that its pursuit of individual advancement was of great importance in expanding the Industrial Revolution, in developing European technology, and, in the long run, in improving the circumstances of daily life for all mankind. There is much to be said for a doctrine that calls for men to be judged by the fruits of their labors rather than by traditional prejudices and the whims of kings and lords. Whatever the defects of the middle-class ethos, it represents a liberating attitude in European culture. The middle-class faith that a man should be judged by the results of his work played a powerful role in removing political disabilities from religious minorities. This attitude could allow the Rothschild family not only to achieve great wealth but also to become socially prominent and could permit Lionel Nathan (1809—1879), a scion of this Jewish banking family, to take a seat in Parliament.

Another bourgeois value was devotion to family. The bourgeoisie adopted the aristocracy's view of the family as the most immediate and important unit of society. They also inherited the puritanical belief that sexual relations were moral only between husband and wife and were justified only by the need to procreate children. Since the middle-class man, in his competitive world, had only his immediate family to rely on, and since the gospel of work made sexual promiscuity seem reckless and improvident, the age-old familial ideal and sexual Puritanism assumed a particular emphasis in middle-class culture.

But devotion to family often contradicted the doctrine of self-help and individual achievement. The bourgeois father fiercely inculcated work habits in his children, but he was as prejudiced in their favor as any noble of the ancien regime. Privilege of birth to high bourgeois families was as advantageous as birth into the landed families. Although the gospel of work and self-help seemed a good argument against aristocracy, inherited status continued to count for a great deal in the supposedly emancipated society of individual achievement. The bourgeoisie tended to blame poverty on personal unworthiness—the poor were held to be lazy, drunken, and sexually promiscuous. In fact, the nineteenth-century poor were usually born poor, and the self-righteous man of property often gained his affluence not by merit but by inheritance.

Middle-class intellectuals sensed this self-serving quality in the middle-class ethos. It was—and still is—the greatest weakness of the Western bourgeoisie that its most sensitive spirits have turned against their class with hatred and contempt. Almost from the start of the industrial era, the alienation of intellectuals, artists, and students was the Achilles' heel of bourgeois power. What incensed the intellectuals most was the materialism of the middle class. To artists and writers, bourgeois values seemed the nadir of the human spirit.

10.6   The Heritage of Socialism

The entrenchment of an industrial economy and mass culture brought social ills as well as human benefits. It was the tragic irony of the late nineteenth century that material and technological progress in some respects aggravate economic crises, the poverty and misery of part of society, and the hatred of various social and national groups for one another. Mass literacy and ease of communication did not necessarily foster public commitment to liberal ideals; on the contrary, the masses were often enthusiastic supporters of aggressive nationalism, militarism, and racism. Democracy did not necessarily bring about an era of human brotherhood; indeed, by 1900 there were indications that it might well usher in an age of fanaticism and violence.

Among the many indices of this menacing trend was the sharp rise in anti-Semitism in all Western countries in the late nineteenth century. This virus had been relatively inert in Western society since the sixteenth century, and early nineteenth century liberalism had strongly condemned such prejudice as unworthy of a civilized society. By 1900 it was evident that many people at all levels of society, particularly among the petite bourgeoisie and the working class, were making Jewish minorities scapegoats for their personal frustrations and national disappointments.

Throughout the Western world, as the second Industrial Revolution moved toward its climax, vast numbers of people still were mired in squalor and hereditary poverty. Few workers were satisfied with their wages or their working and living conditions. They joined militant or revolutionary unions, and they voted for socialist political parties, usually led by middle-class intellectuals more or less hostile to the capitalist system.

In the closing decades of the nineteenth century the merits of the prevailing economic and social system were the subject of heated debate among social theorists—a debate that continues to the present day. A few respectable thinkers, and many industrial and financial magnates used, or misused, social Darwinism to advocate unrestrained power for capitalists. Society was viewed as a primordial jungle in which the strong justifiably ruled and exploited the weak. But the great majority of European intellectuals agreed with the English economist and historian Arnold Toynbee (1889—1975) in unequivocally condemning this variant of the doctrine of the struggle for existence. Among men of good will in all countries, there was an urge for social justice.

But what should be done to prevent the weak from being trampled underfoot? How should the voiceless wrath of the wretched be answered? This was the central issue in the domestic life of most Western states, and social theorists offered a great variety of solutions. Some, particularly in Britain and the United States, still held fast to the principles of early nineteenth-century economic liberalism. The most effective spokesman for this point of view was the eminent Cambridge economist Alfred Marshall (1842—1924), who continued to celebrate the effectiveness of the capitalist free market as the source of technological progress that would eventually abolish poverty.

But even Marshall was concerned about the implications of monopolies and trusts; big business might vitiate the free market that had fostered capitalism's fantastic productivity in the nineteenth century. And another economist of the period, the American Thorstein Veblen (1857—1929), pointed to an even greater defect in the capitalist ethos. As they became a ruling leisure class, he argued, businessmen were no longer interested in technological advance but simply in preserving their own power and status. The business enterprise of his day, Veblen contended, was actually an obstacle to progress.

Whatever the future prospects of laissez-faire capitalism might be, many intellectuals and political leaders at the end of the nineteenth century did not intend to await them; they wanted immediate state interference to improve the conditions of the workers and the poor. In the United States, President Theodore Roosevelt (1858—1919) in the early years of the twentieth century raged against "the malefactors of great wealth". Philosophers quickly sensed the shift in political attitudes; in the late nineteenth century, social theorists like Thomas Hill Green(1836—1882) looked back beyond liberal individualism and recalled Greek, medieval, and Hegelian traditions of the primacy of the community over the interests of the individual.

Chapter 11 Psychoanalysis:
Discovering Man's Inner World

The intellectual and cultural development of Europe and America between 1870 and 1918 was dominated by a reaction against the salient characteristic of the preceding decades—an almost naïve faith in the powers of human reason and the methods of objective science.

Although European economic and political power stood at its zenith, many perceptive and original minds detected sickness, misery, and boredom beneath the glittering façade of affluence. It was becoming apparent that human personality was more complex and ambiguous than the men of mid-century had realized. Scientific objectivity as the cure-all for social and personal ills itself became suspect. The new generation insisted that since all knowledge was human knowledge, it was imperfect and subjective, lacking any absolute or transcendent validity. Instead of deluding himself by clinging to objectivity, man should frankly and joyfully explore the subjective. The focus of intellectual and cultural activity shifted to the inner world of human self-consciousness. Something called the unconscious was discovered. A new view of man emerged.

11.1 Philosophy

Many philosophers of the late nineteenth century reacted against the belief in reason and objectivity that had distinguished the thought of their immediate predecessors. This doubt of accepted values was an important part of the general self-scrutiny occurring throughout Western culture. Philosophers, wondering whether man was indeed a rational animal, came to believe that irrational forces played an important role in his nature. They rejected the claim that science could ultimately explain all aspects of the real world because they questioned the ability of the human mind to apprehend the real world. Indeed, they questioned the very existence of the real world.

In many ways the leading figure of this period was the German philosopher Friedrich Wilhelm Nietzsche (1844—1900). The son of a Protestant minister, Nietzsche spent much of his life in his quasi-adolescent rebellion against Christian values, and in his last years he suffered from mental illness. His writings — such as *Thus Spake Zarathustra* (1885) and *Beyond Good and Evil* (1886)— are informal, somewhat racy, and full of rich metaphor. More a moralist than a systematic philosopher, Nietzsche remains one of the foremost critics of traditional Western values.

With persuasive eloquence, Nietzsche pictured man as an irrational creature. The epitome of irrationality himself, he contended that reason plays little role in human life and held that all ideas are rooted in emotion. Nietzsche believed that man is at the mercy of irrational life forces, and rather than being disturbed by this fact he rejoiced in it. In the *Birth of Tragedy* (1872), he celebrated Dionysian passions that he saw as the mainsprings of human actions and ideas and that found musical expression in the orgiastic music of the German musician Richard Wagner (1813—1883). Nietzsche identified these vital forces as the true source of individual creativity and denounced social and religious constraints upon the individual as the attempt of the majority to smash the creative impulses of the gifted few. At bottom, Nietzsche despised the ordinary person for lacking will, intelligence, and power. The vital, irrational impulses of strong-willed and creative people are repressed by a code of Christian ethics which stresses humility, charity, self-sacrifice; this is the morality of slaves, the ethics of the weak and the mediocre. The notion of a God controlling human affairs was repugnant to Nietzsche, who believed in unbridled individual freedom.

Nietzsche wanted man to be his own God, to work out his own salvation; his writing was a call to ethical action. He urged a thoroughgoing "transvaluation of values" and sought a kind of aristocratic elite of the spirit, who would rise above the ordinary people to be creative and free. Nietzsche spoke in glowing terms of the "Will to Power"—the fundamental drive of life, strength itself. By the exercise of this Will to Power—this innate life force—a few individuals may rise above the masses and become "superior men", truly creative, free, and life-affirming persons.

Nietzsche's worship of the Will to Power and the superior man allowed the Fascists and Nazis later to distort his philosophy for propaganda purposes, but Nietzsche himself would have rejected Fascism and National Socialism as vehemently as he rejected Christianity. The significance of Nietzsche's work lies in his disenchantment with liberal Western culture, his stress upon the irrational, and his view of the totally subjective nature of ethics and of truth itself. If reason and objectivity were the gods of European thought, then it may truly be said that Nietzsche ushered in "the twilight of the gods" of Western philosophy.

But the old gods were not dead yet—nor were all the old philosophers. Various schools of late nineteenth-century philosophy reformulated the ideas of men like Hegel and Kant. The leading figure of the German neo-Kantian school was Wilhelm Dilthey (1833—1911). Dilthey wrote mostly for learned journals, but his work is central to an understanding of thought in this period. He wished to protect history and the other humanities from the claims of metaphysics on the one hand and the exact sciences on the other. His most important work, *Introduction to the Intellectual Sciences* (1883), successfully defends the autonomy of the humanities as disciplines distinct from science. He is also credited with founding intellectual history as an academic discipline.

In contrast to most of earlier philosophers, Dilthey declared that man has no nature or essence but only a history. Each culture has a certain world vision—a constantly changing psychological state containing answers to "the riddles of life". There are no final answers to the riddles of life—no final or correct world view—for that would violate the very nature of history itself. Dilthey's philosophical position is termed "relativistic", for he believed that answers to questions concerning the nature of man and the nature of truth are relative to environment, not absolute, final, or unconditional.

Dilthey is credited with the founding of modern relativism, a leading trend in subsequent intellectual development. Yet he would agree that his own ideas were relative to his own intellectual environment. His stress upon consciousness as the stuff of history was typical of the enormous contemporary interest in psychology. And, like Nietzsche, he was a vitalist, that is, he felt that life was prior to reason or knowledge. Moreover, he distrusted science, contending that the historian must rely upon "sympathetic intuition" rather than the methods of the sciences and must attempt to enter fully into the consciousness or world vision of other ages.

The relativism espoused by Dilthey and others was rejected by Francis Herbert Bradley (1846—1924), the commanding figure in the English neo-Hegelian school of philosophy. The son of an Evangelical preacher, Bradley was associated with Oxford University during most of his life. As a young man, he was deeply influenced by Hegelian idealism, which he used to combat the prevailing doctrines of utilitarianism and empiricism as enunciated by John Stuart Mill. Bradley contended that the only reality is spiritual and that the spiritual world constitutes a harmonious system of experience. In some ways, his emphasis upon the ideal or spiritual world as the only reality distinguished him from other philosophers of his day. Yet, like many of them, he was deeply suspicious of reason and thought and declared that, though his philosophy of absolute idealism was true, it was beyond the power of human intellect to prove or disprove it. A man can understand the reality of the spiritual world only by using his spiritual capacities. In other words, metaphysics could hardly establish itself as an intellectual discipline. Other philosophers, most of them rejecting Bradley's absolute spiritual idealism, eventually came to the same conclusion.

The leading Italian neo-Hegelian, Benedetto Croce (1866—1952), remained much truer to Hegel's original doctrine than Bradley. A leading historian and philosopher of history as well as a literary critic and aesthetician, Croce was the most influential intellectual figure in twentieth-century Italy. He took seriously Hegel's equation of reason and reality, declaring that the subject matter of thought was the mind, life, or spirit, all of which he took to be identical. In true Hegelian fashion, Croce declared that the only reality, the only thing we can know with certainty, is human mental or spiritual activity. In his four-volume *Philosophy of Spirit*, Croce revealed that his conception of mental and spiritual activity included intuition and abstraction as well as economics and ethics. And, since mental and spiritual activity is the subject matter of philosophy, the study of philosophy must involve all these diverse activities. Yet history also embraces the consideration of all these activities. Thus Croce arrived at a truly revolutionary statement: History and philosophy are identical.

Croce was indeed a rationalist in the Hegelian tradition, but his identification of history with philosophy arose from a desire to protect the discipline of history from the claims of the exact sciences. In his insistence that the so-called scientific method was inappropriate to historical research, Croce expressed the anti-rationalist spirit of late nineteenth- and twentieth-century thought. In reaction to historians who claimed that the application of the scientific method to history could produce an objective, ultimate, or universal history, Croce declared that all history is "contemporary history". By this he meant that the writing of history took place within the stream of history itself and that therefore it was motivated by contemporary concerns. History was conditioned by history; the writing of history was relative to the historical environment itself. Somewhat paradoxically, Croce was at once a rationalist and an opponent of scientism, a philosophical idealist and a historical relativist.

The most thoroughgoing attack upon the claims of science came from the French philosopher Henri Bergson (1859—1941), the most popular and influential philosopher of the early twentieth century. His doctrines were much in vogue among writers and artists and much discussed in the fashionable salons of Paris. Bergson believed that the task of the philosopher was to turn his mind inward upon the data of consciousness. He stressed intuition, rather than reason, as a method of knowing reality, and believed that reason was incapable of understanding the true character of human life, since life consisted less in knowing than in willing, feeling, intuiting. Intuition reveals that the inner psychological life is a world of constant changes and everlasting becoming. Intuition thus reveals the nature of inner psychological time and assures us of our freedom as moral beings.

Because Bergson was rather unsystematic, the substance of his philosophy consisted less in his arguments than in the meaning of a few key words and phrases. The central Bergsonian concepts were "intuition" "élan vital" "duration" and "creative evolution". He called the fundamental reality of human nature the "élan vital", or "vital impetus", and a mixture of all of the non-rational faculties. In other words, Bergson was a voluntarist (one who stresses the will) and a vitalist (one who stresses life itself) rather than a rationalist. Bergson believed that life itself was psychological consciousness; it was a unified flow of impulse and experience, a kind of stream of consciousness. The artificial, objective concept of time employed by the physicist cannot be used to understand life and change. Intuition, on the other hand, reveals the nature of real time, or "duration", as purely subjective—as found in the human consciousness. The central task of philosophy is the understanding of time or "duration".

Concerned with the threat to human freedom posed by the popularized doctrines of evolution, Bergson offered his own idea of evolutionary development in *Creative Evolution* (1906), an immediate success. In it, he rejected the mechanistic, deterministic scheme of evolution for one in which the course of evolution was determined by human will. For him, to exist is to change, and to change is to mature, to mature is to go on creating oneself endlessly.

In the last decades of the nineteenth century the United States produced several important thinkers. George Santayana (1863—1952) was born in Spain and eventually became a professor of philosophy at Harvard. A fine literary stylist, he is known best for his *Life of Reason* (1906). Santayana is important chiefly as a moral philosopher. He preferred to consider theology as a body of myth. Far from being a literal account of truth, religion for him was a mythical, allegorical, metaphorical, or poetic rendering of a purely moral truth. Therefore, it should be judged not by rational and scientific standards but by mythical and allegorical ones. A religion may be considered good, though not strictly speaking "true", if its mythology is pleasing to the worshiper.

This concept enabled Santayana to consider himself both an ardent atheist and a devout Catholic; it also had a great influence on twentieth-century philosophers, poets, and novelists, who have been fascinated with the idea of myth. By making the subjective effect of religion upon the devout the criterion of religious truth, Santayana displayed the pragmatic or practical emphasis of American philosophy.

But the true father of American pragmatism was Santayana's Harvard colleague, Charles Sanders Peirce (1839—1914). Little known in his time, Peirce never got around to writing a book; but he was a brilliant thinker, perhaps the greatest philosopher America has ever produced. His famous paper of 1878, entitled "How to Make Our Ideas Clear", enunciated the pragmatic theory of meaning. Essentially, Peirce prescribed certain linguistic tests to determine the precise meaning of general terms and concepts. For him, ideas are what they do or, better, what can be done with them. This was a truly revolutionary way of at looking ideas; it implied that most theological and metaphysical ideas were meaningless from a pragmatic point of view. Ideas like "God" "ultimate reality" and "the secret of the universe" could not pass the necessary pragmatic tests.

If Peirce was the spiritual father of American pragmatism, William James (1842—1910) was its most eloquent spokesman. An eminent psychologist and philosopher, James sought a philosophy that would allow him to be what seemed impossible at the time: an empiricist and a religious man. Beginning in 1898, he revived the ideas of Peirce, transforming them into a philosophy that attempted to mediate between science and absolute idealism and thus to resolve his own inner spiritual difficulties. His book *Pragmatism*, published in 1907, gave classic expression to that distinctively American philosophy.

Whereas Peirce's pragmatic theory concerned itself only with the meaning of concepts, James was interested in the more difficult matter of the truth or falsehood of ideas. He expanded Peirce's theory into the pragmatic theory of truth, according to which an idea is true if it produces good results and false if it does not. To find out if an idea is true, believe in it and see if you get satisfactory results. By declaring those ideas to be true that are personally satisfying, James opened the door to the possibility that many of the theological and philosophical ideas that Peirce declared to be meaningless might actually be true nevertheless.

William James radically transformed the idea of truth as it had existed for centuries in Western philosophy. Since he stressed the practical results of ideas as the criterion for truth, his pragmatism appeared to be empirical and scientific in character. But in fact pragmatism was highly subjective, for the determination of truth rested upon highly individual personal judgment. In the main, pragmatism lacked the substance of prior philosophies; in James's hands philosophy became little more than a technique or a method only.

11.2   Social Sciences

Two distinct trends characterized the political and social thought of the period from 1870 to 1918: reinterpretations of earlier thinkers such as Hegel, Kant, and Darwin, and original thought arising from the newly established "social sciences". Anthropology, sociology, and psychology emerged as academic disciplines, and their rise was both a cause and an effect of the new consciousness. The state, society, and the human mind itself became objects of empirical, "scientific" study. While this emphasis upon science may seem to be at odds with the rather antiscientific spirit of the new philosophy, it is clear that social science functioned as a powerful solvent of traditional Western values. The emergence of modern relativism in anthropology, sociology, and psychology created a crisis in the mind of Western men that continues to the present day. From the field of psychology, moreover, came a revolutionary system of thought which profoundly altered man's view of his nature.

In political theory, one of the most influential developments was the growth of *statism*. The early and middle years of the nineteenth century had witnessed the development of individualistic "classical" or "bourgeois" liberalism. Essentially a negative conception of the state, this philosophy viewed society as a loose collection of individuals. The proper function of the state was to maximize the freedom of action of its constituent parts. Later, under the influence of Kantian and Hegelian political philosophy, some philosophers began to enunciate a more positive conception of the state: the state was conterminous with society, not a mere superstructure atop the social pyramid. Called statism, this view had two main schools. Some thinkers glorified the state and stressed the duty of the individual to it; others stressed the moral obligation of the state to ensure the well-being of individuals. One representative figure from the latter school was Thomas Hill Green. A professor of philosophy at Oxford, Green reformulated English liberalism in terms of the positive, organic conception of the state. The resulting new or collectivistic liberalism became the theoretical basis of the welfare state.

But the most important political ideology in this age of industrial turmoil was socialism. While traditional conservatism was on the decline and liberals like Green were seeking to develop a new collectivist brand of liberalism, the doctrines of Karl Marx were permeating European society. This was also the period when Marx's ideas were being critically examined by leading academicians and his tactics were being modified by leading socialists.

The increasing acceptance of the collectivist principle of state welfare and the beginnings of the melioration of the ravages of capitalism seemed to belie Marx's prophecy that the working class under capitalism was doomed by increasing poverty and misery. Marxist revisionists and moderates like Jean Jaurès (1859—1914) in France and Eduard Bernstein (1850—1932) in

Germany Jaures envisioned the triumph of socialism by democratic political processes and, for the present, approved of the participation of socialist ministers in middle-class liberal governments. Jaures repudiated Marxist materialism; essentially he was a humanist who wished to make available to the working class the finest traditions of Western, and particularly French culture. For Bernstein, constitutional legislation rather than revolutionary violence is best adapted to positive social-political work and the creation of permanent economic arrangements. But the left wing of the Marxist movement would not accept this proposed alliance of socialism and liberalism. Karl Johann Kautsky (1854—1938) insisted that the class antagonisms between the proletariat and the possessing class are so great that the proletariat can never share governmental power with any possessing class. Mikhail Bakunin (1814—1876) condemned the state itself, whether bourgeois or socialist, as a "voracious abstraction". Take away the state, contended Bakunin's disciple Prince Peter Kropotkin (1842—1921), and man's innate love will be liberated; people will spontaneously draw together in "mutual aid". In the syndicalist doctrine of Georges Sorel (1847—1922) in the first decade of the twentieth century, the general strike and revolutionary violence were relished not only for the emancipation they would bring but for their own sake, as life-enhancing acts. Revolution is spiritual redemption, Sorel claimed, a release from the repressions of civilization.

While Marxism was being reexamined, the social implications of Darwinian evolutionary theory were also being explored. Social Darwinists, intoxicated by what they took to be implications of the ideas of Darwin and Spencer, declared that the fittest races not only did survive but deserved to survive by reason of their natural superiority. This vulgarization of evolutionary theory degenerated into wild notion of racial superiority, which was used to justify the most unpleasant aspects of imperialism. Perhaps the most pernicious result of these racist theories was the growth of political anti-Semitism in Europe. Politicians in all countries discovered that they could manipulate popular resentment of Jews to political advantage. In the hands of the ignorant, the cynical, and the prejudiced, evolutionary theory was made to rationalize the dark side of the human spirit. Nor was anti-Semitism confined to the discontented masses. It became fashionable in elite social circles and was given intellectual respectability by some scholars and professors.

Darwinian evolutionary theory also gave birth to the new academic discipline of anthropology. Part natural science and part social science, anthropology involved a naturalistic interpretation of man and human culture. Stated simply, anthropology is the scientific study of human and cultural evolution. Sir Edward Burnett Taylor (1832—1917), an Englishman, wrote the seminal work in this discipline, *Primitive Culture*, in 1871. In a few years there developed a vast literature of anthropology, much of it concerned with aboriginal men and primitive cultures. Very early in its development anthropology divided into two rather distinct areas of scholarly concern: physical anthropology, which dealt with the evolution of man's physiological characteristics, and cultural anthropology, which treated cultural or social evolution.

In addition to its impact on academic scholarship, anthropology exerted at least two discernible influences on European thought and culture. On the one hand, the findings of the physical anthropologists were used by social Darwinists, racial theorists, and anti-Semites to bolster their fanciful ideas about "fittest" and superior races. In general, physical anthropology contributed to that arrogant race consciousness which characterized the mind of Europe and America during this period. On the other hand, the cultural anthropologist contributed to the atmosphere of relativism and skepticism concerning traditional values. Once again, moral values seemed to be little more than adaptations to the environment. The cultural anthropologists pointed out that mores were indeed relative, in the sense that they were constantly evolving to meet the demands of changing social and cultural environments. The study of primitive religions posed an especially serious threat to Christianity. In his seminal work *The Golden Bough* (1890), Sir James Frazer (1854—1941) demonstrated that the practices and beliefs of the Christian religion could be found in many of the "heathen" religions of the world. The findings of anthropology accelerated Europeans' loss of their sense of uniqueness.

The discipline of sociology also contributed to the trend toward relativism. In a general way, sociology may be said to descend from Auguste Comte, who had argued for a science of man and his social institutions. Nineteenth-century thinkers had been deeply concerned with expounding social and political doctrines, but sociology was truly revolutionary in that it treated social institutions as purely natural phenomena, as objects of scientific inquiry.

Although perhaps it's the least mature and the most controversial of academic disciplines, it includes among its practitioners some of the most prominent intellectual figures of the late nineteenth century.

Wilfredo Pareto (1848—1923), the leading Italian sociologist, published an important mathematical analysis of economic and sociological problems in 1916. One of his major contributions to sociological thought was his distinction between fundamental human motivations and the ideas men employ as rationalizations for those motivations. The leading sociologist in France was Émile Durkheim (1858—1917). The son of a Jewish rabbi in Alsace, he was at the University of Paris. Both sociologist and philosopher, Durkheim combined the precision of an empiricist with the boldness of a theoretician. His most important works deal with suicide, the division of labor, and primitive religion. *The Elementary Forms of the Religious Life* (1912) was a highly influential book. One of his most notable contributions to sociology was his concept of collective representation, which concerned the effect of the total societal consciousness upon the individual. Durkheim's study of this phenomenon led him to conclude that stability in a society depends upon the existence of a generally accepted system of values.

In intellectual stature the German sociologist Max Weber (1864—1920) towered over Pareto, Durkheim, and others. It is no exaggeration to suggest that Weber's was the most powerful analytic mind of his time. An invalid during much of his most creative period, Weber was little known outside the academic community, but his work had a profound impact there. Controversial in his day and since, it remained enormously influential.

Weber was the founder of the sociology of religion. He was also profoundly interested in capitalism, which he believed to be unique to Western civilization. In his most famous work, *The Protestant Ethic and the Spirit of Capitalism* (1905) he declared that Protestantism and capitalism were closely related. The key to this affinity of religion and economics lay in the doctrine of predestination, which encouraged a work ethic in the devout Calvinist. Protestantism thus created a frame of mind conducive to the development of capitalism. From these ideas Weber built a monumental analysis of the relationship between religion and work ethics in the major cultures of the world.

Arguing for a radical separation of science and values, Weber wanted sociology to become a pure, empirical science—relativistic and, above all, absolutely dispassionate. But while he wanted sociology to be scientific, he did not believe that it could formulate laws like those of the physical sciences. Rather than trying to establish laws, sociology should concern itself with ideal types—with general concepts like "nationalism" or "the Protestant ethic"— which serve as tools for analyzing empirical data. All twentieth-century Western social science is heavily indebted to Weber's methodology.

Influenced by Hegel, Weber was fascinated by power. He devoted much effort to the scientific analysis of the bases of power in society, producing important studies of bureaucracy and charisma—two antithetical means by which power is obtained and consolidated. To Weber, notions of justice, the common weal, and the like had no place in political analysis. Politics was power, nothing more and nothing less. One could choose to place his faith in one form of government or another, but from a sociological viewpoint no political system enjoyed any special value. For Weber, politics was the study of the techniques of power, and every human institution embodied the Will to Power.

11.3 Freudian Psychology

The third academic discipline that developed in the late nineteenth century was psychology. It is an open question whether this field should be classified as a natural science or a social science. Of all the new disciplines, psychology had the most profound impact upon the general public. Psychology radically altered man's view of himself.

Modern psychology may be said to date from 1879, when the German Wilhelm Wundt (1832—1920) established the first psychological laboratory. Like many later psychologists, Wundt conducted experiments involving animals. In a few years, psychologists all over Europe and the United States were conducting similar experiments and writing articles for learned journals. The dominant trend or "school" of psychology in these years was known as behaviorism. Behaviorist psychologists felt that behavior was the proper object of psychological research. Experimenting with animals and humans, they sought to establish how and why their subjects respond to certain stimuli.

One of the most important early behaviorists was Ivan Pavlov (1849—

1936), a Russian who conducted a series of famous experiments in which he "conditioned" dogs to salivate upon hearing a bell. The work of Pavlov and other behaviorists raised the age-old problem of freedom and determinism. Psychological research implied that men, like dogs, had no freedom of choice at all. All human behavior could be explained scientifically in terms of conditioning or training. Our choices were determined, our purposes were conditioned, and therefore we were not free. The conception of man as a rational, responsible, free moral agent was in great peril.

It was a decidedly non-behaviorist Viennese physician, Sigmund Freud (1856—1939), whose work was most influential in changing Western man's conception of his own nature. Freud was born into a humble Austrian Jewish family. It is said that he was a precocious child of unusual sexual curiosity, deeply attached to his mother. As a young doctor, he specialized in the treatment of nervous disorders called neuroses. He became interested in psychology when he discovered that the traditional ways of treating neuroses did not work. The need for a new method led him to investigate the inner world of mental processes. What emerged from this work was not only a new treatment for neuroses but a new theory of the mind, a new vision of man, and a new interpretation of man's culture.

From talking with his neurotic patients, Freud concluded that the causes of nervous disorders lay in painful past events that were forcibly forgotten, or "repressed" into the subconscious, that part of the human mind that lies below consciousness. The discovery that there were powerful mental processes hidden from the consciousness of men was truly revolutionary. Freud went on to declare that the subconscious was more powerful than the rational realm of consciousness. The subconscious knows no ethical restrictions. It maximizes vital human needs, the most important of which is sex. Freud believed that human motivation was basically irrational and that the sexual drive was the main component of that irrationality.

Freud's theory of the subconscious became the basis of psychoanalysis, the methods he devised for the treatment of neuroses. While the body of Freud's work remained extremely controversial within and beyond the field of psychology, the main outlines of his technique were widely accepted in the 1920s and 1930s. The major element in psychoanalysis is "free association", whereby the patient speaks freely of his thoughts and dreams, enabling the doctor to descend into the depths of the patient's subconscious. The doctor helps the patient to remember repressed episodes by interpreting the patient's dreams, which Freud regarded as products of the subconscious. Freud was quick to admit that psychoanalysis was as much as art as a science, since it depends on the skill of the doctor and the cooperation of the patient.

By far the most controversial and unscientific aspect of Freud's work was his interpretation of human culture. He viewed man's conscious or rational life as the result of repressed instinct, especially sexual instinct. Freud declared everything conscious—all knowledge, art, music, religion—to be the product of repression and sexual frustration. So all-encompassing was the Freudian "system" that Freud felt he could explain all of human history in psychoanalytic terms. In *Totem and Taboo* (1913) he interpreted religion, morality, and social life itself as products of the "Oedipus complex".

Whatever one may think of the Freudian system, it can probably be said that Freud has been the most influential intellectual figure of the twentieth century. His impact on Western culture has been as great as that of Marx or Darwin or even Newton. During his own lifetime, he attracted a host of disciples, some of whom—like Alfred Adler (1870—1937) and Carl Jung (1875—1961)—eventually broke with the master and founded their own schools. He has been criticized severely within the field of psychology for the vagueness of his concepts, but it is surely a mark of his greatness that many of them—"repression" "ego" and the like—have become so much a part of our thinking that they are virtual clichés. Finally, it is easy to do Freud an injustice by emphasizing certain aspects of his thought to the exclusion of others. His *Civilization and its Discontents* (1930) indicates that he was basically a moralist who wanted to help people accommodate themselves to society's repressive regimen.

Under the impact of the relativistic conclusions of the cultural anthropologist, the sociologists, and the behaviorist psychologists, the traditional values, received ideas, and moral homilies of Western man were seriously eroded. After Sigmund Freud, the whole structure of easy, liberal, rational confidence was falling apart.

11.4   Natural Sciences

Thus far, we have observed on the one hand a general reaction against science in the field of philosophy and on the other the application of scientific methods to the new social sciences. Yet the philosophers who decried the scientific method and the social scientists who embraced it were almost totally unaware of what was actually going on in the physical sciences. For during these years there occurred a veritable revolution that eventually changed the scientists' own conception of the nature and function of their work and profoundly altered Western man's view of the material world. Indeed, if the philosophers and social scientists had known of these developments, the philosophers would have been less hostile, the social scientists more humble.

Basic to these changes in the exact sciences were some important developments in mathematics. Between 1910 and 1913 two Englishmen who later became eminent philosophers—Alfred North Whitehead (1861—1947) and Bertrand Russell (1872—1970)—published their *Principia Mathematica*, a systematic derivation of mathematics from pure logic. The significance of the work lay in the fact that it set forth a symbolic logic quite different from traditional Aristotelian logic. Symbolic logic became the analytic tool of important movements in later twentieth-century philosophy.

Among the many important discoveries in the biological sciences, the most significant was in genetics. The origin, nature, and frequency of observable hereditary traits were explained for the first time, in physiological as well as quantitative and statistical terms. The father of genetic theory was Gregor Mendel, an Augustinian monk who conducted a series of important experiments involving the crossbreeding of peas. Mendel hypothesized that inheritance was particulate in character—that is, that hereditary traits were produced by certain tiny particles known as *genes*. These discrete conveyors of inheritable traits combine in certain statistically predictable ways, generating hereditary traits that are similarly predictable. In short, heredity was both explicable and predictable.

Mendel's experimental results fully confirmed his hypothesis, but his revolutionary work went largely unnoticed for three decades. The real breakthrough came in the 1930s, when Walter S. Sutton (1876—1916) demonstrated that Mendel's results could be explained in terms of the cytological behavior of chromosomes. In a few years it became clear to biologists that genes were linked to chromosomes. Mendel and the other formulators of genetic theory had opened up a new field of scientific research.

But the true revolution in science and scientific theory occurred in physics. Since the days of Newton, most educated people had made certain assumptions about the material world, including the following: that certain material causes produced certain material effects; that these causes and effects could be explained in terms of laws which were valid at all times and in all places; that an objective knowledge of these laws was possible, at least in theory; and that space, time, matter, energy, and motion were distinct and absolute. All the previous scientific discoveries of the nineteenth century both accepted these assumptions and confirmed them. Further, it was universally accepted that the basic unit of matter was the indivisible, and indestructible atom. Roughly speaking, these ideas constituted the Newtonian world picture.

The old view began to break down as a result of studies in the field of radiation: Certain experimental results in radiation research could not be explained within the framework of the Newtonian system. Out of radiation research there developed an enormously complicated "new physics", which was concerned with the problems of energy and atomic structure. With each fresh discovery in this new field of scientific endeavor, the crisis in scientific thinking became more acute.

Before 1900 it was thought that energy existed in constantly flowing streams or showers, but in that year Max Planck (1858—1947) of Germany enunciated the famous quantum theory, in which energy was said to exist in small bits or packages called *quanta*. The quantum theory implied that the atom itself was a unit of energy rather than a tangible, continuous piece of matter. This idea was carried one step further in 1911 by Ernest Rutherford (1871—1937) of Great Britain, who compared the structure of the atom to the solar system, and again in 1913 by Niels Bohr (1855—1962) of Denmark, who constructed a nuclear model of the atom.

The leading figure in the new physics was Albert Einstein (1879—1955), who almost single-handedly brought about a fundamental revision of accepted Newtonian concepts. Born to a middle-class German Jewish family, Einstein was not so bright or successful at school and university. But his job in the

Swiss patent office gave him plenty of leisure time to pursue his scientific speculations. In 1905 he announced his "special theory of relativity", in which he challenged traditional concepts of space, time, and motion. Far from being absolute and measurable, observed space, time, and motion are relative to the space, time, and motion of the measurer or observer. Moreover, Einstein rejected the separateness of space and time by positing the existence of a four-dimensional space-time continuum. Mass was not discrete either, since it increases with an increase in velocity. Finally, in his famous equation $E=mc^2$, Einstein declared that matter and energy were interchangeable: energy equals mass times the square of the speed of light.

The implications of Einstein's theory were startling to the scientific community and to the world of thought beyond the laboratory. The concept of a relativity of space, time, and motion bore an obvious similarity to moral relativism, and in general way Einstein's theory of relativity speeded the development of relativism in the other disciplines. The supposedly universal laws of Newton were not valid in the physical world, and as a consequence, thinkers questioned whether universal laws of any sort could or should be formulated. Einstein had remarked at one point that objective knowledge of cause and effect might not be possible even in the exact sciences. In atomic research, he said, the most one could hope for was a high degree of statistical probability. Stimulated by his thought, men in other disciplines began to wonder if an objective knowledge of anything was possible—perhaps they, too, would have to settle for a high statistical probability.

Whether the discoveries in physics have disproved the accepted notions of "causality" and "objectivity" remains questionable, but it is clear that the work of Einstein and other physicists has contributed to the steady decline of these concepts. And it is also clear that the substitution of statistical probability for absolute knowledge as a goal for science profoundly changed the character of scientific thought.

11.5 The Heritage of Fin de Siècle Culture

As we have seen, the shaping of the Western consciousness has been primarily determined by those moments of great upheaval in thought and feeling when men of transcendent insight and sensibility rebel against the reigning ethos, proclaim anew the freedom of the human spirit, and penetrate undiscovered areas of the mind. The closing years of the nineteenth century were such an era of rebellion, spiritual liberation, and intellectual discovery.

Nietzsche was the prophet of the new ethos. He wanted Western man to transcend himself, to become a superior man, who would go far beyond what liberal rationalism and Christian culture had achieved. In a world in which science and technology had achieved so much, Nietzsche announced the perilous yet joyful quest for still greater triumphs, not mechanistic but human, spiritual, aesthetic, and moral. The new culture that will emerge from this quest, said Nietzsche, will transcend the stultifying canons of morality that prevail in contemporary, "descendent" culture. Seldom has a philosopher so perfectly articulated the feelings of liberation and innovation not only of his own generation but of the succeeding century as well. In addition to representing the subjectivist and relativist rebels of the late nineteenth century, Nietzsche anticipated the avant-garde of the twentieth century.

Although the discovery of the unconscious had been anticipated by all manner of creative people—philosophers, painters, poets, novelists and musicians—Freud's was a fourfold achievement. First, he gave scientific authority to the intimations of philosophers and artists. Second, he demonstrated the importance of sex in the subconscious, thereby discrediting Victorian reluctance to consider the implications of sexual drive for morality and personal conduct. He was responsible, before all others, for the gradual extinction of the nineteenth-century image of pure, sexless ladies and gentlemen and for the serious consideration of sexual motivations and mores, as well as for the increasingly major role that eroticism came to play in modern literature and art. His third achievement was his elaborate map of the world of consciousness and unconsciousness, focused on the id, the ego, and the superego, which revealed the inlets of the human psyche that had to be explored. Freud's fourth contribution was to reveal the ambiguity and the tenuousness of polarities and antinomies that had heretofore been taken for granted. The Romantics had claimed that the child is the father of the man, that the child inhabited a world of innocence and that only as he grew up did his mind become contaminated by the adult world. But Freudian psychology questioned whether anyone really grows up and denied the innocence of childhood. He believed that the child has his sexual impulses and activities from the beginning. And if dreams do reflect repressed wishes, there is then little difference between the world of fantasy and the world of conscious reality.

The discovery of the unconscious at the end of the nineteenth century, particularly as it was given scientific respectability and decisive form by Freudian psychology, marks one of the most important turning points in the intellectual history of the West. It produced momentous consequences in the arts, where attempts to evoke the inner realities of the heart and mind led to the proliferation of nonrepresentational painting and sculpture and stream-of-consciousness literature. But the impact of the discovery of subterranean aspects of the human personality went far beyond the arts. It crippled and eroded the faith of modern man in the linear, progressive development of institutions and the moral growth of mankind. The power and tenacity of dreams, myths, and memories shattered the idea of time as a progressive continuum. If it was true that the child continued to live in the man, if the "primitive" could not be expunged from the civilized, many lines that had seemed sharp and clear became blurred. What were the borders between child and adult, between past and present, between human and animal, between sleep and waking?

The rise of the social sciences at the turn of the century was prime evidence that the cold conceptual framework for understanding society was disintegrating and badly in need of revision or reconstruction. The new kind of social theorist was consciously relativistic and pluralistic in his approach. Whereas liberal rationalists of the older generation had believed they could reach conclusions with scientific certainty, Max Weber and his colleagues were satisfied with probability.

This new relativism, which was built into the social sciences from their inception, was intimately bound up with the new subjectivity which insisted that the vantage point of the observer conditioned all perception and experience. Mid-nineteenth-century liberal thinkers had believed that absolute truth about government and society could be predicted. But Weber and the new academic social scientists believed that all concepts, including their own, were socially and culturally conditioned. Thus one view of society could be more sophisticated, more useful, and, for the moment, more probable than another, but no social theory could claim the legitimacy of objective truth.

The rise of the social sciences—sociology, anthropology, and psychology—as formal, academic disciplines marked a new, ambitious attempt to comprehend both individual and collective human experience. But their advent also signaled the erosion of the old-style Western humanism which had sought to understand human life in all its integrity and totality. The social sciences fragmented the old humanistic ideal by apportioning the study of man among a variety of experts and specialists. With the rise of the social sciences came a great deal of new knowledge of human behavior. The price of the new knowledge was the compartmentalizing of the intellect.

The excitement generated by the discovery of the inner world raised again the old question of the proper relationship between the artist and society. Does the life of the mind, however conceived, have any responsibility to the life of the world?

Many thinking people answered in the negative, rejecting the world and choosing to dwell in the inner realm of heightened sensibility. But the new consciousness led others to return to the world with increased sensitivity to social problems; a number of intellectuals and artists adopted the role of social critic. In some cases the new consciousness merged with the new relativism of the natural and social sciences to produce a kind of detachment that differed radically from the easy, self-confident objectivity of the previous period. Sober, disenchanted, acutely conscious of its own limitations, this new clinical attitude involved a cold, hard look at man and society. The social scientist could now offer no concessions to the sentiments of the common man.

The benefits we have derived from Nietzsche's liberating philosophy, from Freudian insight into human nature, and from the analyses of Weber and other social scientists are immeasurable; they have become central not only to our value system but to our institutionalized way of life. Yet the heritage of fin-de-sicèle culture has not been an unmixed blessing. The denial of the validity of traditional Christian ethics and the parallel enthronement of a new elite that fashions its own morality; the breakdown of the distinction between child and adult, between primitive and civilized man, and the revelation of the primacy of erotic impulses in human nature; the undermining of the liberal humanist faith in absolute principles of social and political science, and the substitution of a relativistic attitude toward social values, along with a clinical detachment from the sentiments of the common man—all these currents in twentieth century culture have much to do with the genius of Nietzsche, Freud, Weber, or logical extrapolations from their doctrines. These extrapolations, unfortunately, deprive us of the humanity of the Enlightenment, the moral fervor of the Romantics, and the conscience of liberalism and provide a theoretical basis for totalitarian systems which go far beyond the tyrannies of the past.

Chapter 12   Contemporary Western World: Seeking a Meaningful Existence

Europe began the twentieth century in peace, riding a wave of scientific progress. The peace, however, was uneasy, threatened by German militarism and fragile alliances. Furthermore, new technology—the radio, the automobile, the X-ray—did little to ease the pressing problems of the poor in Europe's crowded, dirty cities. By the end of the nineteenth century, the faith in progress had come to include the ides that the poor need not accept their lot unquestioningly. As the new century began, the old Europe—a world of privilege, elegance, and tradition—was dying; it would be swept away forever by World War Ⅰ.

12.1   The Legacy of War and Revolution

World War Ⅰ (1914—1918), the so-called "war to end all wars", was an unprecedented calamity for Western civilization. By 1917 the war had ceased to have any meaning, purpose, or value for sensitive and liberal men. The war afflicted the Europeans with an acute sense of guilt and futility that accelerated the trend toward irrationality and extremism and further vitiated the moral heritage of liberal rationalism and humanism. The older generation was completely discredited in everything—its politics, its dress, its sexual mores—and there emerged a new insistence on the righteousness of youth, a theme that was to recur again and again in twentieth-century culture.

Everywhere, the standards of social behavior—already in decline—were devastated. If the politicians and generals had treated the millions under their care like animals dispatched to slaughter, then what canons of religion or ethics could any longer inhibit men from treating each other with the ferocity of jungle beasts? The slaughter of the war thoroughly debased the value of human life.

The demoralization of the Western conscience and the destruction of liberal and human values were perceived and described with force and clarity by intellectuals and artists. After the war those politicians who thought they could return to "normalcy" and those capitalists who expected to resume "business as usual", must be judged among the worst fools and dupes in all recorded history.

The war discredited Europe's elite of money and power and crippled its self-confidence. The bastions of masculinity, imperial rule, aristocracy, and capitalism that had seemed so impregnable in 1914 were disintegrating by 1920. During and shortly after the war several groups in European society that had been subjected to exploitation and rigid control claimed the rights and privileges of free citizens and, in their methods and slogans, established a pattern of emancipation for the downtrodden all over the world. World War I inaugurated a new era of social change and egalitarian rebellion as far-reaching in its impact as the French Revolution.

The largest group to benefit from emancipation constituted half of Western society—women. Until the first decade of the twentieth century, the tide of enfranchisement seemed to have stopped at universal manhood suffrage. Only a few humanitarian and liberal men, like John Stuart Mill, and a handful of bold women even dared raise the issue of women's suffrage, and they were greeted with, at best, amused contempt.

Even middle-class women in the nineteenth century were treated by their husbands as household surfs. It is probably true that in Victorian bourgeois society women were less accepted as intellectual equals than they had been during the Enlightenment. Bourgeois reticence about sex kept secret the sadistic aggression of husbands against wives. The double standard flourished: in London of the 1850s one out of every sixteen women was a prostitute. The women's suffrage movement that developed in prewar London was inspired not only by democratic ideals but by deep resentment of male domination.

The suffragettes developed techniques that are still much in use: they marched and petitioned; they disrupted political assemblies; they held sit-ins at the House of Commons; they engaged in hunger strikes; they resorted to occasional violence (including arson) and even martyrdom. These respectable middle-class women were denounced and jailed, but the need for women in offices and munitions plants and on farms during the war added force to their claims for equality. In 1918 the British Parliament gave the vote to women who had reached the responsible age of thirty, and enfranchisement of women followed rapidly in almost every Western country.

Having gained the vote, women showed their inclination toward conservative parties at the polls. But the war brought them more than political emancipation, and conservatism was hardly the rule: They cut their hair, threw away their corsets and crinolines, raised their skirts, smoked, and drank. Some fierce and flaming women even asserted their right to equal promiscuity with men. It is true that women made greater strides toward political and personal freedom in the decade after 1914 than in all the previous centuries of mankind put together.

On Easter Monday of 1916 another submerged group—the Irish—rose in rebellion. Tired of waiting for the British to make home rule effective, a few dozen Dublin poets, teachers, and clerks rose against the world's greatest empire. Their rebellion had all the elements of a comic opera, except for its shocking denouement: The British government proceeded to execute the rebel leaders.

Fired by the example of the martyrs' heroism, a widespread revolution began in 1918. By 1922 most of Ireland was a self-governing republic. Its long-term political leader was Eamon De Valera (1882-1975), who as one of the Easter rebels of 1916 had been spared the death penalty because he happened to be an American citizen. Ireland started the fire of colonial rebellion that was to sweep over Asia and Africa in the next four decades, destroying European empires that in 1914 had seemed eternal. But the most important single consequence of World War I was the replacement of the czarist government of Russia by Lenin's Bolshevik regime. No single event so powerfully affected the destiny of mankind in the next half-century as the Bolshevik take-over in Russia.

12.2 Natural Sciences

Science has profoundly shaped the intellectual history of the twentieth century. It has been a pervasive cult. Men have looked to science, to technology, and to the scientific method for mastery of the material world and for assistance in their attempts to improve the human condition. If any universal symbol does exist, it is surely scientific in character and mathematical in language. Yet the confidence and admiration that caused so many people to place their trust in scientific progress has been sorely tried since 1945. Whether scientists can master their discoveries for the benefit of mankind has become a critical issue.

The most dramatic and revolutionary discoveries of modern physics were made very early in the century. Max Planck developed the quantum theory in 1900, and Einstein announced his special theory of relativity in 1905, his general theory in 1916. Ernest Rutherford, a New Zealander by birth, joined the famous Cavendish Laboratory at Cambridge University in 1895. At the University of Manchester in 1907 he began the work which led to the discovery in 1911 of the atomic nucleus. There Rutherford worked with the Danish physicist Niels Bohr, then a young student, and thus became the intellectual godfather of Bohr's work on atomic structure.

Bohr was responsible for a large share of the modern understanding of the structure of matter. He applied Planck's quantum theory to Rutherford's nuclear atom, in order to make sense of the observable facts about radioactivity. Rohr used spectrum analysis to probe the atom, relating the chemical properties of an element to its spectrographic characteristics and inaugurating the age of nuclear physics. In the 1920s, important discoveries were made with inadequate mathematical tools, quantum mechanics was developed, and Bohr and others contributed to the stockpile of data even while they developed the collateral mathematical theory. Bohr's Institute for Theoretical Physics in Copenhagen attracted young physicists from all over the world.

One of Bohr's associates was the German physicist Werner Heisenberg (1901—1976), whose most notable contribution to quantum mechanics was the revolutionary "uncertainty principle". Heisenberg was the first to state in mathematical language the relativist principle that, on the atomic scale, observation cannot be made without affecting the object or process observed. Whatever measuring device is used, its presence and activity inevitably alter at least one characteristic of the phenomenon under observation; thus one cannot establish both position and velocity (of an electron, for instance) without a definite minimum quantity of uncertainty. This principle is a building stone of modern physics, which (unlike classical physics) accepts the fact that the behavior of an individual particle of matter can never be predicted. However, the behavior of groups of particles can be predicted, and contemporary physics has, in fact, moved forward through the new science of statistics and probability. Scientists can assert with confidence that a certain proportion of a group of electrons will behave in a certain manner, even though no such prediction can be made for any individual electron.

One aspect of Einstein's special theory of relativity, its statement of the convertibility of mass and energy, hinted at the enormous forces contained within the atomic nucleus. Rutherford produced the first laboratory nuclear reaction in 1919; after the discovery of the neutron by James Chadwick (1891—1974) in 1931, nuclear reactions were produced by the Italian Enrico Fermi (1901—1954) and others, but it seemed impossible at first to apply the liberated energy to any purpose. Not until the Germans Otto Hahn (1879—1968) and Fritz Strassmann (1902—1980) produced barium by splitting the uranium atom in 1938 was there any real possibility of practical fission.

Their accomplishment was known to Bohr because an associate of Hahn and Strassmann had fled from Nazi persecution to Copenhagen. Bohr took the news to the United States in 1939 and discussed it with Einstein, Fermi, and others who feared the military implications of work with fission in the laboratories of Nazi Germany. Fermi was the first to understand the possibilities of chain reaction and was chiefly responsible for the first nuclear reactor in a squash court at the University of Chicago in 1942. The production of self-sustaining nuclear energy was a scientific triumph of the greatest significance, and it was turned at once to military purposes. Bohr and Einstein knew that Werner Heisenberg was at work in Germany on a uranium pile, and Einstein wrote to President Roosevelt in 1939 to warn him of the German effort. After appeals to the President by other distinguished scientists, the Manhattan Project, whose purpose was to develop the military possibilities of atomic energy, was authorized.

In 1943 the Manhattan Project laboratory at Los Alamos, New Mexico, with Julius Robert Oppenheimer (1904—1967) as its director, was assigned the task of developing an atomic bomb. The first test at Alamogordo on July 16, 1945, was an outstanding success (the desert sand was fussed to glass for hundreds of yards around the site). In August two atom bombs were dropped on Hiroshima and Nagasaki of Japan.

Hiroshima inaugurated not only a new age of science but a new kind of scientist—the government servant whose knowledge and talent is an important part of the national arsenal. Furthermore, scientists were now much more conscious of their social position and responsibilities. This was true in all advanced industrial countries, but particularly in the United States and the former Soviet Union. Presumably, Soviet scientists were satisfied to follow the dictates of government leaders, but after World War II Oppenheimer and other American scientists entered into a great debate over the human, political, and social implications of atomic science and a profound searching of their own conscience. Oppenheimer resisted the building of the hydrogen bomb—a much more devastating weapon than the bombs used against Japan—in the early 1950s, and he made important enemies. When Oppenheimer's security clearance was withdrawn in 1954, a great outcry from his colleagues expressed more than personal indignation. Certain branches of scientific research are not only secret today; they are expensive secrets: the cyclotrons and reactors of the 1960s are far beyond the means of any university or other institution without government support.

Although rockets have been used in war since the early nineteenth century, they were never very effective before the days of modern electronics and nuclear warheads. Modern rocketry began in Germany, where the V-2 robot bomb that contributed to the horrors of the Nazi blitz against London during World War II was developed under the direction of Wernher von Braun (1912—1977) in the 1930s and early 1940s. The sophisticated rockets of the next quarter-century were used both for long-range ballistic missiles and in the exploration of outer space. Intercontinental missiles could be armed with nuclear or thermonuclear warheads; in fact, they were so expensive to build that the destructive capacity of a conventional warhead would not justify the cost. The development of solid fuels and inertial guidance systems made it possible to devastate a target anywhere on earth with a missile shot from a plane, a surface vessel or submarine, or a silo. The very existence of such weapons, of course, encouraged the development of equally complicated and expensive defensive systems like SDI, or antimissile missiles like PAC-3; the possibilities for escalation of weaponry became endless.

As missile-carrying rockets grew more sophisticated during the arm race of the 1950s, it became obvious that it was possible to build a rocket powerful enough to escape the earth's gravitational field. The first artificial satellite (Sputnik I) was put into orbit by the former Soviet Uninon on October 4, 1957. This scientific and engineering triumph produced a panic among government officials and military men in the United States (with repercussions in American education), and the humiliation was shortly compounded by Yuri Gagarin's orbiting the earth in April 1961. The American Mercury, Gemini, and Apollo programs were conceived and put into execution as fast as possible, and the astronaut Alan Shepard went suborbital flight in May 1961, inaugurating the American manned space program, which caught up with and then surpassed the Russian program shortly thereafter. In 1968 and early 1969, American manned spacecraft circumnavigated the moon, preparing for a landing on the moon's surface. On July 20, 1969, the American astronauts Neil A. Armstrong and Edwin A. Aldrin, Jr. landed on the moon near the Sea of Tranquility and spent a couple of hours walking on the surface collecting rock samples. In the opinion of many, this feat inaugurated a new era in the history of mankind. It was at least a superb tribute to the achievement of post-World War II science and technology.

Spy satellites permit the major powers to scan one another's terrains, and weather satellites provide a great deal of information to meteorologists. Communications satellites allow instantaneous intercontinental telecasting. But few economic or social assets can be expected from men on the moon, and in space exploration as in nuclear physics. Scientists and laymen debate the value and expediency of the programs. Can the enormous cost in money, materials, and brains be justified in a world where so many basic human needs are not met yet?

The early twentieth century saw the greatest changes in the physical science since the Age of Newton. In the mid-twentieth century, the biological sciences experienced a revolution of comparable importance. The most dramatic discovery was that of the structure of the molecule of DNA (deoxyribonucleic acid) by Francis H. C. Crick (1916—2004) and James D. Watson (1928—2012) in Cambridge, England, in the early 1950s. DNA is the fundamental genetic material, and the new understanding of its structure was expected ultimately to reveal the working of the genetic code and even permit men to interfere in the process of heredity. The result has been an explosion in biochemistry which has transformed the science.

Modern medicine has extended human life, chiefly through the incredible range and variety of new drugs and techniques in chemotherapy and surgery. Sulfanilamide was synthesized from coal tar in the 1930s; it was the first drug to act specifically against streptococcal infections and was used widely in the treatment of wounds during World War II. The effectiveness of penicillin—the first and perhaps the greatest of the antibiotics—was first noticed by Alexander Fleming (1881—1955) in 1928; the strain was isolated during the 1930s, and wartime needs propelled it into production. Penicillin and related drugs have lengthened human life and incidentally added to the burdens of twentieth-century man, one of whose major problems is overpopulation.

Viruses are not as susceptible to drugs as bacteria, but in certain instances they have succumbed to the growing science of immunology. The most important recent advance in this field was the development by the Americans Jonas Salk (1914—1995) and Albert Sabin (1906—1993) of vaccines that provided immunity to polio. Insulin, discovered by two Canadians, Frederick Banting (1891—1941) and Charles Best (1899—1978), has made it possible for diabetics to live normal lives. Rheumatoid arthritis has been ameliorated, though not cured, by cortisone. The discovery and isolation of vitamins has made it possible to eradicate deficiency diseases such as scurvy and rickets. Modern insecticides, beginning with DDT, can rid the world of malaria, but the effects of insecticides upon human life and the planetary ecology are now well understood. Even while streptomycin reduced TB mortality, cigarette smoking and air pollution affected the mortality rate, and though modern medical research has been concentrating on cancer for many years, no cure has been found.

Surgical techniques have become immensely ambitious and complex since the development of anesthesia and asepsis. The first organ transplant in the late 1960s revealed a need for the study of immune reaction (the body's rejection of foreign material); since then, transplants of almost every major organ, including the heart, have been accomplished. Here again, technical and scientific achievements have created a new concern over their social and moral implications.

The basic scientific knowledge that lies behind what was first called wireless telegraphy and the then radio had largely been attained by the early years of the twentieth century. Radio was first applied to ship-to-shore communication and then, in the 1920s and early 1930s scientists and engineers in both Britain and the United States experimented with television broadcasting; a few stations already were in operation in 1939. After World War Ⅱ television became a prime source of information and entertainment in all industrialized countries. The development of transistors to take the place of large, cumbersome vacuum tubes allowed radio and television sets to become lighter, less bulky, and much cheaper.

Between 1935 and 1938 a team of British scientists headed by Robert Alexander Watson-Watt (1892—1973) developed radar, which allowed the presence of ships and planes to be detected at long distances. Further research made radar a serviceable military weapon, and after World War Ⅱ it greatly contributed to air safety. The most important change in air transportation resulted from the invention of the jet engine, developed almost simultaneously in Germany, the United States, Great Britain, and the Soviet Union at the close of the war. Jet engines greatly increased air speed and made the building of much larger planes feasible.

The decades after 1940 comprised another era of revolution in transportation and communication, which enormously increased the opportunity for communicating knowledge and providing education and entertainment for the masses. In the late 1950s British television followed the pattern already set by the United States; its main purpose was popular entertainment. But in some other countries, television, like the press, was more often than not an instrument for political indoctrination. Nowhere was television's potential as a vehicle for raising the level of public taste and public understanding of political issues consistently pursued. Once again the twentieth-century pattern was repeated by which scientist abdicated responsibility for the social applications of their discoveries.

Perhaps the most revolutionary of all the technological inventions of the twentieth century is the computer. Early computers, which required thousands of vacuum tubes to function, were large and took up considerable space. The development of the transistor and then the silicon chip provided a revolutionary new approach to computers. In 1971, the invention of the microprocessor, a machine that combines the equivalent of thousands of transistors on a single, tiny silicon chip, opened the road for the development of the personal computer.

The computer is a new kind of machine whose chief function is to store and produce information, now considered a fundamental asset of our fast-paced civilization. By 2000, the personal computer had become a regular fixture in businesses, schools, and homes. The Internet—the world's largest computer network—provides millions of people around the world with quick access to immense quantities of information. Not only does the computer make a host of tasks much easier, but it has also become an important or indispensable tool in virtually every area of modern life.

Although computers have greatly enhanced many aspects of human life, they also carry dangers. Computer surveillance and database have the power to dramatically erode our privacy if they are not regulated. As more and more aspects of individuals' lives are recorded on computer—from financial information to their medical records—care must be taken to maintain confidentiality. In addition, replacing human workers with computers carries implications for society—both for the workers who must retrain and adapt themselves to the changing conditions, and for consumers who find that contact between people is increasingly replaced by interactions with computers. The challenge we face is to preserve the impressive benefits and reduce the impact of the problems the computer has brought us.

12.3 Social and Behavioral Sciences

One of the most significant changes in the pattern of higher culture since World War I has been the expansion and proliferation of the social and behavioral sciences, their entrenchment in universities as full-fledged academic disciplines, and their substantial influence on public policy.

Economics, the oldest and most firmly established of the social sciences, experienced in the twentieth century a transformation in methodology and doctrine. The direction of this transformation was strongly determined by a charismatic figure, a single individual whose bold ideas changed theory and practice alike. John Maynard Keynes (1883—1946) was one of the rare revolutionaries of the social sciences. His work was a watershed in the history of economics. Keynes, a Cambridge don who was also a member of the Bloomsbury intellectual group of prewar and postwar London, served as Britain's financial representative at the peace conference in 1919. His condemnation of reparation policy made him unpopular in government circles, and he returned to Cambridge, where his teaching influenced a generation of British economists. At Cambridge, he wrote his major work, which, particularly after World War Ⅱ, revolutionized public policy as well as academic economic theory. *The General Theory of Employment, Interest and Money* (1936) set forth Keynes's belief that man is not necessarily a helpless victim of the business or industrial cycle, that unemployment and depression can be controlled by reasonable government action. This view departed from classical economics and Marxism as well.

The General Theory is an attack on the old notion that capitalistic systems automatically adjust themselves to the most favorable level of employment and of prices and wages. Keynes denied the nineteenth-century principle that demand follows production—that as businesses spend more on labor, the wages that pay out enable workmen to buy more goods. He also rejected the prevailing belief that any workman can be employed if he will simply accept a lower wage, that unemployment is essentially voluntary.

Keynes explained unemployment by the theory of aggregate demand, which says in effect that although one businessman may increase demand for his product by cutting prices (and costs, including wages paid to labor), this does not work when all businessmen cut prices and wages. In that situation, demand declines along with wages because workers can then buy fewer goods of any kind. Thus the level of aggregate demand determines the level of employment. How can the level of aggregate demand be raised? Keynes asserted that investment is a major factor in economic expansion.

Keynes was certain that government monetary policy could effect significant changes in the rate of economic growth and employment levels, but that public works (which could be financed by government deficits and which Keynes and most other social theorists hoped could be of social value) were even more effective. Government investment—in a war or in public works—was as effective as, or more effective than, private investment. Tax reduction served a similar purpose by encouraging spending; but it did not assure that the spending would take socially desirable forms.

Keynes's radical ideas made him a public figure. In the United States, his theories influenced the economic thinkers of the New Deal although President Roosevelt himself was never a convinced Keynesian. It was World War Ⅱ —not the New Deal—that seemed fully to substantiate Keynesian theory. The enormous wartime public spending and deficit financing led to economic boom, which brought about full employment and unheard-of economic expansion. Keynesian analysis of statistics (on employment, prices, wages, interest rates) became part of the routine work of any modern government financial department, and analysis occupied a large part of the time of theoretical economists as well. Further, the desirability of deficit financing—the ultimate denial of the old Puritan virtue of thrift—was widely accepted. Post-Keynesian economists accept the deficit and believe that government can and should stimulate the economy, but they argue over whether this should be done by tax reform (as most conservatives believe) or by expansion of government into ever larger areas of social welfare. The latter view is held by the influential American economist John Kenneth Galbraith (1908—2006), whose book *The Affluent Society* (1958) expresses the view that economic growth should be redirected from the production and consumption of a surplus of consumer goods into needed public services.

The modern economist deals with quantitative matters and with the mathematical relationships of various economic circumstances. He uses statistical techniques; the subspecialty of econometrics is concerned entirely with statistical measurements. Computers handle the mass of available information, and economics itself is approaching the stage where it can be communicated as well as in mathematical symbols as in words, if not better.

In the 1920s and 1930s European sociologist—working in the tradition of Marx, Weber, and Durkheim—continued to search for the universal truths that might allow them to understand increasingly complex human institutions. In *Ideology and Utopia* (1931) Karl Mannheim (1893—1947) wrote of the "structure" of social reality and the inevitability of social planning in the complicated modern world. American sociologists on the whole avoided the search for comprehensive patterns, but Talcott Parsons (1902—1979) of Harvard developed a universal theory of social action that was intended to transcend differences among specific societies.

In the 1920s and 1930s, however, the main trend of American sociology was in the direction of empirical research, involving the careful accumulation of data. Scholars left their armchairs for field work on the streets of Chicago or in the vineyards of California, and their published work was heavily statistical and non-ideological. Simultaneously, statistics itself became a science. Testing methods, demographic surveys, and ultimately computers all became more sophisticated, and sociological data was put to use by insurance companies, advertising agencies, political parties, and government bureaus responsible for the supply of goods and services.

In the 1940s and 1950s sociologists insisted that their work was a science, that their findings were not speculative theories but verifiable facts, like the findings of physicists. Underlying all their activity was the assumption that group behavior can be predicted—that, in this instance, a social scientist can predict the behavior of a group of people, if not that of an individual. Just as in physics the measuring process affects the behavior of atomic particles, so in sociology the announcement of a poll or rating may alter the voting pattern or buying habits of the object of study.

By the late 1950s emerged a trend away from amoral, purely descriptive studies. Sociological began to return to the reforming spirit and moral commitment of early twentieth-century social science. The Swedish sociologist Gunnar Myrdal (1898—1987) had already provided an arsenal of facts and figures for the American civil rights movement in his study *An American Dilemma: The Negro Problem, and Modern Democracy* (1944). David Riesman's *The Lonely Crowd* (1950) used data gained from empirical research to portray contemporary values and life styles. By the 1960s this kind of liberal and critical sociological literature was competing with the novel as a vehicle for providing the educated public with an awareness of its group habits and ideals. In 1968 Myrdal published a detailed analysis of Southeast Asian society, *Asian Drama*; his conclusions were tinged with Malthusian pessimism about the viability of efforts made in the postwar period to bring these countries from the agricultural to the industrial stage. Charles Wright Mills (1916—1962), a Columbia University professor, contributed to this growing body of sociological critiques with *The Sociological Imagination* (1959), in which he criticized theorists like Talcott Parsons as too abstract and general to be meaningful. Mills claimed that most twentieth-century sociology defeated itself by excessive empiricism. The sociological imagination, he believed, should apply itself to building a better society.

Between 1920 and 1950 it was fashionable for academic historians to sneer at sociologists, whom they frequently regarded as arrogant fabrications of unfounded theories. The overwhelming majority of professional historians remained oblivious to the tremendous upheaval in thought that had begun in the late nineteenth century. With passionate and ignorant conservatism, historians avowed their loyalty to mid-nineteenth-century positivism—if only enough documents were studied and enough facts gathered, somehow a meaningful interpretation of the past would ultimately emerge. Understandably, history steadily moved away the interest of the intellectual public.

There were, however, some significant exceptions to academic positivism. A few historians, such as George M. Trevelyan (1876—1962) in Britain and Allan Nevins (1890—1971) in the United States, perpetuated the liberal and romantic traditions of nineteenth-century historiography and commanded a wide audience. Some important scholars presented broad interpretations predicted on the Marxist view that the basis of political and social change is economic and that class struggle is inevitable and perpetual. Charles Beard (1874—1948) viewed American history in this way, Richard H. Tawney (1880—1962) perceived the development of sixteenth-century England in this framework, and Michael Rostovtzeff (1870—1952) found this pattern in Roman history. The two celebrated philosophers of history of the interwar era, the German Oswald Spengler (1880—1936), in his *The Decline of the West*, and the Englishman Arnold Joseph Toynbee (1889—1975), in his multivolume *A Study of History*, both revived the cyclic theory of the development of civilizations, to which Greek and Roman thinkers had been devoted—Spengler with the mystical tone of German Romanticism, Toynbee with the analytical acumen of British scholarship.

Meanwhile, in the 1930s isolated efforts were made to apply ideas derived from the behavioral and social sciences to historical interpretation. Lewis B. Namier (1888—1960), convinced by the Freudian view of human nature, undertook a realistic analysis of the functioning of eighteenth-century British politics. At the same time, the eminent French medievalist Marc Bloch (1886—1944) was applying Durkheim's sociology to his analysis of feudal society. Bloch was killed by the Nazis while he was fighting in the resistance, but after the war several of his disciples, notably Fernand Braudel (1902—1985), developed a major French school of sociological history. In the late 1950s a similar trend began to emerge in the United States and Britain, and by the late 1960s, far from sneering at sociology, leading historians of the younger generation were applying the insights and theories of all the social and psychological sciences to the understanding of the pattern of historical change.

As was the case with all sciences in their early stage of development, anthropology has had a difficult time deciding what its subject matter and purpose are. Physical anthropology, which was developed mainly in German universities in the early years of the twentieth century, concentrated on human biology and genetics, on the characteristics of various racial groups, and on human evolution. There can be no doubt that this branch of anthropology, when it has confined itself to the subject of prehistory, has been a particularly careful and empirical science. But in their study of racial groups, the physical anthropologists achieve only modest results. They never reached agreement on what constitutes a race or whether the term is valid at all. The pernicious racist doctrines of the Nazis effectively discouraged further inquiry into the subject.

The other branch of anthropology—cultural or social anthropology—set out to establish nothing less than the patterns of human institutions: kinship and family life, political system, economic practices, religious beliefs and organizations, and language patterns. Partly because of the Darwinist assumption that the laws of social behavior can best be observed among primitive people who had not yet evolved to more sophisticated and complex forms of behavior, and partly because sociologists had already preempted the study of advanced societies, anthropologists during the first two decades of the twentieth century committed themselves to detailed field work among extremely primitive peoples, particularly in Asia and Africa. Essentially, cultural anthropology has never advanced beyond this subject matter.

The founder of scientific analyses of primitive peoples still extant was Franz Boas (1858—1942) of Columbia University, who sent his students to conduct ethnographic studies in the Americas and Asia. Boas was not only hostile to evolutionary doctrines, social Darwinism, and racist theories but also to the effort to establish any pattern or laws in social development. A thorough empiricist, he exercised a very important influence on anthropological thought. It is difficult, however, for a science to develop with no general theory. Since 1920 anthropologists have devoted a great deal of time and energy trying to find a substitute for the earlier evolutionary theory. Boas's own students Ruth Benedict (1887—1948) and Margaret Mead (1901—1978) tried to impose an interpretative pattern on their studies, respectively, of Indians of the American

Southwest and of Pacific islanders. Their well-written, imaginative books were highly popular but received a decidedly mixed reaction from their anthropological colleagues.

Among the welter of interpretations offered by twentieth-century anthropologists, three schools have gained the widest adherence. The "structural-functional" approach developed in Britain in the 1920s and 1930s by Alfred Radcliffe-Brown (1881—1955) and Bronislaw Malinowski (1884—1942) tried to show how institutions developed in response to basic human needs. The French school of cultural anthropology has used linguistic analysis and empirical social data to demonstrate that institutions develop in response to mental structures and reflect psychological types. The leading exponent of this school has been Claude Levi-Strauss (1908—2008). Yet a third school of anthropological interpretation gave precedence to material and environmental factors. In the work of the Australian-born British scholar V. Gordon Childe (1892—1957), an authority on the prehistory of the ancient Near East, this cultural materialism was openly associated with Marxist doctrine. The American school of cultural materialism—to which Julian Steward (1902—1972) and Marvin Harris (1927—2001), among others, made important contributions—was more empirical and less schematic in its approach.

Psychologists, particularly in the United States, shared the general scientism (the emphasis on verifiability and objectivity) that characterized the social sciences during much of the twentieth century. Even while Freud's disciples were working out new schools in which both consciousness and the unconscious were used in psychoanalysis, American psychologists turned away from consciousness on the grounds that it could be known only by introspection and was therefore unreliable. J. B. Watson (1878—1958) inaugurated psychological behaviorism, which remained dominant in the United States until the late 1940s. Watson defined psychology as an objective, experimental, natural science that should be restricted to the relation of observable, measurable stimuli and responses.

The behaviorists, who based their work on Pavlov's experiments with conditioned responses in animals, believed that environmental forces are crucial in the development of behavior. Watson's was essentially an optimistic view—of child-raising, at least—and thousands of American parents brought up their children in the confidence that they could be trained by stimuli to develop proper patterns of behavior. Later neo-behaviorists such as Clark L. Hull (1884—1952) and B. F. Skinner (1904—1990) redefined and extended classical behaviorism.

The Gestalt school of psychology originated in Germany and became active in the United States after most of its leading representatives fled Hitler's regime. Gestalt psychologists were particularly concerned with perception, stressing the organization of sense data by the brain in the Kantian tradition, which held that mind imposes structure upon experience. They provided an alternative to behaviorism, but the psychology laboratories developed during the 1920s and 1930s still flourished in the 1960s. New applications—in industry, in the military, in motivational research, and in educational and vocational testing—required a great deal of complicated apparatus and made psychology a big business.

Even while behaviorism predominated in the United States, European psychologists continued to work out Freud's ideas in new schools. Some of Freud's disciples continued in the strict Freudian traditions; others broke away; but none shed Freud's influence entirely. Alfred Adler, an Austrian psychiatrist, worked with Freud from 1902 until 1911, when he left to found his own school. He differed from Freud in emphasizing the drive for superiority, a sociogenic drive that may be expressed in either productive or antisocial attitudes. For Adler, the crucial determining factor in mental health was not Freud's biological necessity but individual, subjective response to a particular social situation, including the family.

Carl Gustav Jung, a Swiss associate of Freud's between 1907 and 1921, founded an important school of psychological interpretation in Zurich. Jung divided men into introverts and extroverts, depending on the predominance of thought, emotion, sensation, or intuition in the individual personality. He emphasized the immediate conflicts of his neurotic patients instead of concentrating on their childhood experiences. Jung's most important contribution was his theory of the "collective unconscious" inherited by all men from primitive ancestors; this theory was both a reflection of, and further inducement to, the great resurgence of interest in myth and legend and in primitive or preliterate societies.

Another influential social psychologist Erik Erikson (1902—1994) stresses the importance of interpersonal relationships in creativity and personality. In

Childhood and Society (1950) Erikson studied the development of the healthy personality, which he described as a series of crisis in the concept of self. The reinforcement of traditional, social and sexual identification is essential to this process, particularly in the crisis of identity that accompanies adolescence. Much of Erikson's work suggests the desirability of a stable, traditional society in which the "generation gap" is not too large to allow the young to identify with adult models.

Obviously Freud's theories are basic to modern psychological thought, but the practice of psychoanalysis which he inaugurated seems destined to play a reduced role in the treatment of mental illness. Analysis became a quasi-religion among intellectuals of the 1930s and 1940s; it was an inherent part of up-to-date artistic and social theory, and its techniques, assumptions, and jargon were closely bound into the higher culture of the era. However, as medical practice it was simply too expensive, too slow, and too elitist to be very useful. Research in the late 1950s seemed to establish a biochemical basis for schizophrenia, and this discovery has provided the greatest existing hope for the future treatment of mental illness. Group therapy is becoming more and more common, though Freudian analysis is still used in certain cases and Freud's theories have had a permanent influence in all the fields of thought that require insight into the human personality.

Rarely has an eminent philosopher directed his attention to the nature and problems of education—although Plato and Rousseau did. The main issue in the early twentieth century was the continued utility of traditional, humanist, classical education in an industrial and technological society. This was the problem to which John Dewey (1859—1952) addressed himself. Dewey, who, with William James and Charles Sanders Peirce, was one of the American pragmatist trinity, established the famous Laboratory School at the University of Chicago. In 1904 he went to Columbia, where he taught philosophy until 1930. His philosophy of education was derived both from his interpretation of the psychology of learning and from his analysis of modern society. Thinking, he believed, is an activity of inquiry undertaken to solve problems and to deal with the situations of uncertainty. Learning is a process that occurs when experience provides new situations which our customary responses do not handle satisfactorily. Education, then, must begin with experience—a student must experience (do, see, touch, taste) a problem—actively and tangibly, if possible—in order to reason out and understand its solution. The second plank in Dewey's platform of educational reform was his conviction that an education suitable to the nineteenth century was not adequate in the scientific society of the twentieth.

Dewey was fascinated by methods, by the concept of "instrumentality", believing that art, scientific techniques, and ethical principles are tools with which men impose order on a chaotic universe. Like Peirce and James, he saw philosophy as an active agent in culture and society. Dewey himself was a staunch supporter of personal liberty and social justice.

These attitudes were combined in the theory that education must be organized around students—or rather their problems—instead of around subjects, that the traditional learning by memorizing and reciting must give way to experience-based learning by thinking and doing in schools which were essentially models of the outside world. Education should pattern itself on scientific investigation; problems should be examined on their merits as they presented themselves to students through experience; there was no good reason to turn to the past for authoritative beliefs, although what former generations have learned and passed on to us is the only resource we have except our own ability to learn from experience. These ideas were enthusiastically received by "progressive" educators, especially in the United States. Education through activity—learning by doing—became a cherished tenet of American educational theory.

In the 1950s progressive theories were blamed for a great many failings of American education. Some of these failings might have been better blamed on the population explosion, or even on the concept of mass education. Dewey's progressive program—by which the school was a reflection of the democratic and industrial society and was itself a quasi-democratic community—was the most important educational innovation of the twentieth century.

In European countries the democratization of the secondary schools was never attempted. Whether public or private, they remained elitist institutions in which the superior intellectual minority was given rigorous training in the traditional literary curriculum, with appropriate mathematical and scientific additions. The same was true of European higher education, which remained an elitist system, both in terms of the rigorous standards required for matriculation and graduation and in terms of the small percentage of the college-age population that had the opportunity and qualifications for university study.

Down to the mid-1960s the main trend in universities throughout the Western world was neither curricular experimentation nor democratization of the institutional structure. Rather, it was the proliferation and expansion of graduate and professional schools and research institutions. In the period after World War II this trend was accelerated everywhere, as governments and business corporations lavishly endowed research in the natural, biological, social, and behavioral sciences. The underside of the coin was the general neglect of the interests of the undergraduate college in favor of the more prestigious and prosperous branches of the university. Many universities, particularly in France and Germany, but also to a somewhat lesser degree in Britain and the United States, were notoriously overcrowded. This general neglect of the teaching function of the university, as compared with its scholarly and research functions, provided a seedbed for discontent which, inflamed by left-wing agitation against capitalism and war, exploded into student rebellion all over the Western world in the late 1960s.

12.4 Philosophy and Theology

Modern philosophy divides quite naturally into two separate schools of thought. One group, centered in Great Britain and the United States (although some of its original leaders were Germans), concentrated on logic and theory of knowledge; the other—Continental European—on ethics and metaphysics. Anglo-American philosophers, impressed by the achievements and methods of modern science, have disdained what they regard as the intuitive insights of metaphysics, particularly the vestiges of Romantic idealism. They have accordingly turned to mathematicians, physicists, and linguists; they criticize what men believe by analyzing what men say and how they know.

The patriarch of modern Americanism and British philosophy is Bertrand Russell. Russell's early work on the foundations of mathematics led him into a philosophy he described as "logical atomism". After his collaboration with Alfred North Whitehead on *Principia Mathematica* (1913), Russell continued to focus on mathematical logic as the instrument of meaningful thought about the world. To Russell, knowable truths were like those of pure mathematics, ascertainable only by rigorous intellectual analysis that owed nothing to experience or experiment. In contrast, beliefs about "the external world" could be probable at best, based on very complicated interferences from our sensations.

Russell's aim was to establish modern science on a firm logical foundation, to achieve complete clarity by choosing a mathematical language that could not mislead us. Much of Russell's confidence in an "ideal" symbolic language has been rejected by later philosophers, but his contribution to the philosophy of mathematics makes him one of the great figures in the history of modern thought.

Russell's work was influential in the development of logical positivism, which appeared as a philosophical school in the "Vienna Circle" of the early 1920s. The chief spokesman for logical positivism was Rudolf Carnap (1891—1970), who left Vienna for the United States in 1935 and taught at the University of Chicago and the University of California. He and his colleagues shifted the emphasis of scientific philosophy from understanding nature to understanding the way we talk about nature. Every meaningful statement must be verifiable, just as a scientific hypothesis must be verifiable—its meaning lies in its verifiableness. The logic positivists hoped to remove all the obscure or irrational elements of science by perfecting and clarifying scientific language. Because all scientific knowledge has the same formal linguistic structures and is advanced by the same experimental and logical methods, the philosophers of the Vienna circle hoped to unify all the sciences in a single encyclopedic system that would easily distinguish real science from the "pseudo-science" of metaphysicians and other "poetic" and "mystical" thinkers.

Ludwig Wittgenstein (1889—1951) also influenced the development of logical positivism although his own work grew beyond it. Wittgenstein was an Austrian by birth, but he was a member in good standing of the modern Anglo-American philosophical tradition. In 1921 he published *Tractatus Logico-Philosophicus*, his own version of logical positivism, which stated that language reflects the real world of fact and experience and cannot express ethical or metaphysical speculation. The world *is*, and can be described, but religion and value systems and most of the important and interesting things do not lead themselves to explicit and meaningful statement.

Since the only meaningful philosophical discussion was confined to mathematical logic and empirical science, philosophy itself—like much of the poetry and painting of the 1920s, rapidly became inaccessible to the layman. Philosophers could not and did not attempt to communicate their ideas except in technical language. Wittgenstein himself, concluding that discourse about important matters was not possible, followed his own logic and retired to Austria to teach kindergarten. Later he accepted a post at Cambridge University. In his *Philosophical Investigations*, published posthumously in 1953, Wittgenstein modified the emphasis of much of his earlier thinking but concentrated again on the place of language in thought. The meaning of words is settled through usage, which reflects "a form of life", he said. It is the philosopher's analysis of the meaning of common terms and his untangling of puzzles that arise when we "stretch" language beyond its limits that make his work useful.

Wittgenstein's later work was essential to the formation of the "new Oxford movement", the contemporary philosophical school whose chief concern is analyzing and understanding the language and concepts we use in ordinary life. Its members departed from their logical positivist teachers after World War II made the older philosophy seem narrow and remote, unable to help solve the desperate problems of human life. No statements, they say, is absolutely verifiable, because there is none that will not change its meaning in altered circumstances. Everything depends on context, and thus neither ethics nor metaphysics in any timeless or absolute form is a suitable subject for philosophical thought. In a discussion of good and evil, it is our various uses of these concepts that are studied—not any inherent, permanent meaning of the words. These English thinkers, whose chief spokesman was John Austin of Oxford until his death in 1960, have moved a long way from the belief that exact mathematical language is the ultimate goal of philosophy, but their concern is still with knowledge and language.

A figure who bridged the opposed interests of the Anglo-Saxon and Continental schools was Alfred North Whitehead, an Englishman who spent his later years in America. Whitehead had worked with Russell in logic and mathematics and was so well versed in physics that he formulated a distinctive theory of relativity, but he turned to metaphysics during his years at Harvard in the 1920s and 1930s. *Process and Reality* (1929) stated his organic philosophy of "process". Just as the physicists had abolished the empty universe and substituted a field of force and energy, so Whitehead saw man's world of nature and society as alive and continuous. He sought a synthesis of scientific, social, moral, and aesthetic categories, hoping that an organic philosophy could unify and illuminate the interrelated aspects of experience.

Another transitional figure was the German philosopher Edmund Husserl (1859—1938), the founder of phenomenology. Like his French predecessor Henri Bergson, Husserl was neither a pure intuitive idealist in the German tradition nor a complete empiricist. Husserl thought that everyday experience must be reduced to its base elements by subtracting all presuppositions and interpretations of experience (such as scientific laws) from consciousness. The phenomenological philosopher must examine all kinds of experience, subjecting them to his own analyses to reveal elements of pure consciousness or intuition. Husserl's emphasis on intuition was extremely influential in Continental philosophy.

In striking contrast to the Anglo-American school, the Continental philosophies were expressions of moral, historical, and metaphysical understanding, not reflections of preoccupation with science. These philosophers demanded social or political commitment. They regarded the detachment of a linguistic analyst as immoral and in fact impossible in the modern world. Martin Heidegger (1889—1976), a German, was much influenced by Husserl's emphasis on intuition and by Kierkegaard's grounding of philosophy on the fear and certainty of death. In *Being and Time* (1927) Heidegger explored the meaning of Being in relation to its corollary—Death. Being is temporal; it is "becoming"; and man can realize himself only by accepting this basic fact. This kind of tragic humanism makes Heidegger a forerunner of the existentialist school.

Existentialists assert that "existence precedes essence"—that, in other words, man has no determinate nature but creates himself after he comes into the world. He forms his own essence by the choices he makes. Thus men differ from manufactured products, which come into the world according to a preconceived plan in the mind of a creator or designer. In atheistic existentialism there is no Creator; men choose for themselves and for all men, thus contributing to the human essence. Man is doomed to the anguish of responsibility for his choices. God and prescribed value systems have been abandoned in modern secular society, and human life is nothing but the sum of individual actions. Man is condemned to a life of perfect freedom, for which he cannot avoid responsibility by suicide or by yielding to a belief in superhuman values to guide him.

The chief spokesman for existentialism was Jean-Paul Sartre (1905—1980), a novelist, dramatist, journalist, and leader of the French left-wing intelligentsia. Sartre's fictional heroes are antiheroes who knew only their own consciousnesses and cannot form meaningful relationships with others. Often their anguish prevents any action except violence, which liberates them from anxiety and doubt. Sartre reconciles existentialism and Marxism on the basis that man must make a choice and do what he can—acting through violence, if necessary, to express his freedom.

On the latter point Sartre differed from Albert Camus (1913—1960), a playwright, novelist, and journalist whose writings have an important place in contemporary religious thought and philosophy. Camus was a French Algerian of working-class origin. His major theme was human freedom, which all men have in this absurd, irrational, and meaningless universe. God is dead, and so are absolute values. In the absence of eternity, human life on earth must be cherished. Like Sartre, Camus felt that the artist had a duty to speak out for human rights—to be engaged—but unlike Sartre, he would not accept any ideology.

In *The Myth of Sisyphus* (1942) Camus attempted to find an individual solution to the problem posed by the death of God: if the universe is irrational, why live at all? He had been described as nihilist, but in fact his recognition of meaninglessness was only a starting point from which he began to search for positive values. Confessing the terror of mortality from which man cannot escape, Camus hoped to reveal the value of life. In *The Rebel* (1951) Camus described the artist as the perfect rebel who tries to impose order on natural disorder. Ends cannot justify means in a world which is not moving anywhere and in which only humanism and aesthetics provide any value.

Something like existentialism has had a place in Christian theology since St. Augustine, but the Death-of-God attitude appeared only with Nietzsche and achieved wide influence only in the mid-twentieth century. Before atheistic existentialism was clearly formulated after World War II, Christian theology enjoyed a renaissance in the form of a reaffirmation of the Augustinian doctrine of a transcendent God. The Protestant movement was sparked by thinkers like Karl Barth (1886—1968), a Swiss theologian who in the 1920s led a reaction to nineteenth-century liberal theology. Barth rediscovered divine grace and "Christology", claiming that the death and resurrection of Jesus Christ was the only reality. Barth's "theology of crisis" intended to describe God, not men's idea of God. Barth's contemporary, Rudolf Bultmann(1884—1976), attempted to "demythologize" the New Testament. He believed the Gospels to be statements of the Christian message and Jewish tradition, not accurate biographies of Jesus, which were in any case unnecessary. Both Barth and Bultmann were influenced by a Christian existentialism which found in God's grace the source of hope and in the life of Jesus a model for human action. Paul Tillich (1886—1965), who became an important figure in American theology after he was expelled from Germany by Hitler in 1933, believed that new forms and interpretations would arise out of the old, making Protestantism relevant to every age.

Certain French thinkers have maintained the orthodox Roman Catholic position while making significant contributions to contemporary theology. Jacques Maritain (1882—1973) had devoted much of his life to the study of Thomas Aquinas. In the liberal Thomist spirit, Maritain urged the Church to abandon conservatism and concern itself with the needs of industrial society. Pierre Teilhard de Chardin (1881—1955) developed an evolutionary Christ-centered philosophy, contending that all human history would ultimately converge in Christ. An upheaval in Catholic theology, relating traditional doctrine to the problems of contemporary society, began in the late 1950s, particularly in Germany, Austria, and Holland. This trend was greatly accentuated during the pontificate of John XXIII (1959—1963), who favored the reform and renewal of the Roman Church, and by the Second Vatican Council that Pope John summoned. The Council, which opened in 1962, had a mixed record of accomplishment but undeniably sparked Catholic thought on all kinds of subjects. It fostered a renewed emphasis on Scripture, thereby bringing the Roman Church closer to the Protestant, and it inaugurated cooperation with other Christian faiths. Pope John's encouragement of free thought, free speech, and ecumenism opened the Church to a great wave of questioning in all aspects of doctrines and established practice, including the relevance of Christianity to modern society.

12.5   The Heritage of the Twentieth Century

In the twentieth century, most forms of higher thought have been absorbed into the university, and in the 1950s and 1960s, especially in the United States, even many artists and writers did their work on the campus. Nearly every major thinker after 1920 became, if he did not start out as, a university professor. The university has been called upon to solve every social problem, from management of the business cycle to racial conflict to the development of new technology for both peace and war. Indeed, the university and academics have never played such a central role in Western culture or taken such a lead in formulating new ideas.

The academicization of thought, which was already under way at the beginning of the twentieth century but which was intensified with each passing decade and sharply accentuated in all Western countries after World War II, brought with it obvious benefits. Research in the natural and biological sciences was no longer undertaken by isolated geniuses. Rather, it was pursued by teams of scientists at leading universities who commanded vast resources. Their hypotheses and discoveries were immediately reported at academic meetings—often international in character—and subjected at once to scrutiny, testing, and amplification by other scientists. Thus a breakthrough achieved at one university triggered a whole series of additional discoveries in the same field at other research centers in several countries. The development of atomic physics since the early 1900s is a prime example of this phenomenon. In the following decades similar accelerated progress occurred in other disciplines as well.

The social and behavioral sciences likewise benefited. Theories of social action and individual behavior, which until the end of the nineteenth century had been the province of philosophers, theologians, and poets, by the mid-twentieth century, were subjected to the rigorous academic scrutiny that had come to prevail in the natural and biological sciences. Anyone who set out to answer the age-old questions "What is human nature?" and "How does society function?" could not gain a hearing in serious intellectual circles unless he could express his theories in the technical vocabulary of sociology, psychology, and anthropology and display awareness of the data these disciplines have made available.

Twentieth-century academic thought has, however, exhibited the defects of its qualities. The compartmentalization of the intellect that began in the late nineteenth century has been greatly intensified. With scholars dissecting and scrutinizing the various parts of the human experience, who could speak for the whole man—for the good life of man and society in their integrated wholes?

One of the grim paradoxes of the twentieth century has been the simultaneous dissemination of fantastic and vicious myths by the extreme Left and Right and the accumulation in the universities of verifiable information on social and individual behavior which thoroughly contradicts these myths. But the extremists provided total views of human nature and social change which the academics, with their enthusiasm for analysis, generally failed to offer. The academic brought into question the old ethics, the old humanism, the old liberalism, but they were tardy and negligent in developing holistic social theories that were both scientifically verifiable and comprehensible and attractive to the common man. Consequently, extremist ideologies proved fatally popular, even to some intellectuals and professors.

In English-speaking countries, the social and behavioral sciences have had a devastating impact on philosophy, which used to provide an integrated view of life. In the face of the vast and often confusing data that these sciences provided, British and American philosophers simply abdicated their social responsibility. They abandoned ethics, metaphysics, and social and political theory as their province and confined themselves to linguistic analysis. Valuable as this scrutiny of terms and the meaning of conceptual phrases has been in clarifying communication, it leaves men with nothing to communicate about—nothing to believe in, no value system to govern their lives—and therefore vulnerable to emotional commitment to extremist dogmas. The abdication by the "analytic" philosophers of philosophy's traditional role has been a calamity for the twentieth century. If philosophers will not tell us what is justice and virtue, to whom shall we turn?

A third characteristic of twentieth-century culture has been the perpetuation of modes of thought and feeling that were the product of the new consciousness of the late nineteenth century. The relativism and irrationalism of the age of Nietzsche, Freud, and Weber reached its zenith (or nadir) in the 1920s and 1930s. The motto of these decades might well have been "nothing sacred, nothing true, and nothing good". Moral and social standards were regarded either as the product of class consciousness or as suppressed, unconscious, or semi-conscious personal drives. No interpretation of the past was supposed to have a claim to objective validity; it was at best the view of the particular moment, subject to immediate change, or at worst merely a class or national ideology or a private myth. Human nature was regarded as a miscellany of atavistic urges, and human action was viewed as so completely determined by physical and sexual drives as to make a mockery of the Enlightenment view of man as rational and the Romantic faith in the quest for moral and spiritual fulfillment.

The mass murders, unprecedented in human history, perpetuated by the Nazis and the like demonstrated the pragmatic dangers of extreme relativism and irrationalism. If nothing was good and sacred, how could any ideology, no matter how vicious, be condemned as false? And how could any aggressive act—murder, rape, or pillage—be condemned as inhuman? Freud had tried to show how civilization could absorb and cure its discontents. But the doctrines of relativism and irrationalism of the 1930s perverted Freud's moral intentions—they eroded the dichotomy between reason and unreason; they abandoned the distinction between civilization and savagery. Auschwitz was the consequence, and in the postwar world a quest for the reaffirmation of human values—a search for some principles of good and truth in human life— was launched.

Essentially, the leading thinkers of the contemporary world have tried to regain a kernel of the faith of liberal humanism and rationalism without ignoring the more sophisticated understanding of human nature and society that was the product of the new consciousness or the horror of the two world wars. Many of these thinkers, as exemplified by Albert Camus and Jean-Paul Sartre, subscribed to a faith called existentialism, which is simply a sadder and wiser, more tragic and less naïve version of traditional Western humanism. We are painfully aware of the "absurdity" of human life, the conflict between irrationality and our longing for peace and justice. We cannot deny this awful crisis of the human condition; we have to make the best of it.

Even before Sartre and Camus reaffirmed the old faith in man's nobility, a group of Christian existentialists had revived Augustinian theology. Whether this gave individual man any more external support in his quest for peace and happiness than the secular existentialists allowed him is still being debated. In the formulation of Christian existentialism by Karl Barth, man's situation was bleak indeed, but Jesus' life and death is both the means of divine grace and the model for human life. Dietrich Bonhoeffer (1906—1945), the Lutheran theologian martyred by the Nazis, advocated a revived Christian activism that seeks to transform the world through personal commitment to the highest moral act in a particular situation.

The main point of the postwar existentialism, whether secular or Christian, was toward a vision of liberated individuals joining together in mutual respect and love to build a better society that would take account of the social and behavioral sciences and the horrible lessons of modern history and transcend all of these in a new world community.

References

[1] BALDICK C. 2000. Oxford dictionary of literary terms[M]. Shanghai: Shanghai Foreign Language Education Press.

[2] BEATTY J L, JOHNSON O A, REISBORD J. 2004. Heritage of Western civilization[M]. Beijing: Peking University Press.

[3] BENTLEY J H, ZIEGLER H, STREETS H E. 2008. Traditions and encounters: a brief global history [M]. New York: The McGraw-Hill Companies, Inc.

[4] BLACKBURN S. 2000. Oxford dictionary of philosophy[M]. Shanghai: Shanghai Foreign Language Education Press.

[5] BURNS E M, MEACHAM S, LERNER R E. 1993. Western civilizations [M]. 12th ed. New York: W. W. Norton & Company, Inc.

[6] COLLINSON D. 1987. Fifty major philosophers: a reference guide[M]. London: Croom Helm.

[7] KAGAN D, OZMENT S, TURNER F M. 2004. The Western heritage [M]. 8th ed. New York: Pearson Education, Inc.

[8] KISHLANSKY M, GERY P, O'BRIEN P. 2007. A brief history of Western civilization[M]. 5th ed. New York: Pearson Education, Inc.

[9] LAMM R C. 1996. Humanities in Western culture[M]. 10th ed. New York: The McGraw-Hill Companies, Inc.

[10] LERNER R E, MEACHAM S, BURNS E M. 1993. Western civilizations [M]. 12th ed. New York: W. W. Norton & Company, Inc.

[11] MACK M. et al. 1992. The Norton anthology of world masterpieces [M]. 6th ed. New York: W. W. Norton & Company, Inc.

[12] RIETBERGEN P. 2006. Europe: a cultural history[M]. 2nd ed. London: Taylor & Francis.

[13] ROGERS P M. 2008. Aspects of Western civilization[M]. 6th ed. New York: Pearson Education, Inc.

[14] SHERMAN D. 2006. Western civilization: sources, images, and interpretations [M]. 7th ed. New York: The McGraw-Hill Companies, Inc.

[15] SPIELVOGEL J J. 2005. Western civilization: a brief history[M]. 3rd ed. Beijing: Peking University Press.

[16] STAVRIANOS L S. 2004. A global history: from prehistory to the 21th century[M]. Beijing: Peking University Press.

[17] STEARNS P N, ADAS M, SCHWARTZ S B, GILBERT M J. 2001. World civilizations: the global experience[M]. 3rd ed. New York: Addison-Wesley Educational Publishers Inc.

[18] STEVENSON L, HABERMAN D L. 2009. Ten theories of human nature [M]. 5th ed. Oxford: Oxford University Press.

[19] STUMPF S E, FIESER J. 2003. Socrates to Sartre and beyond: a history of philosophy[M]. 7th ed. New York: The McGraw-Hill Companies, Inc.

[20] SULLIVAN R E, HARRISON J B, SHERMAN D. 1994. A short history of Western civilization[M]. New York: The McGraw-Hill Companies, Inc.

[21] 陈刚.2000.西方精神史[M].南京:江苏人民出版社.

[22] 姜守明,等.2004.西方文化史[M].北京:科学出版社.

[23] 李世安.2000.世界文明史[M].北京:中国发展出版社.

[24] 刘建军.2006.外国文化导论[M].天津:南开大学出版社.

[25] 刘文荣.2010.西方文化史[M].上海:文汇出版社.

[26] 孟节省,等.2002.西方文化漫谈[M].北京:红旗出版社.

[27] 沈之兴,等.1997.西方文化史[M].广州:中山大学出版社.

[28] 徐新,等.2002.西方文化史[M].北京:北京大学出版社.

[29] 朱寰,等.2005.西方文化要览[M].北京:中国青年出版社.

[30] 庄锡昌.1989.世界文化史通论[M].杭州:浙江人民出版社.

Index